CLASS
AND SCHOOLS

Is school reform the answer?

Opinion on the charter school movement?

What would it mean to close the achievement
gap? — within social class, or
overall?

Role for families?

With all the attention & effort, why does the achievement
gap still exist?

Why does the black community seem relatively
complacent about the achievement gap?

CLASS
AND SCHOOLS

Using Social, Economic, and Educational Reform to Close the Black–White Achievement Gap

◆

Richard Rothstein

TEACHERS COLLEGE
COLUMBIA UNIVERSITY

ECONOMIC POLICY INSTITUTE

About the author

Richard Rothstein is a research associate of the Economic Policy Institute and a visiting lecturer at Teachers College, Columbia University. From 1999 to 2002 he was the national education columnist for *The New York Times*; he is now a senior correspondent for *The American Prospect*. Mr. Rothstein's recent publications include *The Way We Were? Myths and Realities of America's Student Achievement* (Century Foundation Press 1998), *All Else Equal: Are Public and Private Schools Different?* (with Luis Benveniste and Martin Carnoy; RoutledgeFalmer 2003), and *Where's the Money Going? Changes in the Level and Composition of Education Spending* (EPI 1995, 1997).

Mr. Rothstein welcomes readers' comments about this book. He can be contacted at rr2159@columbia.edu.

This research was funded by The William and Flora Hewlett Foundation. We thank them for their support. The William and Flora Hewlett Foundation has been making grants since 1966 to help solve social and environmental problems at home and around the world. The Foundation concentrates its resources on activities in education, environment, performing arts, population, conflict resolution, and U.S.-Latin American relations. In addition, the Hewlett Foundation has initiatives supporting neighborhood improvement, philanthropy, and global affairs.

Table of contents

Prefaces

In this book, Richard Rothstein asks us to view the black–white and low- to middle-income achievement gaps with a wider lens. His revealing and persuasive analysis of how social class shapes learning outcomes forces us to look at the differences in learning styles and readiness across students as they enter school for the first time. Further, he prods us to consider the influence of income, health, safety and other gaps affecting students as they proceed through school. Even the racial and income gaps facing adults play a role, particularly as students look to their elders for signs of a payoff to education and sometimes find the evidence lacking. Consequently, according to Rothstein, addressing the achievement gap requires no less than a significant transformation of social and labor policy along with extensive school reform.

Such an analysis provides little room for easy answers and leaves few institutions off the hook. A few inspiring, dedicated teachers will not do the trick. Nor will higher expectations, in isolation, yield big payoffs for those left behind. In fact, school reform itself must be supplemented by a comprehensive compensatory program in the early years of school, along with after-school, summer, and pre-kindergarten programs. Holding schools accountable may be part of the answer, but what schools can do, even when they are at their best, will solve just part of the problem.

One can hope and expect that Rothstein's analysis will catalyze a broader discussion of how to enhance learning in our society and, even more hopefully, inspire a broader commitment to addressing the gross inequalities that pervade American life. One can also hope that researchers will pursue empirical examination of many of Rothstein's conjectures so that our understanding of education and the learning process deepens further.

The Economic Policy Institute is proud of its long association with Richard Rothstein, who has been an EPI research associate for over a dozen years, and pleased to publish this pathbreaking work along with Teachers College at Columbia University

— Lawrence Mishel
President, Economic Policy Institute

Two important things happened at Teachers College in 2004. First, the college completed a two-year strategic planning exercise and determined that we would focus our resources – people, programs, and dollars – on what we believed to be the most urgent issue facing education – educational inequity, which is popularly called "the achievement gap" – the chasm in access, expectation, and outcomes in education between low-income and high-income populations; whites/Asians and blacks/Hispanics; urban and suburban residents, etc.

We are convinced this problem is to education the equivalent of AIDS or cancer in health care. It is a scourge that robs children of their futures. Today's information economy demands more education and higher levels of skills and knowledge for employment than ever before in history. Children on the lower end of the achievement gap without adequate skills, knowledge, and education have little chance for economic well-being in this country. When a quality education is denied to children at birth because of their parents' skin color or income, it is not only bad social policy, it is immoral.

Teachers College chose to focus on educational equity as an affirmation of our historic mission of serving urban and disadvantaged populations. We believed, too, that our faculty, embracing three major fields – health, psychology, and education – had the capacity to study the issue comprehensively because it involves not only schools, but also families, communities, and social services such as health care.

The second important happening is that Richard Rothstein, an eminent scholar and former education columnist for *The New York Times,* came to Teachers College as the Sachs Lecturer. He gave three extraordinary lectures on the achievement gap. Rich with data, they comprehensively outlined the causes of the gap, identified the fallacies and misperceptions regarding the gap, redefined the meaning of the achievement gap, and offered proposals to narrow the gap. The lectures were mesmerizing, drawing a crowd even during a blizzard. They became the talk of the college, providing content not only for classes, but also for sidebar conversations at meetings on administrative matters and lunch discussions around tables in the cafeteria.

Given TC's new focus, we asked Richard Rothstein if we could publish an extended version of his lectures. We thought his work both groundbreaking and fundamental to understanding educational equity. Accordingly, we wanted it to be our inaugural publication on the subject.

Four things make Richard Rothstein's book unique.

First, recent years have brought an avalanche of publications on the achievement gap, characterized much too often by simplistic sound bites and ideological blinders. In contrast, Richard Rothstein's book, drawing on a wealth of previous research, provides the most intelligent, compelling, and comprehensive analysis of the causes of the achievement gap I have ever read. He demonstrates that the problem cannot be attributed simply to variations in the quality of the schools attended by children of different races and economic classes. He shows that schools alone cannot provide a remedy. Along the way, the author presents evidence debunking the popular myth that there are super-schools capable of eliminating the gap. Presenting study after study, Rothstein highlights the far greater impact of health care, nutrition, parents, home, and community.

The author makes a second invaluable contribution in this volume. He enlarges upon the traditional conception of the achievement gap, which has almost universally focused on disparities in cognitive or academic achievement. Rothstein makes the case that non-cognitive outcomes – attitudes and behaviors – must be incorporated as well. He presents data to show both that these affective outcomes are important to employers, and that an achievement gap exists in this area as well.

Third, Richard Rothstein makes a series of policy recommendations on how to narrow the gap, focusing on education, health, housing, and income differentials. He proposes earned income tax credits, policies to stabilize family housing, school–community health clinics, early childhood education, after-school programs, and summer programs.

Fourth, based on his recommendations, the author does something very unusual. He matches his ideas with dollars, determining the cost of significantly reducing the achievement gap.

In sum, Richard Rothstein has written a unique and powerful volume that needs to be read by scholars, policy makers, and practitioners who have the capacity to shape tomorrow.

I am enormously grateful to Larry Mishel and the Economic Policy Institute for making this volume possible. He joined the college in publishing this book. He produced the volume in only a few months, warp speed in academic publishing, and disseminated it to the leading policy makers and practitioners in this country.

— Arthur E. Levine
President, Teachers College, Columbia University

Introduction

The 50th anniversary of the Supreme Court's school desegregation order has intensified public awareness of the persistent gap in academic achievement between black and white students. The black–white gap is partly the difference between the achievement of all lower-class and middle-class students, but there is an additional gap between black and white students even when the blacks and whites come from families with similar incomes.

The American public and its political leaders, along with professional educators, have frequently vowed to close these gaps. Americans believe in the ideal of equal opportunity and also believe that the best way to ensure that opportunity is to enable all children, regardless of their parents' stations, to leave school with skills that position them to compete fairly and productively in the nation's democratic governance and occupational structure. The fact that children's skills can so clearly be predicted by their race and family economic status is a direct challenge to our democratic ideals.

Policy makers almost universally conclude that these existing and persistent achievement gaps must be the result of wrongly designed school policies – either expectations that are too low, teachers who are insufficiently qualified, curricula that are badly designed, classes that are too large, school climates that are too undisciplined, leadership that is too unfocused, or a combination of these.

Americans have come to the conclusion that the achievement gap is the fault of "failing schools" because it makes no common sense that it could be otherwise. After all, how much money a family has, or the color of a child's skin, should not influence how well that child learns to read. If teachers know how to teach reading, or math, or any other

1

subject, and if schools emphasize the importance of these tasks and permit no distractions, children should be able to learn these subjects whatever their family income or skin color.

This common-sense perspective, however, is misleading and dangerous. It ignores how social class characteristics in a stratified society like ours may actually influence learning in school. It confuses social class, a concept that Americans have historically been loath to consider, with two of its characteristics, income and, in the United States, race. For it is true that low income and skin color themselves don't influence academic achievement, but the collection of characteristics that define social class differences inevitably influences that achievement.

Recognizing social class and its impact on learning

This book tries to explain how social class differences are likely to affect the academic performance of children. For example, parents of different social classes often have different styles of childrearing, different ways of disciplining their children, different ways of communicating expectations, and even different ways of reading to their children. These differences do not express themselves consistently or in the case of every family; rather, they influence the average tendencies of families from different social classes.

That there would be personality and childrearing differences, on average, between families in different social classes makes sense when you think about it: if upper-middle-class parents have jobs where they are expected to collaborate with fellow employees, create new solutions to problems, or wonder how to improve their contributions, they are more likely to talk to their children in ways that differ from the ways of lower-class parents whose own jobs simply require them to follow instructions without question. Children who are raised by parents who are professionals will, on average, have more inquisitive attitudes toward the material presented by their teachers than will children who are raised by working-class parents. As a result, no matter how competent the teacher, the academic achievement of lower-class children will, on average, almost inevitably be less than that of middle-class children. The probability of this reduced achievement increases as the characteristics of lower-social-class families accumulate.

Many social and economic manifestations of social class also have important implications for learning. Health differences are among them. Lower-class children, on average, have poorer vision than middle- class children, partly because of prenatal conditions, partly because of how their eyes are trained as infants. They have poorer oral hygiene, more lead poisoning, more asthma, poorer nutrition, less adequate pediatric care, more exposure to smoke, and a host of other problems. As will be discussed in this book, each of these well-documented social class differences is likely to have a palpable effect on academic achievement, and, combined, the influence of all of these differences is probably huge.

The growing unaffordability of adequate housing for low-income families is another social class characteristic that has a demonstrable effect on average achievement. Children whose families have difficulty finding stable housing are more likely to be mobile, and student mobil- ity is an important cause of low student achievement. It is hard to imag- ine how teachers, no matter how well trained, could be as effective for children who move in and out of their classrooms as teachers can be for children whose attendance is regular.

Differences in wealth between parents of different social classes are also likely to be important determinants of student achievement, but these differences are usually overlooked because most analysts focus only on annual income to indicate disadvantage. This practice makes it hard to understand, for example, why black students, on average, score lower than white students whose family incomes are the same. It is easier to understand this pattern when we recognize that children can have similar family incomes but be ranked differently in the social class structure, even in economic terms: black families with low income in any year are likely to have been poor for longer than white families with similar income in that year. White families are likely to own far more assets that support their children's achievement than are black families at the same current income level.

Throughout this book, the term "lower class" is used to describe the families of children whose achievement will, on average, be predict- ably lower than the achievement of middle-class children. American sociologists once were comfortable with this term, but it has fallen out of fashion. Instead we tend to use euphemisms like "disadvantaged" students, "at-risk" students, "inner-city" students, or students of "low-socioeconomic status." None of these terms, however, capture the central characteristic of lower-class families: a collection of occupational, psychological, personality, health, and economic traits that interact, predicting performance not only in schools but in other institutions as well that, on average, differs from the performance of families from higher social classes.

The critique in this book tries to show that much of the difference between the average performance of black and white children can probably be traced to differences in their social class characteristics. But there are also cultural characteristics that likely contribute a bit to the black–white achievement gap. These cultural characteristics may have identifiable origins in social and economic conditions – for example, black students may value education less than white students because a discriminatory labor market has not historically rewarded black workers for their education – but values can persist independently and outlast the economic circumstances that gave rise to them.

One of the bars to our understanding of the achievement gap is that most Americans, even well-educated ones, are inexpert in discussions of statistical distributions. The achievement gap is a phenomenon of averages, a difference between the average achievement of lower-class children and the average achievement of middle-class children. In human affairs, every average characteristic is a composite of many widely disparate characteristics. For example, we know that lead poisoning has a demonstrable effect on young children's I.Q. scores. Children with high exposure to lead, from fumes or from ingesting paint or dust, have I.Q. scores, on average, that are several points lower than the I.Q. scores of children who are not so exposed. But this does not mean that every child with lead poisoning has a lower I.Q. Some children with high lead levels in their blood have higher I.Q. scores than typical children with no lead exposure. When researchers say that lead poisoning seems to affect academic performance, they do not mean that every lead-exposed child performs more poorly. But the high performance of a few lead-exposed children does not disprove the conclusion that lead exposure is likely to harm academic achievement.

This reasoning applies to each of the social class characteristics that are discussed in this book as well as to the many others that, for lack of space or the author's ignorance, are not discussed. In each case, social class differences in social or economic circumstance likely cause differences in the average academic performance of children from different social classes, but, in each case, some children with lower-class characteristics perform better than typical middle-class children.

Good teachers, high expectations, standards, accountability, and inspiration are not enough

As is argued in this book, the influence of social class characteristics is probably so powerful that schools cannot overcome it, no matter how well trained are their teachers and no matter how well designed are their instructional programs and climates. But saying that a social class achievement gap should be expected is not to make a logical statement. The fact that social class differences are associated with, and probably cause, a big gap in academic performance does not mean that, in theory, excellent schools could not offset these differences. Indeed, there are many claims today, made by policy makers and educators, that higher standards, better teachers, more accountability, better discipline, or other effective practices can close the achievement gap.

The most prominent of these claims has been made by a conservative policy institute (the Heritage Foundation), by a liberal advocacy group (the Education Trust), by economists and statisticians who claim to have shown that better teachers do in fact close the gap, by prominent educators, and by social critics. Many (although not all) of the instructional practices promoted by these commentators are well designed, and these practices probably do succeed in delivering better educations to some lower-class children. But a careful examination of each claim that a particular school or practice has closed the race or social class achievement gap shows that the claim is unfounded.

In some cases, the claim fails because it rests on the misinterpretation of test scores; in other cases, the claim fails because the successful schools identified have selective student bodies. Remember that the achievement gap is a phenomenon of averages – it compares the average achievement of lower- and middle-class students. In both social classes, some students perform well above or below the average performance of their social class peers. If schools can select (or attract) a disproportionate share of lower-class students whose performance is above average for their social class, those schools can appear to be quite successful. Many of them are excellent schools and should be commended. But their successes provide no evidence that their instructional approaches would close the achievement gap for students who are average for their social class groups.

The limitations of the current testing regime

Whether efforts to close the social class achievement gap are in-school or socioeconomic reforms, it is difficult to know precisely how much any intervention will narrow the gap. We can't estimate the effect of various policies partly because we don't really know how big the achievement gap is overall, or how big it is in particular schools or school systems.

This lack of knowledge about the merits of any particular intervention will be surprising to many readers because so much attention is devoted these days to standardized test scores. It has been widely reported that, on average, if white students typically score at around the 50th percentile of achievement on a standardized math or reading test, black students typically score at around the 23rd percentile. (In more technical statistical terms, black students score, on average, between 0.5 and 1.0 standard deviations below white students.)

But contrary to conventional belief, this may not be a good measure of the gap. Because of the high stakes attached to standardized tests in recent years, schools and teachers are under enormous pressure to raise students' test scores. The more pressure there has been, the less reliable these scores have become. Partly, the tests themselves don't really measure the gap in the achievement of high standards we expect from students because high standards (for example, the production of good writing and the development of research skills and analysis) are expensive to test, and public officials are reluctant to spend the money. Instead, schools use inexpensive standardized tests that mostly, though not entirely, assess more basic skills. Gaps that show up on tests of basic skills may be quite different from the gaps that would show up on tests of higher standards of learning. And it is not the case that a hierarchy of skills are gained sequentially by students. Truly narrowing the achievement gap would not require children to learn "the basics" first. Lower-class children cannot produce typical middle-class academic achievement unless they learn basic and more advanced skills simultaneously, with each reinforcing the other. This is, in fact, how middle-class children who come to school ready to learn acquire both basic and advanced skills.

The high stakes recently attached to standardized tests have given teachers incentives to revise the priorities of their instruction, especially for lower-class children, so that they devote greater time to drill on basic skills and less time to other, equally important (but untested) learning areas in which achievement gaps also appear. In a drive to raise test scores in math and reading, the curriculum has moved away not only from more advanced mathematical and literary skills, but from social studies, literature, art, music, physical education, and other important topics where test scores do not result in judgments of school quality. We don't know how large the race or social class achievement gaps are in these subjects, but there is no reason to believe that gaps in one domain are the same as the gaps in others, or that the relationships between gaps in different domains are consistent at different ages and on different tests. For example, education researchers normally expect that gaps in reading will be greater than gaps in math, probably because social class differences in parental support play a bigger role for reading than for math. Parents typically read to their very young children, and middle-class parents do so more and in more intellectually stimulating ways, but few parents do math problems with their young children. Yet, on at least one test of entering kindergartners, race and social class gaps in math exceed those in reading.

Appreciating the importance of non-cognitive skills

We also don't know how large are the social class gaps in non-cognitive skills – character traits like perseverance, self-confidence, self-discipline, punctuality, communication skills, social responsibility, and the ability to work with others and resolve conflicts. These are important goals of public education; in some respects, they may be more important than academic outcomes.

Employers, for example, consistently report that workers have more serious shortcomings in these non-cognitive areas than in academic proficiency. Econometric studies show that non-cognitive skills are a stronger predictor of future earnings than are test scores. In public opinion surveys, Americans consistently say they want schools to produce good citizens and socially responsible adults first, and high academic proficiency second. Yet we do a poor job, actually no job at all, in assessing whether schools are generating such non-cognitive outcomes. And so we also do a poor job of assessing whether schools are successfully narrowing the social class gap in these traits, or whether social and economic reform here, too, would be necessary to narrow these gaps.

There is some evidence that the non-cognitive social class gaps should be a cause for concern. For very young children, measures of anti-social behavior mirror the academic test score gaps. Children of lower social classes exhibit more anti-social behavior than children of higher social classes, both in early childhood and in adolescence. It would be reasonable to expect that the same social and economic inequalities that likely produce academic test score gaps produce differences in non-cognitive traits as well.

In some areas, however, it seems that non-cognitive gaps may be smaller than cognitive ones. In particular, analyses of some higher education affirmative action programs find that, when minority students with lower test scores than white students are admitted to colleges, the lower-scoring minority students may exhibit more leadership, devote more serious attention to their studies, and go on to make greater community contributions. This evidence reinforces the importance of measuring such non-cognitive student characteristics, something that few elementary or secondary schools attempt. Until we begin to measure these traits, we will have no insight into how great are the non-cognitive gaps between lower- and middle-class students.

Moving forward

Three tracks should be pursued vigorously and simultaneously if we are to make significant progress in narrowing the achievement gap. First is school improvement efforts that raise the quality of instruction in elementary and secondary schools. Second is expanding the definition of schooling to include crucial out-of-school hours in which families and communities now are the sole influences. This means implementing comprehensive early childhood, after-school, and summer programs. And third are social and economic policies that enable children to attend school more equally ready to learn. These policies include health services for lower-class children and their families, stable housing for working families with children, and the narrowing of growing income inequalities in American society.

Many of the curricular and school organizational reforms promoted by education critics have merit and should be intensified. Repairing and upgrading the scandalously decrepit school facilities that serve some lower-class children, raising salaries to permit the recruitment of more qualified teachers for lower-class children, reducing class sizes for lower-class children (particularly in the early grades), insisting on higher academic standards that emphasize creativity and reasoning as well as basic skills, holding schools accountable for fairly measured performance, having a well-focused and disciplined school climate, doing more to encourage lower-class children to intensify their own ambitions – all of these policies, and others, can play a role in narrowing the achievement gap. These reforms are extensively covered in other books and in public discussions of education and are not dwelt upon in this book. Instead, the focus here is the greater importance of reforming social and eco- nomic institutions if we truly want children to emerge from school with equal potential.

Readers should not misinterpret this emphasis as implying that better schools are not important, or that school improvement will not make a contribution to narrowing the achievement gap. Better school practices can probably narrow the gap. School reform, however, is not enough. In seeking to close the achievement gap for low-income and minority students, policy makers focus inordinate attention on the improvement of instruction because they apparently believe that social class differences are immutable and that only schools can improve the destinies of lower-class children.

This is a peculiarly American belief – that schools can be virtually the only instrument of social reform – but it is not based on evidence about the relative effectiveness of economic, social, and educational improvement efforts. While many social class characteristics are impervious to short-term change, many can be easily affected by public policies that narrow the social and economic gaps between lower- and middle-class children. These policies can probably have a more powerful impact on student achievement (and, in some cases, at less cost) than an exclusive focus on school reform, but we cannot say so for sure because social scientists and educators have devoted no effort to studying the relative costs and benefits of non-school and school reforms. For example, some data presented in this book suggest that establishing an optometric clinic in a school to improve the vision of low-income benefits to taxpayers of our achievement gap.

role of experiment
children would probably have a bigger impact on their test scores than spending the same money on instructional improvement. We can't be certain if this is the case, however, because there have been no experiments to test the relative benefits of these alternative strategies.

Proposals to increase the access of lower-class families to stable housing should also be evaluated for their educational impact, as should proposals to improve all facets of the health of lower-class children, not their vision alone.

(U.S.)
Incomes have become more unequally distributed in the United States in the last generation, and this inequality contributes to the academic achievement gap. Proposals for a higher minimum wage or earned income tax credit, designed to offset some of this inequality, should be considered educational policies as well as economic ones, for they would likely result in higher academic performance from children whose families are more secure.

role of family
Although conventional opinion is that "failing" schools contribute mightily to the achievement gap, evidence indicates that schools already do a great deal to combat it. Most of the social class difference in average academic potential exists by the time children are three years old. This difference is exacerbated during the years that children spend in school, but during these years the growth in the gap occurs mostly in the after-school hours and during the summertime, when children are not actually in classrooms.

So in addition to school improvement and broader reforms to narrow the social and economic inequalities that produce gaps in student achievement, investments should also be made to expand the definition of schooling to cover those crucial out-of-school hours. Because the gap is already huge at three years of age, the most important focus of this investment should probably be early childhood programs. The quality of these programs is as important as the existence of the programs themselves. To narrow the gap, early childhood care, beginning for infants and toddlers, should be provided by adults who can provide the kind of intellectual environment that is typically experienced by middle-class infants and toddlers. This goal probably requires professional care givers and low child–adult ratios.

Providing after-school and summer experiences to lower-class children that are similar to those middle-class children take for granted would also likely be an essential part of narrowing the achievement *the nature of the program matters.*

gap. But these experiences can't comprise just after-school or summer remedial programs where lower-class children get added drill in math and reading. Certainly, remedial instruction should be part of an adequate after-school and summer program, but only a part. The advantage that middle-class children gain after school and in the summer likely comes mostly from the self-confidence they acquire and the awareness they develop of the world outside their homes and immediate communities, from organized athletics, dance, drama, museum visits, recreational reading, and other activities that develop their inquisitiveness, creativity, self-discipline, and organizational skills. After-school and summer programs can be expected to have a chance to narrow the achievement gap only by attempting to duplicate such experiences.

Provision of health care services to lower-class children and their families is also needed to narrow the achievement gap. Some health care services are relatively inexpensive, like a school vision clinic. Dental clinics likewise can be provided at costs comparable to what schools typically spend on less-effective reforms. A full array of health services, however, will cost more, but can't likely be avoided if there is a true intent to raise the achievement of lower-class children. Some of these costs, however, are not new; they can be recouped by school clinics with reimbursements from other underutilized government programs, like Medicaid.

For nearly half a century, the association of social and economic disadvantage with a student achievement gap has been well known to economists, sociologists, and educators. Most, however, have avoided the obvious implication of this understanding – raising the achievement of lower-class children requires amelioration of the social and economic conditions of their lives, not just school reform. Perhaps this small volume can spur a reconsideration of this needlessly neglected opportunity.

Main point

CHAPTER 1

Social class, student achievement, and the black–white achievement gap

The legacy of the Coleman report

The 50th anniversary of the Supreme Court's desegregation decision in *Brown vs. Board of Education* has directed renewed attention to the persistent achievement gap between black and white students. The court's ruling was an early hint that American public education should be judged on whether schools produce racially equal outcomes. When it relied on sociological reasoning, particularly that of Kenneth Clark, to show that segregation inevitably led black students to achieve less, the court spurred a debate in which Americans continue to engage.[1] If equal resources do not produce equal achievement, what will?

By 1964, 10 years after the court decision, the achievement gap remained huge. Many districts resisted integration. Advocates of equality were convinced that a gap persisted simply because, whether segregated or integrated, black children continued to attend more poorly financed schools.

So Congress then ordered a study to prove, once and for all, that blacks attended inferior schools and that this caused their relatively low achievement. Most people thought the proposed study was somewhat silly; after all, why prove once again that blacks attended inferior schools? But James S. Coleman, a sociologist then at Johns Hopkins University, accepted the charge and concluded, to his own consternation, that variation in school resources had very little – almost nothing – to do with what we now term the test score gap between black and white children. Instead, the family backgrounds of black and white students, their widely different social and economic conditions, accounted for most of the difference.[2]

13

Since the Coleman report, refuting this conclusion has been an obsession of education research. Surely, there were flaws in Coleman's analysis. He found, for example, more variation in achievement within schools than between them, but left mostly unexplored whether relative teacher effectiveness might explain this variation more than student background. Nonetheless, scholarly efforts over four decades have consistently confirmed Coleman's core finding; no analyst has been able to attribute less than two-thirds of the variation in achievement among schools to the family characteristics of their students.

Yet no matter how often confirmed, the claim remains counter-intuitive. Why should poverty mean a child can't learn to read, write, and compute? Surely, a good teacher can guide any child, regardless of skin color or family income, to do these things. Surely, throughout our history, poor children have used education to rise in the United States, and poverty was no fatal impediment. If today there is an achievement gap, common sense says that schools must not be doing for blacks what they did for immigrants and other poor youngsters since the nation's founding.

This book endeavors to show why socioeconomic differences *must* produce an achievement gap between students from different social classes, why these differences have always produced such a gap (myths about a golden age of immigrant achievement notwithstanding), and why this unpleasant reality actually makes the most compelling common sense. Children from lower social classes and from many racial and ethnic minorities, even in the best schools, will achieve less, on average, than middle-class children.

Some common misunderstandings about the achievement gap

Three misunderstandings about the achievement gap cloud public discussion about the pathways by which social class influences learning.

First, the Coleman report's finding that families are a much bigger influence than school quality on achievement is too easily misinterpreted as the notion that "schools don't make a difference." Since it is apparent that schools make a big difference – as the late Senator Daniel Patrick Moynihan (and a co-author, Frederick Mosteller) quipped, "children don't think up algebra on their own"[3] – we are tempted simply to dismiss Coleman's claim. But what the Coleman report argued is not that schools don't influence achievement but rather that the quality of schools attended by black and white children has little influence on *the difference* in average achievement between black and white students. If we describe *average* achievement, schools clearly have the biggest influence of all. This is common sense, and it is not wrong. Whether children learn math is schools' responsibility, but you will be better at predicting *which* children do better in math, and which do worse, if you know their social class backgrounds.

Think of Coleman's finding this way: all students learn in school, but schools have demonstrated limited ability to affect differences in the rate at which children from different social classes progress. Children from higher social classes come to school with more skills and are more prepared to learn than children from lower classes. All children learn in school, but those from lower classes, on average, do not learn so much faster that they can close the achievement gap.

A second misunderstanding stems from the loose way that the "achievement gap" is described in public discourse. Scholars and educators used to portray the gap in relative, or "norm-referenced" terms. A description of this type leads to the conclusion that average black achievement is from one-half to a full standard deviation below average white achievement. In other words, if average white students are at about the 50th percentile of a national test score distribution, then average black students would be somewhere between about the 16th and the 31st percentile in that distribution.[4]

In contrast, policy makers now typically report achievement in "criterion-referenced terms" – they ask not how students rank in comparison to national averages (or norms), but whether they passed a specific point on a scoring scale. This point is usually termed "proficiency." So instead of asking how black students achieve, on average, relative to whites, policy makers ask what percentage of blacks passed the cut point, and how this compares to the percentage of whites who did so.

This shift in measurement causes great mischief because the gap now depends on how difficult the cut point is. If very simple skill levels are judged proficient, most students of both races can pass the test. If more skill is required, fewer will pass. The simpler the level, the smaller the gap.[5] Effective schools can ensure that close to 100% of students, regardless of race or social class, pass simple tests. These schools can then claim to have closed the gap because both blacks and whites pass the proficiency point equally. But if the same students took somewhat more difficult tests, achievement gaps would re-appear.

As Chapter 2 discusses further, many claims by those who now brag that their particular approaches can close the gap have been based on this statistical sleight of hand – if you set a cut score low enough, you can eliminate the gap without in any way changing average achievement of students from different social classes. (And as Chapter 3 describes more fully, this is a strategy that federal law now invites states to adopt.)

So to be clear: when the following pages describe why differences in social class *must* produce a big achievement gap, they refer to a gap in *average* achievement in the wide range of skills that schools should produce – not only basic math and literacy, but also the ability to reason and create; an appreciation of history, science, art, and music; and good citizenship, self-discipline, and communication skills.

The third misunderstanding is to equate group averages and the performance of all individuals within the group. We all know highly successful students from lower-class backgrounds, and it is tempting to conclude that their success proves that social class cannot be what impedes most disadvantaged students. But there is a distribution of achievement in every social group, and these distributions overlap. While average achievement of lower-class students is below average achievement of middle-class students, there are always some middle-class students who achieve below typical lower-class levels. And there will always be some lower-class students who achieve above typical middle-class levels.[6] Demography is not destiny, but students' social and economic family characteristics are a powerful influence on their relative *average* achievement.

These three clarifications should be kept in mind in any discussion of causes of the achievement gap between white and black students or between middle-class and low-income students. First, schools do make a big difference in the level, if not in the variation, of achievement. Second, socioeconomic differences are less of a bar to closing the achievement gap if the gap is measured only as the difference between groups in low-level proficiency. And, third, the power of social class to predict average performance is not inconsistent with high achievement of some students from lower classes. Any average includes relatively higher and relatively lower performance of some in the group.

If these three misunderstandings are not permitted to cloud our think-ing, then the Coleman report's conclusion seems not at all counter-in-tuitive; indeed, it makes perfect sense that the economic, educational, and cultural characteristics of families have powerful effects on learn-ing, effects that even great schools cannot obliterate, on average.

Genetic influences

A family's economic, educational, and cultural traits are influenced by the genetic traits of the parents. This places some limits on how mal-leable to policy are a family's social class characteristics.

Because of genetic potential, children whose parents have more innate ability are more likely to have more innate ability themselves. This has been confirmed by "adoption studies," in which children brought up in different socioeconomic environments from their biological par-ents are more similar in their academic achievement to their biological parents than to their adoptive parents.[7] The importance of genetic makeup to academic achievement is rarely discussed in America today, partly because the atmosphere has been poisoned by those who claim that there are differences in academic ability, attributable to genes, between average black and average white students. There is no reasonable basis for such a claim, and there is every reason to believe that the genetic potential within races is identical, or nearly so. Blacks did not become over-represented in the lower class in America because their genetic makeup was inferior, but because they were enslaved, then segregated and barred from equal opportunity for more than another century.

The purpose of the rest of this chapter is to explore the influence of families' social and economic conditions on their children's achieve-ment, and to suggest that, to narrow the achievement gap, greater atten-tion should be paid to ameliorating these conditions. We should not devote our attention exclusively to school reform.

This book does not dwell on the possible genetic contributions to the social class achievement gap because, given the state of current knowledge, genetic endowment that affects academic achievement is not reasonably amenable to policy influence, whereas socioeconomic conditions or school practices are. It may be that some day more will be known about the interaction of genes and the social and economic envi-ronment, and it will then be possible to have a reasoned discussion of how a balanced policy should not only mix social, economic, and educational reform, but also how these reforms might be made more effective by biological interventions.

We do a little bit of this now. For example, some children, because of their genetic inheritance, have more difficulty seeing print than other children. In such cases, we believe we should offset the effects of genetic makeup on student achievement by providing these children with eyeglasses. In the case of dyslexic children, their difficulty stems not from sight itself but from a genetically influenced tendency to process visual images in ways that make reading more difficult. Here, we agree that the effects of genes on student achievement should be remediated by using different instructional techniques from those used for children without this genetic disability. Increasing attention is also being paid to providing children with different (probably genetically influenced) learning styles with opportunities to learn and to excel in different ways.[8]

The research on genetic contributions to academic achievement is even more preliminary than research on the social and economic contributions. There are even fewer "adoption studies" than there are studies of social and economic influences on achievement. But there is growing understanding by scholars that genetic potential and environmental influence are not distinct but interactive. How genes influence biological development is influenced by environmental conditions, nutrition being the most obvious example. Some people may have a greater genetic disposition to obesity, but whether and how this genetic disposition is expressed depends on the type and quantity of food available. Similar interactions affect academic achievement and the readiness to learn.[9]

If, however, we were to inquire deeply into how social class influences academic achievement, part of the explanation would be socioeconomic and part would be genetic. This being the case, fully closing the social class achievement gap is probably not a theoretically desirable goal. However, we are far from being in danger of having too small a gap. Fully closing the black–white achievement gap *is* both desirable and feasible, but will first require social and economic reforms that would result in distributing black and white students equally between the social classes.

Social class differences in childrearing

To take full advantage of school, children should enter ready to learn, and their after-school, weekend, and summer activities should reinforce their learning. But children differ in how ready they are to learn when they enter school, and these differences are strongly influenced by their social class backgrounds.

Parents of different social classes tend to raise children somewhat differently. More educated parents read to their young children more consistently and encourage their children to read more to themselves when they are older.[10] Most parents with college degrees read to their children daily before the children begin kindergarten; few children whose parents have only a high school diploma or less benefit from daily reading. White children are more likely than blacks to be read to or told stories in pre-kindergarten years.[11] Young children of college-educated parents are surrounded by more books at home while children of less-educated parents see fewer books.[12]

A five-year-old who enters school recognizing some words and who has turned pages of many stories will be easier to teach than one who has rarely held a book. The second child can be taught, but, with equally high expectations and effective teaching, the first will more likely pass a reading test than the second. So the achievement gap begins.

As discussed earlier, this is not a determinist description. Some low-income children are naturally quick learners, take to school well, and respond so well to high expectations that after a few years of school they read better than typical middle-class children. Some middle-class children get no support for learning from troubled families, and some low-income parents organize life around a dream of college. But *on average*, a typical middle-class child who began to read at home will have higher lifetime achievement than a typical low-income child who was taught only in school, even if each benefits from good curriculum, effective teaching, and high expectations. If a society with such social class differences wants children, irrespective of social class, to have the same chance to achieve academic goals, it should find ways to help lower-class children enter school having the same familiarity with books as middle-class children have.

By kindergarten, almost all upper-class children, about half of middle-class children, and fewer than one in five lower-class children

have used computers.[13] This difference is not due solely to expense –
lower-class families have televisions, and they could obtain computers
if they were valued – but rather to differences in how parents from different social classes use computers themselves. If parents routinely sit
at computers, toddlers will sit on their parents' laps and play with the
mouse and keyboard. If computers are rarely used by parents, their children will be less proficient, even with computers at home. Some school
reform proposals include distributing computers to children's families,
expecting that this will help close the achievement gap. But while it
may help a little, such a distribution will not do much. If schools filled
kindergartens with computers, or even distributed them to families, the
advantages of children who also learned at home would persist, because differences in computer literacy practices that parents model will
not have been affected.

Some people acknowledge the impact of such differences on student achievement but find it hard to accept that good schools should
have so difficult a time overcoming them. This challenge would be easier
to understand if Americans had a broader international perspective on
education. Although many countries' students do better on academic
tests, on average, than Americans, class backgrounds influence *relative*
achievement everywhere. The inability of schools to overcome the disadvantage of less literate home backgrounds is not a peculiar American
failure but a universal reality. The number of books in students' homes,
for example, consistently predicts scores within almost every country.[14]
Turkish immigrant students suffer from an achievement gap in Germany, as do Algerians in France, as do Caribbean, African, Pakistani,
and Bangladeshi pupils in Great Britain, and as do Okinawans and low-
caste Buraku in Japan.[15]

An international reading survey of 15-year-olds, conducted in 2000,
found a strong relationship in almost every nation between parental occu-
pation and student literacy. The gap between literacy of children of the
highest-status workers (like doctors, professors, lawyers) and the lowest-
status workers (like waiters and waitresses, taxi drivers, mechanics) was
even greater in Germany and the United Kingdom than it was in the United
States. In France the gap was about the same as in the United States,
while in the Scandinavian countries and Korea it was smaller. There were
similar disparities between other social classes. The gap between the literacy of children of middle-class workers (like teachers, accountants,

engineers) and of children of lower-status workers was about the same in the United States and the United Kingdom, greater in Germany than in the United States, and slightly smaller in France than in the United States.[16] After reviewing these results, a U.S. Department of Education summary concluded that "most participating countries do not differ significantly from the United States in terms of the strength of the relationship between socioeconomic status and literacy in any subject."[17] Remarkably, the department published this conclusion at the same time that it was guiding a bill through Congress that demanded every school in the nation abolish social class differences in achievement within 12 years. It was enacted as the "No Child Left Behind" law.

Just as giving away computers won't overcome these gaps, so urging less-educated parents to read to children can't fully compensate for differences in school readiness. If children see parents read to solve their own problems or for entertainment, children are more likely to want to read themselves.[18] Parents who bring reading material home from work demonstrate by example to their children that reading is not a segmented burden but a seamless activity that bridges work and leisure.[19] Parents who read to children but don't read for themselves send a different message.

How parents read to children is as important as whether they do; more educated parents read aloud differently. When working-class parents read aloud, they are more likely to tell children to pay attention without interruptions or to sound out words or name letters. When they ask children about a story, questions are more likely to be factual, asking for names of objects or memories of events.[20] Parents who are more literate are more likely to ask questions that are creative, interpretive, or connective, like "what do you think will happen next?" "why do you think this happened?" "does that remind you of what we did yesterday?"[21] Middle-class parents are more likely to read aloud to have fun, to start conversations, to provide an entree to the world outside. Their children learn that reading is enjoyable and are more motivated to read in school.[22]

Stark social class differences arise not only in how parents read but in how they converse. Explaining events in the broader world to children, in dinner talk, for example, may have as much of an influence on test scores as early reading itself.[23] Through such conversations, children develop vocabularies and become familiar with contexts for reading in school.[24] Educated parents are more likely to engage in such talk and to begin it with infants and toddlers, conducting pretend conversations long before infants can understand the language. Typically, middle-class parents "ask" infants about their needs, then provide answers for the children ("Are you ready for a nap, now? Yes, you are, aren't you?"). Instructions are more likely to be given indirectly: "You don't want to make so much noise, do you?"[25] This kind of instruction is really more an invitation for a child to work through the reasoning behind an order and to internalize it. Middle-class parents may not think of themselves as conducting academic instruction for infants, but that is what they are doing with this indirect guidance.

Yet such instruction is quite different from what policy makers nowadays consider "academic" for young children: explicit training in letter and number recognition, letter-sound correspondence, and so on. Such drill in basic skills is unlikely to close the social class gap in learning.

Beginning in 1998, the federal government surveyed a national sample of kindergartners and their parents. The government intends to continue monitoring this sample of children as they move through school. Results so far illustrate how complex are the social class differences in children's academic preparation.

The survey includes data on family income, mother's education, father's education, mother's occupational status, and father's occupational status. Families, mothers, and fathers were ranked on these measures and then the five measures were averaged to create a composite called socioeconomic status, or SES. All children can then be divided into five SES quintiles, with those from the highest 20% of families by SES in the top quintile, and those from the lowest 20% of families by SES in the bottom quintile.[26]

As you would expect, entering kindergartners from higher social classes have more books in their homes and are read to more frequently by their parents. Yet surprisingly, smaller proportions of parents from higher SES quintiles than from lower SES quintiles believed that their children should know how to count when they first entered kindergarten. Smaller proportions of parents from higher SES quintiles believed that their children should know the alphabet letters before kindergarten.

Similarly in this government survey, black parents were more likely than white parents to believe that their children should count and know the alphabet when they entered kindergarten.[27]

In a few years, the government will report survey results on this group of kindergartners when they have third grade test scores. It is probably safe to predict that the average math and reading scores of higher-SES children, fewer of whose parents believe that their children should know the alphabet and count before kindergarten, will, in third grade, be higher than the average scores of children whose parents expected them to master the mechanics of reading and math before kindergarten. These parents from higher social classes were confident that raising children in an environment where literacy was valued and modeled would be a more important determinant of children's own literacy than drilling these children in the basics.

This relative lack of concern among higher-SES and white parents about very young children's mastery of the mechanics of reading and arithmetic does not mean that middle-class parents do not expect their children to absorb a familiarity with letters and numbers more naturally. "Touch and feel" books are among middle-class children's first toys. Later, alphabet blocks, magnetic letters on refrigerator doors, and labels taped on walls or objects are commonplace. Adult conversations vary by social class and become part of infants' and toddlers' background environments. When educated parents speak to each other in children's presence, even if the children are not being addressed directly, these parents use larger vocabularies and more complex sentences than less-educated parents do. Although middle-class preschoolers don't use advanced vocabulary words or sentence constructions themselves, they have an advantage when they hear their college-educated teachers speak or when these words and constructions are first encountered in books.

Soon after middle-class children become verbal, parents typically draw them into adult conversations so children can practice expressing their own opinions. Inclusion this early in adult conversations develops a sense of entitlement in children; they feel comfortable addressing adults as equals and without deference. Children who want reasons rather than simply submitting to direction on adult authority develop intellectual skills upon which later academic success in school will rely. Certainly, some lower-class children have such skills and some middle-class children lack them. But, on average, a sense of entitlement is social class-based.[28]

Working-class parents typically maintain firmer boundaries between adult and child worlds and are less likely to conduct conversations with pre-verbal children. Except when it is necessary to give a warning or issue other instructions, these parents less often address language directly to infants or toddlers. Unlike middle-class parents, working-class parents are less likely to simplify their language (using "baby talk") to show pre-verbal children how to converse, before the children are naturally ready to do so. If children need instruction, the orders are more likely to be direct, undisguised in question form.[29]

Working-class adults are more likely to engage in conversation with each other as though their infants, even older children, were not present. These parents make less of a deliberate effort to name objects and develop children's vocabularies. Such parents assume that children will learn to talk naturally. The children do, but not with the same sophistication as middle-class children. One study of black and white working-class families in the rural South in the 1970s found that black parents made a deliberate effort to teach pre-verbal children to name objects and to speak, but then were more likely than white working-class parents to abandon this activity once the children began talking; the black parents were more likely to view the job of teaching children to speak as having now been accomplished.[30]

The point here is not that there are childrearing practices, specific to the social classes, that are identical over time and geography. Rather, it is that such patterns do exist, and that they are bound to have an influence on how children learn, at what rate they learn, and what instructional approaches will be most effective in schools.

Today, these social class differences may help to explain why schools have more success in narrowing the achievement gap at lower grades, only to see it widen later on. In the upper grades, when posing more open-ended questions increasingly becomes a way to learn, middle-class children do what comes naturally to them. Lower-class children may succeed with direct instruction when learning basic skills, but are less prepared for the inquiry learning that is more important to academic success in upper grades. Tests in primary years have more questions of fact, identification, or simple recall, questions like those that children of lower-class families are used to answering when stories are read to them. But tests in the later grades contain more questions requiring abstract reasoning or conceptualization, the kinds of questions about stories that lower-class children are unused to answering but with which middle-class children have more experience.[31]

Social classes also differ in the responsibility children take for learning. Parents whose professional occupations entail authority and responsibility believe more strongly that they can affect their environments and solve problems. At work, they explore alternatives and negotiate compromises. They naturally express these personality traits at home when they design activities where children figure out solutions for themselves. Even the youngest middle-class children practice these traits that make academic success more likely when they negotiate what to wear or to eat. When middle-class parents give orders, the parents are more likely to explain why the rules are reasonable.

But parents whose jobs entail following orders or doing routine tasks exude a lesser sense of efficacy. Their children are less likely to be encouraged to negotiate clothing or food.[32] Lower-class parents are more likely to instruct children by giving directions without extended discussion. Following orders, after all, is how they themselves behave at work. So their children are also more likely to be fatalistic about obstacles they face, in and out of school.

The specific details of how childrearing practices tend to vary by social class can change from era to era, yet differences in average achievement of children from different social classes persist. It seems, for example, that while middle-class parents are today more "permissive" than working-class parents, the reverse used to be the case; current patterns began to be established in the second half of the 20th century. However, broad patterns continue, in ways that are little understood. A study based on surveys of parents in both the United States and Italy concluded, over 30 years ago, that parents whose occupations required creativity and decision making were less likely to punish their children for actions where the children's intent was desirable, even if matters did not work out as intended. Parents whose occupations were routine and who were closely supervised were more likely to base punishment on the children's actions themselves, regardless of intent.[33] In both countries, disciplinary practices varied by social class and in particular by whether parents (fathers in particular) had more or less autonomy and opportunities for creativity in their own work. This study provided further confirmation that achievement gaps by social class are not a peculiarly American phenomenon. They have persisted and are likely to continue in any society where the occupational structure requires vastly different skills and work habits for employees in different strata.

Differences in childrearing practices by social class extend not only to how behavior is rewarded or punished but to differences in conceptions of appropriate behavior. Middle-class parents' behavioral expectations are typically aligned with those of schools, while lower-class parents' expectations are sometimes in conflict. Lower-class children, for example, are often expected by their parents to fight back and defend themselves physically when they are provoked, and are ridiculed or punished if they fail to do so. Yet the opposite response is sanctioned in school.[34]

Middle-class children's self-assurance is enhanced in after-school activities that sometimes require large fees for enrollment and almost always require parents to have enough free time and resources to provide transportation. Organized sports, music, drama, and dance programs build self-confidence (with both trophies and admiring adult spectators) and discipline in middle-class children. Lower-class parents find the fees for such activities more daunting, and transportation may also be more of a problem. In many cases, such organized athletic and artistic activities are not available in lower-class neighborhoods, so lower-class children's sports are more informal and less confidence-building, and offer less opportunity to learn teamwork and self-discipline.[35] For children with greater self-confidence, unfamiliar school challenges can be exciting; such children are more likely to be from middle-class homes, and they are more likely to succeed than those who are less self-confident.[36]

Homework has been controversial for the last century, partly because educators observed that homework exacerbated the academic differences between middle- and working-class children, largely because middle-class parents are more likely to assist effectively with homework. In 1916, a North Carolina professor visited homes in Durham to record the help that middle- and working-class children got with their homework, and how this help influenced their grades in school. "Where the parents are capable of guiding the child and are inclined to supervise the home study, their children succeed in school," he observed, but because factory workers are less likely to supervise homework than are middle-class parents, schools "reproduce social inequality."[37] In 1940, a New Rochelle school official led a national campaign to abolish homework and compensate for it by extending the school day – partly because, he observed, children from lower-income families did not benefit from parental support for homework as did middle-class students.[38]

Homework would increase the social class achievement gap even if all parents were able to assist their children with homework. Parents from different social classes supervise homework differently. Consistent with overall patterns of language use, middle-class parents – particularly those whose own occupational habits require problem solving – are more likely to assist children by posing questions that decompose problems and that help children figure out the correct answers. Lower-class parents are more likely to guide their children with direct instructions. Children from both strata may go to school with the correct answers to homework problems, but middle-class children will have gained more in intellectual power from the exercise than do lower-class children.[39]

Again, remember, these traits are not perfectly correlated with social class; there is overlap between the average characteristics of lower- and middle-class children. Some lower-class children have more self-confidence than typical middle-class children. Some middle-class parents have more authoritarian styles, and some working-class parents want their children to practice working their way out of difficulties and to understand the reasons for rules the children must follow. But, on average, good schools and teachers will have more academic success with middle-class children whose parents feel confident they can shape their environments, and who do not have the habit of blind obedience but rather believe that rules are only as legitimate as they are reasonable.

There is no suggestion here that the childrearing practices of middle-class parents are morally superior to those of lower-class parents, nor that middle-class childrearing practices develop children who are more psychologically well-adjusted or who function better in all adult roles. Taken to an extreme, many middle-class childrearing practices described here can result in selfish and otherwise "spoiled" children. The only suggestion here is that children who are raised with self-confidence and a sense of entitlement, whether spoiled or not, can have an advantage when called upon to master difficult academic material in school.

Twenty years ago, two researchers from the University of Kansas visited the homes of families from different social classes to monitor conversations between parents and toddlers. The researchers found that, on average, professional parents spoke over 2,000 words per hour to their children, working-class parents spoke about 1,300, and welfare mothers spoke about 600. So by age 3, children of professionals had vocabularies that were nearly 50% greater than those of working-class children and twice as large as those of welfare children. Indeed, by three years of age, the *children* of professionals had larger vocabularies themselves than the vocabularies used by *adults* from welfare families in speaking to their children. Cumulatively, the Kansas researchers estimated that by the time children were four years old, ready to enter preschool, a typical child in a professional family would have accumulated experience with 45 million words, compared to only 13 million for a typical child in a welfare family.[40]

Grandparents' social class backgrounds can also have a direct effect on student achievement. This may widen the black–white achievement gap because black children typically have more contact with their grandparents than do white children. This difference is partly due to a higher rate of single and teenage motherhood in the black than in the white community, and a tradition in the black community of close ties between nuclear and extended families, dating in part from the difficulty of maintaining the integrity of nuclear families during slavery.[41] So childrearing often falls to grandmothers when mothers are at work. Although black grandparents are more mature than teen mothers, and children being raised by grandmothers benefit from this greater maturity, it is also the case that black grandparents have significantly less education than white grandparents or black parents. As a result, because black children are raised by grandparents to a greater extent than are white children, black children's verbal fluency, vocabulary, and later academic achievement will partly reflect the lower education level of their grandparents.[42]

Deficits like these cannot be made up by schools alone, no matter how high the teachers' expectations. For all children to achieve the same goals, those from the lower class would have to enter school with verbal fluency similar to that of middle-class children.

The Kansas researchers also tracked how often parents verbally encouraged children's behavior, and how often parents reprimanded their children. Toddlers of professionals got an average of six encouragements per reprimand. Working-class children received two. For welfare children, the ratio was reversed, an average of one encouragement for two prohibitions. It seems reasonable to expect that when these children later go to school, their teachers cannot fully offset these differences from early interactions. Children whose initiative was encouraged from an early age are probably more likely, on average, to take responsibility for their own learning.

If you live in a diverse urban area, you can easily conduct your own ethnographic research on this topic and need not rely on the rich sociological literature to which this chapter makes reference. When I wrote these words, I was a visiting professor at Teachers College at Columbia University in Manhattan; I discussed with my students how, by riding the Broadway subway line or by taking the bus, they could come to a more profound understanding than most policy makers possess of the gap in achievement between middle-class and lower-class children. As my students traveled from the immigrant community of Washington Heights into mostly black West Harlem and then into the affluent white Upper West Side, they could observe middle- and working-class mothers, black and white, with young children. These mothers' behaviors, highly correlated with their social class, were easy to spot – middle-class mothers in non-stop conversations with their pre-verbal infants or toddlers, commenting on surroundings, recounting events of the day, and giving indirect instructions; working-class mothers, mostly black and Hispanic, speaking to children mostly when instructions were needed, and then with direct language: "Get up, now," not "Isn't this our stop?" Of course, as always, there were exceptions to these generalizations. But after a few hours of observation, clear patterns emerged, patterns that can fairly accurately be used to predict differences in these children's average achievement when they later go to school.

Social class differences in role modeling also make a social class achievement gap almost inevitable. If adults perform jobs requiring little academic skill, their children's images of their own futures are influenced. Again, beware of deterministic simplification: some lower-class children, despite few educated role models, succeed in school, perhaps as the first children in their families to attend college. But on average, these children must struggle harder to motivate themselves to achieve than children who assume that, like their parents' social circle, the only roles are doctor, lawyer, teacher, social worker, manager, administrator, or businessperson.

For typically, and predictably, middle-class professional parents tend to associate with, and be friends with, similarly educated professionals. Working-class parents have fewer professional friends. One survey of parents from different social classes found that 93% of middle-class parents had a friend or relative who was a teacher, compared with 43% of working-class parents and 36% of poor parents. Medical doctors were identified as friends by 70% of middle-class parents, 14% of working-class parents, and 18% of poor parents.[43] These adult friendships reinforce how children imagine their future roles, and what they strive to achieve.

In middle-class homes, "what do you want to be when you grow up?" is a frequent question, posed in a way that assumes choices are limitless. Low-income families ask the question less often; because parental occupational roles have had more to do with economic conditions than with choice, parents assume their children will face similar constraints.

Even lower-class children now usually say they plan to attend college. College has become such a broad rhetorical goal that black eighth-graders tell surveyors that they expect to earn college degrees as often as white eighth-graders respond in this way.[44] But despite these intentions to pursue education, fewer black than white eighth-graders actually graduate from high school four years later (72% vs. 82%),[45] fewer black than white eighth-graders eventually enroll in college the year after high school graduation (44% vs. 58%),[46] and even fewer persist to get bachelor's degrees (17% vs. 35%).[47]

A bigger reason than affordability is that, while lower-class students *say* they plan on college, they don't feel as much parental, community, or peer pressure to take the courses or to get the grades to qualify and to study hard to become more attractive to college admission offices. Lower-class parents say they expect children to get good grades, but they are less likely to reinforce these expectations behaviorally. Middle-class youth are more likely to be punished by their parents for poor grades, or rewarded for good ones, and black parents are less likely to reinforce high expectations than are white parents at a similar income level.[48] Teachers and counselors can stress doing well in school to lower-class children, but such lessons compete with children's own self-images, formed early in life and reinforced daily at home.

These class distinctions are not of recent origin. Fifty years ago, sociologists at the Harvard University "Mobility Project" observed that upper-class children with high test scores were likely to attend college, while lower-class children with similarly high test scores were not likely to do so. The researchers anticipated this finding. But they puzzled about why some lower-middle-class children with high test scores actually made it to college, while other lower-middle-class children with equally high test scores did not. Surveying these youths and their families, the researchers concluded that the difference was mostly attributable to the aspirations of parents for their children to rise in the social structure, and the pressure these parents placed on their children to do so.[49] Not much has changed since then. When schools succeed with some children from lower in the social structure but fail with others, we are too quick to conclude that the teachers or schools of the first group must be superior. This assumption may be accurate in many cases. But in others the difference is beyond the reach of schools, due to the range of parental ambition even within a particular social class.

While watching soccer games or waiting for piano lessons to end, middle-class parents consult one another about the experiences their children share at school.[50] When parents want to influence a school policy (for example, if they prefer that their children be assigned to a different teacher's classroom, if they want their children admitted to a "gifted" program, or if they seek special education services for children who are having difficulty), middle-class parents are more confident about challenging administrators and more likely to have support from other parents with similar concerns or with expertise to share.[51] No matter how attentive school administrators are to individual children, youngsters whose parents intervene will have an edge; on average, which children get this edge is predictable by parents' social class. This difference also adds to the gap in academic achievement between lower- and middle-class children.

The best schools try to address the alienation of many lower-class parents from their children's schooling, because if parents get more involved they can help raise their children's expectations of themselves. Parental involvement in schools is one way of counteracting the dissonance that children perceive between their parents' professed support for academic achievement and their parents' actions, which often send the opposite message. So educators often try to get parents more involved in school, by observing classrooms, helping teachers, ushering field trips, or becoming active in the PTA. But while these forms of parental involvement may help a little, they can't do much to narrow the class-based achievement gap because the forms taken by parental involvement are also class-based. Parents whose own jobs are routine, where they are expected to follow well-defined roles, often assume that schools should operate similarly. "Education," they think, falls under the job classification of teacher and it is not a parent's place to question how teachers perform their assigned tasks. Middle-class parents, in contrast, more easily assume a right to collaborate with teachers because these parents' own professional roles often place a premium on making suggestions to others whose formal responsibilities differ. In more affluent middle-class communities, where teachers have educations no greater, and perhaps substantially less, than the parents' own, parents' confidence about intervening grows even stronger.

Several years ago, I participated in a research team that conducted a series of interviews of parents and teachers in public and private schools in California. We were trying to determine if there was something public school administrators could learn from educators in the private sector, so that the public school leaders could duplicate the widely reported greater parental involvement in private schools. What we found was that, contrary to popular belief, parental involvement did not vary by whether a school was public or private but rather by whether the school's parents were lower or middle class.

In parochial schools in low-income neighborhoods, for example, we found teachers who complained about the lack of parental involvement as much as teachers in any public school. These private school teachers blamed the lack of parental involvement for their pupils' low test scores. In these schools, if the principal was able to get parents involved, it was mostly to help with fundraising, by selling candy, for example.

In public schools in affluent communities, in contrast, we found parental involvement that exceeded anything experienced in typical private schools. Teachers in these public schools complained to us that parents were so intrusive that it was impossible to deliver a coherent curriculum. One teacher reported that each week she received a curricular suggestion from a parent of nearly every child in her class. The involvement of parents was so burdensome in one middle-class public school that it had a high turnover of teachers; they often quit to find work at schools where parents were less involved.[52]

Cultural influences on achievement, black underachievement, and racial discrimination

Parents from some immigrant cultures express even greater deference toward teachers than do American-born lower-class parents. These immigrant parents fear (sometimes accurately) that their grammar will not earn teachers' respect or that they will not understand what teachers say. Cultural differences influence achievement in other ways as well. Immigrant students from Asia often achieve more in American schools (again, only on average) than similarly low-income blacks or Latin Americans. Too often, commentators assume that the cause of these differences must be that teachers and schools have lower expectations of Latin American or black students. While low expectations may play a role, it is not a complete explanation.

The religious values of some immigrant groups may have an impact. Asian students with Confucian traditions are often taught obligations to serve their parents with academic achievement.[53] Latin American and Asian immigrant families may have similar incomes and be similarly close-knit, but where the former expect children to serve by assisting with chores, the latter expect them to do so by studying.[54] Lending further support to the idea that culture plays a role is the fact that students whose mothers were born in Asia typically have higher academic achievement than Asian students with American-born mothers who are more likely to be culturally assimilated and less likely to place intense pressure on children to achieve academically.[55]

Similar cultural differences have shown up in the past. Many American believe that public schools did a better job of educating and assimilating immigrants a century ago than they do now. This impression is not confirmed by historical fact. In truth, the children of some immigrant groups a century ago did relatively well in school while the children of other groups did relatively poorly, just as is the case today. For example, although Eastern European Jewish and Southern Italian immigrants arrived in the United States at roughly the same time, had similar poverty, and were both non-English speaking, their children performed very differently in school, with Jews posting higher achievement and attainment. The hand-wringing of a century ago about the high failure and dropout rates of children from Italian and some other immigrant groups is remarkably similar to concerns commonly expressed today about the children of peasant immigrants from Latin America. In the early 20th century, schools were engines of mobility only for some groups and not for others. After one generation in this country, typical children of some ethnicities went to college in large numbers, but children of other ethnicities took two and sometimes three generations to experience similar attainment.[56]

Cultural traits can have complex causes. Partly, a black community culture of underachievement may help to explain why even middle-class black children often don't do as well in school as other children from similar socioeconomic backgrounds. On average, middle-class black students don't study as hard as white middle-class students, and blacks are more disruptive in class than whites from similar income strata. Low expectations that teachers have of black students may be unfair to those who desire to excel, but these expectations are partly based on the real experiences of teachers with black students who, more than whites, perform below their potential. When such students get to high school, their potential may no longer be visible.[57]

This culture of underachievement is easier to understand than to cure. Throughout U.S. history, many black students who excelled in school were not rewarded in the labor market for their effort. Although a black professional class (doctors, teachers, lawyers) served segregated black communities, many well-educated black adults could only find work as servants (Pullman car porters, for example) or, in business and clerical fields, as assistants to less-qualified whites. Some commentators have publicized the idea that these practices have entirely disappeared in the United States and that black and white workers with similar test scores now have similar earnings and occupational status.[58]

It is certainly true that blacks who excel academically are rewarded in the labor market more than used to be the case.[59] But it is also true that labor market discrimination, even for black workers whose test scores are comparable to those of white workers, continues to play an important role. Racial discrimination against black workers with adequate cognitive skills is more pronounced for high school graduates and for males than it is for college graduates and for females. In fact, strong evidence suggests that black college graduates and black females now can expect to earn as much, if not more, than white college graduates and white females whose test scores are similar. But against black males with only a high school education, discrimination persists.[60]

Evidence of ongoing discrimination comes from the continued success of employment discrimination cases. For example, in a prominent 1996 case Texaco settled for a payment of $176 million to black employees after taped conversations of executives revealed pervasive racist attitudes, presumably not restricted to executives only of this corporation. Other evidence comes from studies that find black workers with darker complexions have dramatically less labor market success than black workers with lighter complexions but with identical education, age, and criminal records.[61] Still more evidence comes from audit studies in which black and white applicants with similar qualifications were sent out to apply for job vacancies; the white applicants were far more successful than the black applicants. Indeed, in one recent study where young, well-groomed, and articulate black and white college graduates, posing as high school graduates with identical qualifications, applied for entry-level jobs, whites who reported criminal records on their applications got positive responses more often than blacks who reported no criminal records.[62]

It does not take a lot of discrimination for the effects to accumulate. Young workers tend to change jobs frequently, so if young black workers experience discrimination, the attitudes toward employers of some of these workers may become more mistrusting, and future employers may treat these workers less favorably because of the workers' less cooperative attitudes. This compounding of an initial experience of discrimination can lead to a lifetime of reduced earnings for black workers whose skills are similar to those of white workers.[63]

So the expectation of black students that their academic efforts will not be rewarded to the same extent as the efforts of their white peers is rational for the majority of black students who do not expect to complete college. Some will reduce their academic effort as a result. We can say that they should not do so and, instead, should redouble their efforts in response to the greater obstacles they face. But as long as racial discrimination persists in the labor market, the average academic achievement of black students will be lower than the average achievement of white students, simply because many black students (especially males), who see that academic effort has less of a payoff for them than it has for whites, can be expected to respond by reducing their effort.

Even if discrimination were suddenly to end completely, and clearly it has not, community expectations that academic prowess will be

unrewarded, based on 150 years of reality, would not disappear over-
night. The culture of many black families is one where anticipation of
mistreatment remains prevalent. The grandparents and in some cases
the parents of today's black workers entered the labor market at a time
when explicit "whites-only need apply" hiring practices were prevalent, even in Northern cities where the practices were nominally unlaw-
ful.[64]

In a recent survey in four major cities, two-thirds of black adults
said they believed they still experienced "a lot" of discrimination.[65] When
black students who say they value education are pressed harder by in-
terviewers to state what they really believe, they respond affirmatively
to statements like "people in my family haven't been treated fairly at
work no matter how much education they have."[66] It should be expected
that black students will absorb this anticipation from their homes and
communities, and that it will not be erased simply by insisting that teachers hold high expectations for black students.

So it is not surprising that black students whose parents were born
in the Caribbean perform better, on average, than black students whose
parents were born in the United States. Unlike parents born here, immigrant blacks believe that education offers opportunity for mobility, and
they have not become cynical from generations of frustrated ambitions.
Immigrant parents from Caribbean cultures, like Asian parents, place
greater pressure on their children to succeed academically.[67]

It is commonplace for blacks to say they have to be twice as good
as whites to qualify for the same position.[68] Some black students respond to this folk wisdom by working twice as hard. But more respond
with lassitude. Inspirational teachers may push some students from the
second group into the first, but even the best teachers are unlikely to
succeed with all black students. Failing only with a few explains part of
the gap in achievement between black and white students, on average.

There is also an oppositional culture in the black community, in
which dignity and self-respect have been earned by opposition to majority institutions, including public schools, that were oppressive or worse.
This attitude should also be understood historically; generations of black
adults have maintained their dignity by withholding respect, however
privately it was necessary to do so, from white institutions. Perhaps
today that oppositional culture is no longer a rational reaction to American institutions as they presently operate. But it would be naive to ex-

pect black students, raised in nearly homogenous de-facto segregated communities, suddenly to enter school without pride in their mistrust of majority institutions, including educational ones. This too contributes to the achievement gap.[69]

Again, these cultural explanations are not determinist. Some black students succeed despite cultural pressures not to do so. And, at best, cultural factors explain only part of the difference between black and white student achievement, most of which is attributable to the fact that black families, on average, have lower social class characteristics than white families.

Health differences and school performance

Despite these big race and social class differences in childrearing, role modeling, and cultural characteristics, the poor achievement of lower-class students may not mainly be caused by these differences. Childrearing practices, role modeling, and values play a role, but even more important may be differences in the actual social and economic conditions of the classes.

Vision
Overall, lower-income children are in poorer health. Their greater incidence of vision problems has the most obvious impact on their relative lack of school success. Children with vision problems have difficulty reading and seeing what teachers write on the board. Trying to read, their eyes may wander or have difficulty tracking print or focusing. Tests of vision show that these problems are inversely proportional to family income; in the United States, poor children have severe vision impairment at twice the normal rate.[70] Juvenile delinquents especially have extraordinarily high rates of such problems; difficulties in seeing and focusing may contribute to their lack of mainstream success.[71] Foster children, who experience even more stress than most disadvantaged children, also have unusually high vision failure rates.[72]

Fifty percent or more of minority and low-income children have vision problems that interfere with their academic work.[73] A few require glasses, but more need eye-exercise therapy to correct focusing, converging, and tracking problems. Some studies find that test scores of lower-class children who get therapy and free glasses rise relative to those of children whose vision does not need support. In one experiment where therapy or lenses were provided to randomly selected fourth-graders from low-income families, children who received optometric services gained in reading achievement beyond the normal growth for their age, while children in the control group, who did not get these services, fell farther behind. [74]

Children who are believed to have learning disabilities are also more likely to have vision impairment. Disproportionate assignment of low-income black children to special education may partly reflect a failure to correct their vision. Often, when children seem to have puzzling difficulties learning to read, the explanation is no more complex than that they cannot see. Sometimes, vision difficulties remain undiagnosed in middle-class children as well, leading also to inappropriate special education placement. But more often, the failure to diagnose is a problem of the poor.

Lower-class children are more likely to suffer from vision problems because of their less adequate prenatal development than are middle-class children whose pregnant mothers had better medical care and nutrition.[75] Visual deficits also arise because poor children are more likely to watch too much television, activity that does not train the eye to develop hand-eye coordination and depth perception; 42% of black fourth-graders watch six hours or more of television a day, compared to 13% of whites.[76] Middle-class children are also more likely to have manipulative toys that develop visual skills, what is commonly termed hand-eye coordination.[77]

Vision screening in schools usually only asks children to read charts for nearsightedness. Most schoolchildren are never tested for farsightedness or for difficulty with tracking, the problems that are most likely to affect academic performance.[78] Even when testing leads to optometric referrals, low-income children are less likely to follow up. When they get prescriptions for lenses, they less frequently obtain them or wear them to school. Partly, even subsidized costs seem like an unnecessary expense to parents, especially because their children seem to function normally in everyday life; it is only in the reading of print that children's vision deficiencies may become problems. Frames, even in subsidized programs, are typically unfashionable, and children are unwilling to wear them to correct difficulties that impede reading but that don't interfere with most other functions.[79]

Hearing

Lower-class children also have more hearing problems.[80] These may result from more ear infections that occur in children whose overall health is less robust. But though ear infections are easily treatable for middle-class children with access to good pediatric care, lower-class children whose hearing is less acute will achieve less, on average, in school. If poor children simply had as much medical treatment for ear infections as middle-class children, they could pay better attention and the achievement gap would narrow a bit.[81]

Oral health

Children without dental care are more likely to have toothaches; untreated cavities are nearly three times as prevalent among poor as among middle-class children.[82] Although not every dental cavity leads to a toothache, some do. Children with toothaches, even minor ones, pay less attention in class and are distracted more during tests, on average, than children with healthy teeth. So differences in dental care also contribute another bit to the achievement gap between lower- and middle-class children.

Lead exposure

Children who live in older buildings have more lead dust exposure that harms cognitive functioning and behavior.[83] High lead levels also contribute to hearing loss.[84] Low-income children have dangerously high blood lead levels at five times the rate of middle-class children.[85]

Indeed, lead poisoning now exacerbates the achievement gap more than it used to. A generation ago, all children suffered declines in I.Q. from breathing leaded fumes from auto exhaust. For middle-class children, this was the main source of lead exposure. With gasoline now unleaded, middle-class children have less lead exposure, but other sources remain for low-income children who continue to suffer cognitive impairment from lead in wall and house paint to which they are exposed. Although lead-based paint was banned from residential construction in 1978, low-income children more likely live in buildings constructed prior to that date and in buildings that are not repainted often enough to prevent old layers from peeling off. Urban children are also more likely to attend older schools, built when water pipes contained lead. New York City, Baltimore, and Washington, D.C. have recently found it necessary to shut off school drinking fountains because lead exceeded dangerous levels.[86]

Low-income children are also more likely to live in areas where leaded paint peels from fire escapes or steel beams of elevated trains.[87] Compounding the problem further for immigrant children, their families often come to this country with lead poisoning because they migrate from countries where lead-based paint is still used for dishes and pottery, or in remedies and cosmetics.[88] Not only is the cognitive harm already done when these children arrive in the United States, but consumption of such products sometimes continues in immigrant communities here, which import the products from the home country.[89]

Asthma

Lower-class children, particularly those who live in densely populated city neighborhoods, are also more likely to contract asthma – the asthma rate is substantially higher for urban than for rural children, for children whose families are on welfare than for non-welfare families, for children from single-parent than from two-parent families, and for poor than for non-poor families.[90] A survey in New York City found that one of every four children in Harlem suffers from asthma, a rate six times as great as that for all children.[91] A Chicago survey found a nearly identical rate for black children and a rate of one in three for Puerto Ricans.[92] The disease is provoked in part from breathing fumes from low-grade home heating oil and from diesel trucks and buses (school buses that idle in front of schools are a particularly serious problem), as well as from excessive dust and allergic reactions to mold, cockroaches, and secondhand smoke.[93] In the Chicago neighborhoods with the highest asthma rates, nearly half the children suffering from the disease live in homes where adults smoke.[94]

Asthma keeps children up at night, and, if they do make it to school the next day, they are likely to be drowsy and less attentive. Middle-class children typically get treatment for asthma symptoms, while low-income children get it less often. Asthma has become the biggest cause of chronic school absence.[95] Low-income children with asthma are about 80% more likely than middle-class children with asthma to miss more than seven days of school a year from the disease.[96] Children with asthma refrain from exercise and so are less physically fit. Drowsy and more irritable, they also have more behavioral problems that depress achievement.[97]

Asthma's relatively greater effect on low-income children adds another bit to the explanation of why poor children's school achievement, on average, is lower. Probably because of environmental factors, asthma seems to be growing rapidly – the asthma rate for all children increased by 50% from 1980 to 1996 and doubled for African Americans.[98] If these rates are accurate, the effect of the increase is to offset, to some slight extent, efforts to raise achievement for disadvantaged children.[99]

Medical care

Children without regular medical care are also more likely to contract other illnesses, some serious, others minor, that keep them out of school. Despite federal programs to make medical care available to low-income children, there remain gaps in both access and utilization. Many eligible families are not enrolled because of ignorance, fear, or lack of belief in the importance of medical care.

Under the 1996 federal welfare reform law, recipients who went to work at low-wage jobs that provided no health insurance continued to be eligible for Medicaid. But the bureaucratic difficulties of enrolling in Medicaid, including the fact that welfare officials in many states discouraged working welfare recipients from enrolling, has meant that many low-income children are still not enrolled. The federal Child Health Insurance Program, adopted in 1997 and intended to extend health care to all low-income children, has helped, but many low-income children are still uninsured.[100] Twenty percent of poor children are without consistent health insurance, compared to 12% of all children; 13% of black children are without insurance, compared to 8% of white children.[101] This too adds to the achievement gap.

Even with health insurance, low-wage work interferes with the utilization of medical care. Parents who are paid hourly wages lose income when they take their children to doctors. Parents who work at blue-collar jobs risk being fired for excessive absence, so are likely to skip well-baby and routine pediatric care and go to doctors only in emergencies. Salaried middle-class parents have more flexibility to schedule doctor visits, for themselves and for their children, without loss of job or income.

Lower-class families with health insurance who attempt to use it also confront huge disparities in medical facilities. An analysis of California communities found that urban neighborhoods with high poverty and high concentrations of black and Hispanic residents had one primary

care physician for every 4,000 residents. Neighborhoods that were neither high poverty nor high minority had one primary care physician for
every 1,200 residents.[102] At the extremes, one low-income minority Los
Angeles neighborhood has one primary care physician for every 13,000
residents, while a nearby high-income neighborhood has one for every
200 residents.[103] These gaps are mirrored nationwide. Low-income families, with or without insurance, are more likely to use emergency rooms
and less likely to use primary care doctors, even for routine care.

As a result, black preschoolers are one-third less likely than whites
to get standard vaccinations for diphtheria, measles, and influenza.[104]
This ongoing difference in regular pediatric care is probably the reason
why poor children lose 30% more days from school than the non-poor,
on average.[105] The difference in school attendance, attributable to differences in access to health care alone, causes a difference in average
achievement between black and white children. Good teaching can't do
much for children who are not in school.

Use of alcohol

Youngsters whose mothers drank during pregnancy have more difficulty with academic subjects, are less able to focus attention, have poorer
memory skills, less ability to reason, lower I.Q.'s, less social compe-
tence, and more aggression in the classroom.[106] On into adolescence,
these children continue to have difficulty learning.[107]

Fetal alcohol syndrome, a collection of the most severe cognitive,
physical, and behavioral difficulties experienced by children of prenatal drinkers, is 10 times more frequent for low-income black than for
middle-class white children.[108] Data are not available for disparities by
social class for less severe symptoms of prenatal alcohol consumption,
but it can be presumed that here, too, the consequences are greater for
the lower class. Although affluent women actually consume more alcohol than lower-class women, the affluent tend to drink more evenly.[109]
Low-income women tend to drink more heavily in binges that apparently do more harm to a developing fetus.[110]

Smoking

Smoking in pregnancy also contributes to lower achievement. Children
of mothers who smoked prenatally do more poorly on cognitive tests,
their language develops more poorly, they have more serious behav-

ioral problems, more hyperactivity, and more juvenile crime.[111] Because secondhand smoke also causes asthma, children whose mothers smoke after pregnancy also more likely have low achievement.

Maternal smoking behavior adds another bit to the gap; 30% of poor women smoke, compared to 22% of non-poor women.[112] During pregnancy, one-fourth of high school dropouts smoke, 50% more than the rate for high school graduates and 13 times more than that for college graduates.[113]

Birth weight

Partly from mothers' prenatal smoking, low-income children are more likely to be born prematurely or with low birth weights and to suffer from cognitive problems as a result; low-birth-weight babies, on average, have lower I.Q. scores and are more likely to have mild learning disabilities and attention disorders.[114] Thirteen percent of black children are born with low birth weight, double the rate for whites.[115] Even if all children benefited from equally high-quality instruction, this difference alone would ensure lower average achievement for blacks.

Recent studies of low-income, mostly Puerto Rican and black women in East Harlem found that exposure to commonly used domestic pesticides was associated with children being born with smaller head circumference and much lower weight (as much as 6 ounces smaller birth weight from exposure). Head circumference, along with low birth weight, is associated with children's lower I.Q. and more behavioral problems. The Environmental Protection Agency has banned these pesticides and they are being phased out, but they are still being sold in minority and low-income communities, sometimes in violation of the ban. As a result of the ban, however, fewer women are now exposed to these pesticides, and their children are being born healthier.[116]

Low birth weight is only partly caused by inadequate prenatal care, exposure to urban pollutants, diet, smoking, and drinking. The interaction of poor health habits with other stresses exacerbates children's adverse outcomes. Maternal stress has hormonal consequences that interfere with the absorption of nutrients on which a healthy fetus depends.[117] Partly for this reason, low birth weight, alcohol consumption, and smoking all have greater negative effects on poor children than on middle-class children who were exposed to similar risks. Poor women, with greater stress and less adequate nutrition, can tolerate less smoke and alcohol and still deliver a healthy baby than women whose better over-all health conditions can protect their fetuses from the effects of alcohol or smoking.[118] Perhaps also, middle-class children can more easily overcome earlier health shocks or disadvantage, rebounding when they later experience healthier environments after exposure to risk.[119]

Nutrition

Poor nutrition also directly contributes to an achievement gap between lower- and middle-class children. Hunger is not nearly as serious here as in Third World countries where children are so nutrient-deprived that brain growth is impeded, but moderate under-nutrition of the kind found in the United States does affect academic performance, particularly if it is sustained over long periods of time.[120]

Low-income kindergartners whose height and weight are below normal for children their age tend to have lower test scores.[121] Iron deficiency anemia also affects cognitive ability; 8% of all children suffer from anemia, but 20% of black children do so.[122] Anemia also makes it more probable that children will absorb lead to which they have been exposed.[123] Compared to middle-class children, the poor also have deficiencies of other vitamins and minerals.[124] In experiments where pupils received inexpensive vitamin and mineral supplements, test scores rose from that treatment alone.[125]

Indeed, the relationship between good nutrition and achievement is so obvious that some school districts, under pressure recently to increase poor children's test scores, boosted the caloric content of school lunches on test days. Districts that pursued this strategy posted bigger score gains than those that did not.[126] This does not suggest that children in schools without this caloric boost were hungry or were insufficiently nourished, but only that, following mothers' conventional wisdom, children should "eat a good breakfast" (or lunch) to perform to their potential.

For low-income children, hunger does make a small contribution to the achievement gap, and lack of good nourishment probably makes a somewhat larger contribution.[127] In 2002, at least 2% of children from low-income families seem to have experienced real hunger at some time in the year, even if briefly.[128] Needs for food aid have grown so that many cities operating community pantries have reduced the amount of food distributed per family, and more families with emergency needs are now being turned away from food distribution centers because of insufficient supplies.[129]

Welfare-to-work policies seemed to make sense as a way to encourage poor parents to take more responsibility for supporting their children, but the policies may have had a perverse effect for hunger. Food stamp use has fallen because many welfare-to-work participants were either misled or wrongly concluded that they became ineligible. In 1994, 86% of eligible children were in families getting stamps; by 1998, the figure dropped to 69%.[130] New York City, for example, distributes food stamps to only half of those eligible.[131] In light of these trends, it would be astonishing if the academic achievement gap did not grow between well-nourished and poorly nourished or hungry children.

The government subsidizes free breakfast and lunch programs for low-income children; most enroll for lunch, but few for breakfast. Even with the best of intentions, breakfast programs are hard for schools to organize. Arranging to supervise breakfast before classes begin is one problem. Another is scheduling buses to bring eligible children, but not others, to school early.

The result is that only a minority of eligible children get subsidized breakfast in school. In New York State, for example, only 35% of children who get lunch also get breakfast to which they are entitled. Texas with 50%, and California with 40% don't do much better.[132] Urban participation is lower still: in New York City, only 26% of children who get subsidized lunch also get subsidized breakfast.[133]

Yet breakfast programs affect achievement. School nutrition programs mostly assume that children can learn well even if they have to wait until lunch time for a nutritious meal. Evidence from school breakfast programs confirms the folly of this approach. Poor children who get school breakfasts have better test scores and attendance and are better behaved – less hyperactive, for example – than similar children who are not fed.[134]

Like social class differences in childrearing and literacy practices, each of these differences in health – in vision, hearing, oral health, lead exposure, asthma, use of alcohol, smoking, birth weight, and nutrition – when considered separately has only a tiny influence on the academic achievement gap. But together, they add up to a cumulative disadvantage for lower-class children that can't help but depress average performance.

Housing and student mobility

Other socioeconomic differences also add up. Housing is one. Urban rents have risen faster than working-class incomes. Even families where parents' employment is stable are more likely to move when they fall behind in rent payments. In some schools in minority neighborhoods, this need to move boosts mobility rates to over 100%: for every seat in the school, more than two children were enrolled at some time during the year.[135] The lack of affordable housing is not the sole cause of lower-class children's high mobility – bouts of unemployment and family breakup are among the others – but it is almost certainly one of the important causes.

A 1994 government report found that 30% of the poorest children (those from families with annual incomes of less than $10,000) had attended at least three different schools by third grade, while only 10% of middle-class children (from families with annual incomes of over $25,000) did so. Black children were more than twice as likely as white children to change schools this much.[136] Schools with high mobility are often disrupted by the need to reconstitute classrooms to avoid placing all newcomers together, or because classes get too large or too small from new arrivals and departures.[137]

So high mobility depresses achievement not only for children who move – each move means readjusting to teachers, classmates, and curriculum – but also for stable children in these schools whose classes are reconstituted and whose teachers use more discrete units and are thus unable to integrate instruction over time. Teachers with mobile students are more likely to review old than introduce new material, and less able to adjust instruction to the individual needs of unfamiliar students. A recent statistical analysis concluded that if black students' average mobility were reduced to the level of white students' average mobility, this improvement in housing stability alone would eliminate 14% of the black–white test score gap. Reducing the mobility of low-income students (those eligible for lunch subsidies) to that of other students would eliminate 7% of the test score gap by income.[138]

Middle-class children usually have a quiet place at home, perhaps their own bedrooms, to read or do homework. Children in more crowded housing can less often escape television, conversation, or siblings. Earlier, this chapter discussed how homework itself exacerbates the achievement gap because less-educated parents are less able to help their children think through the problems homework poses. For children with inadequate housing without quiet study space, homework creates further disadvantage.

An achievement gap between stable and mobile or poorly housed pupils is inevitable, on average, even though some mobile children overcome their hardships and some stable children fail to take advantage of their opportunities.

Social class differences between blacks and whites with similar incomes

An aspect of the black–white gap that puzzles many observers is its persistence even for whites and blacks from families whose incomes are similar. Poor whites perform, on average, better than poor blacks, and middle-class whites better than middle-class blacks. How can this be, people wonder? Even if differences in social and economic conditions affect learning, why should there be a gap when income is similar? Surely, many people speculate, even if school efforts are frustrated by children's poverty, why should schools be less effective with poor children from one racial group than from another?

As discussed above, cultural differences explain part of this added black–white gap, after controlling for income, but probably only a small part. The most important reason to expect achievement differences for black and white children whose families have similar incomes is that income is an inexact proxy for the many social class characteristics that differentiate blacks from whites whose current-year income is the same. For example, blacks whose incomes are near the poverty line are more likely to have been poor for several years than whites whose poverty is more often episodic. Children from permanently poor black families will have more obstacles to learning than white children with the same income in the current year, but who are only temporarily poor.[139] For example, both children and adults are in poorer health the longer they have lived in poor families.[140]

Partly, the length of time spent in poverty affects student achievement because income affects learning differently at different ages. For adolescents, family income has little effect once their prior achievement is taken into account. What matters most, even for subsequent achievement, is family income in early childhood.[141] Family income of children below 5 years of age has a bigger impact on whether these children complete high school than their family income later when they are actually in high school.[142] This makes sense in light of the importance of early childhood nutrition, health, and nurturing, discussed earlier in this chapter. Families who are poor for longer periods are more likely to have had low income in their children's early years. So the achievement of black children would typically be lower than that of white children from families with similar current low incomes, because the black families were likely to have experienced longer bouts of poverty.

When parents suffer unemployment, children's achievement tends to suffer. Parents under stress from unemployment are more likely to discipline children arbitrarily, leading to more misbehavior. When their parents lose work, adolescents are more likely to be delinquent, use drugs, lose faith in the future, and suffer from depression.[143] Recovery from these effects is rarely instantaneous. Between black and white families whose current incomes are similar, black workers are more likely to have suffered recent job loss than whites, even if they are now re-employed.

There are also differences between blacks and whites with middle-class incomes. Here again, many observers are puzzled that black middle-class students do more poorly than white middle-class students whose families have similar current incomes. Partly, this difference occurs because black middle-class families are more likely than white families at the same current income level to have poor extended family members to whom some support is given; as a result, black middle-class families are likely to have less income available to spend on children than white families with the same total income. Black families are also larger on average than white ones.[144] Families with fewer children have more income to spend per child than families with more children.

Children from small families have higher average achievement than those from large ones, not only because of more income per child. Parents in smaller families have more time to devote to each child because, like income, attention need not be divided so finely.[145] In the 1970s and 1980s, the black–white achievement gap narrowed in part because average black family size decreased faster than average white family size.[146] This trend may also help to explain why class size reductions in early grades seem to have a bigger impact on achievement of low-income black

FIGURE 1   Ratio of black to white wealth and income

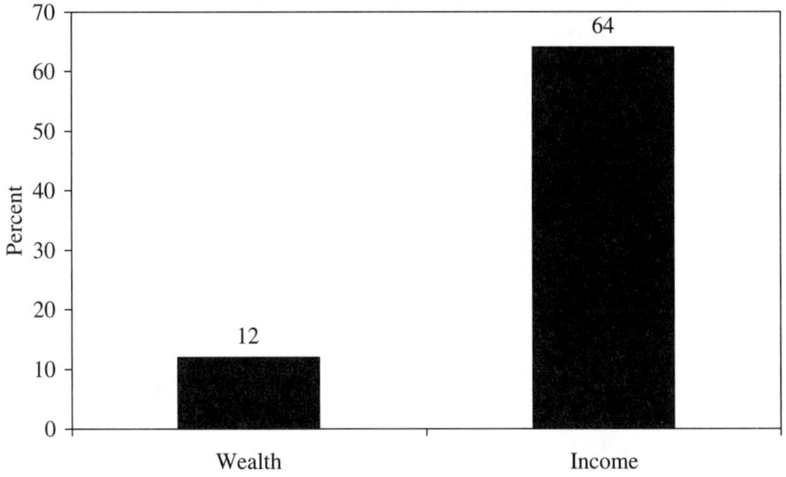

Source: Mishel et al. (2003).

than middle-income white children: for children from large families, class size reduction increases the intensity of adult attention proportionally more than a similar reduction for children from smaller families.[147]

Assets as well as income affect achievement, and help to explain the gap between middle-class black and white children. Families with similar annual incomes can still have different social class positions because of differences in their wealth, or the assets they control. As **Figure 1** shows, the asset gap is huge. Median black family income is about 64% of median white family income, but median black family net worth is only 12% of white family net worth.[148] In practical terms this means that white middle-class families are more likely than black middle-class families to have adequate and spacious housing, even when annual incomes are similar, because white middle-class parents are more likely to have received capital contributions from their own parents – for a down payment on a first home, for example. Black middle-class parents are more likely to be the first generation in their families to have middle-class status, and their own parents are less likely to have been able to help in this way.[149] As with all these examples, not all middle-class whites get first-time home down payments from their parents, and not all middle-class blacks fail to get them. But on average, more whites than blacks with similar incomes get them, and this contributes to average differences in neighborhood resources and in housing quality, which in turn contributes another bit to the test score gap.

Asset differences also influence how much families save for children's college educations. Once enrolled in college, family home equity is a strong predictor of whether students graduate.[150] Children's awareness that their families have resources for college can also influence the confidence with which those children assume that college attendance is within their grasp. So between black and white middle-class children whose families have similar current incomes, it would be reasonable to expect the white children to be more confident about their ability to afford college, and thus more dedicated to working hard in high school. Furthermore, white middle-class children are more likely to consider college a routine part of growing up because not only their parents but many adults known to them are likely to have attended college; the result is another bit added to the pressures creating an achievement gap between black and white middle-class children.

Being the first middle-class generation in a family may well have consequences for educational values and parenting practices, as well as for economic security. If high educational aspirations are more a middle- than a working-class value, then families who are the first generation to be middle class might be expected to have less entrenched attachment to education than families whose previous generations were well-educated. It probably takes at least two generations, on average, for changes in the economic characteristics and educational attainment of parents to be fully reflected in how they raise children, including whether they take children to museums and other intellectually stimulating locations outside the home, engage in reading activities, organize other literacy experiences in the home, and adopt less punitive disciplinary styles.[151]

So black children's lower scores, on average, even when family income is the same as whites', is not all that hard to understand when we recognize that differences in a particular year's income do not fully describe more complex social class differences.

Does culture or social class explain the black–white achievement gap?

Because of the sensitivity of race in American political history, and because of its ongoing sensitivity and politicization, excessive attention is paid in public debate to the extent to which lower test scores for black students are attributable to race-neutral socioeconomic characteristics or, instead, to the culture of underachievement in the black community. The motivation for this debate is that some conservatives want to show that economic reforms are relatively unimportant and that moral and cultural self-help is the best antidote to low achievement. Some liberals, in contrast, want to deny that cultural factors play a role, partly because they confuse cultural explanations with genetic ones. Yet it should be apparent that the existence of historically rooted cultural differences between black and white Americans does not in any way suggest that blacks and whites have different genetic capacities.

Some liberals also argue that if only economic reforms were implemented, blacks would quickly do as well as whites in school. These liberals fear that acknowledging the role of cultural factors, no matter what their origin, implies that problems of black students in U.S. schools are the "fault" of blacks, not whites, and that therefore the broader society bears little responsibility for remedying inequality.

Things are clearly more complicated – if black students expect their academic efforts to be unrewarded, it is because the weight of historical experience has been that black efforts in fact have been unrewarded. Nonetheless, black students' force of will and determination have to play a role in overcoming the weight of this history; teachers and schools cannot transplant ambition into students who are not yet ready to adopt it.

The debate about whether the low achievement of black students is rooted in culture or economics is largely fruitless because socioeconomic status and culture cannot be separated. On the one hand, if black families value education less because their historical experience has been that education has not paid off in economic mobility, then the undervaluing of education won't likely be eliminated simply with cultural appeals, and social and economic reforms (like non-discrimination enforcement and affirmative action) will also be needed. On the other hand, even if we could develop a complex measure of socioeconomic status that included, along with family income, measures such as family assets, persistence of poverty, savings for college, grandparents' assets, and so on, and even if this measure fully explained all differences in educational outcomes between blacks and whites, it would not eliminate the possibility that cultural factors play a role. After all, if there were a culture of underachievement in the black community, that could lead families to accumulate less savings for college. If parents strove to achieve less in school, and this resulted in lower family incomes, then a child's family income itself would be partially a cultural effect, not entirely a socioeconomic factor. Similarly, the number of books in a child's home is considered by many social scientists as a measure of social class. But parents can purchase books not only because the parents are well educated and can afford the purchases, but because parents value literacy more highly, a cultural characteristic.

These interactions between culture and social class make it harder to interpret the studies demonstrating that when other background characteristics – such as parents' educational level and mothers' own test scores, parents' occupational status, family size, number of books in the home, and children's birth weight – are added to long-term family income in analyzing test scores, few differences remain between the achievements of socioeconomically similar black and white students.[152]

In 1994, *The Bell Curve*, a book by Richard Herrnstein and Charles Murray, ignited a national controversy by arguing that the black–white achievement gap resulted, in part, from genetic differences between the races. Partly, they reasoned that the black–white achievement gap was so large that it could not be explained by social and economic differences. Their argument, however, fell prey to the commonplace oversimplification of these differences. If black–white social and economic conditions differed only in current income and parental education levels, the social and economic gap may indeed seem too small to explain the achievement gap. But if the full array of socioeconomic differences are considered, the plausibility of the Herrnstein-Murray argument disappears.[153]

Data on the vocabulary and intellectual development of four- and five-year-olds, from the government's ongoing survey of 1998 kindergartners (mentioned above in the section, "Social class differences in childrearing"), provides further evidence for this judgment that social class matters more than race.

The new data are useful for this discussion because with such young children cultural factors can play a role in student achievement only indirectly, through values expressed subtly by parents. After all, black four-year-olds do not suppress their own achievement because they believe hard work won't pay off in higher earnings. So while it is not possible to separate culture from socioeconomic status entirely, we can probably come closer to doing this with very young children.

The data show that there remains a race gap for children of the same SES quintile, but these remaining skill differences between black and white children are relatively small, especially in reading. Most of this racial skill gap is explained by socioeconomic factors – in this case, family income, parental education, and parental occupational status.

Figure 2A displays the reading skills of average four- to five-year-old black students in comparison to white students. Before taking SES into account, there is a big racial gap, with black children scoring about 16 percentile points below white children.[154] But, as **Figure 2B** shows, most of this gap is eliminated for children of similar SES. Middle-class whites (in the middle quintile) scored at about the 49th percentile, while middle-class blacks scored at about the 43rd percentile.[155]

Affluent white children (those in the top SES quintile) scored at about the 74th percentile, and affluent black children scored at about the 62nd percentile. So a race gap remained, even after controlling for SES. But the race gap at the top end is also small relative to the SES gap; these affluent top-quintile black children still scored higher than white students in the next highest (upper-middle-class, or fourth) quintile, who were at about the 59th percentile.

The same pattern is true at the low end. Black children in the lowest socioeconomic class (bottom quintile) scored at about the 29th percentile, while white children in this lowest class did better, scoring at about the 32nd percentile. But lower-middle-class blacks from the next lowest (second) SES quintile still scored better (at about the 38th percentile) than whites from the lowest SES quintile.

In math, the racial gaps are bigger, compared to the SES gaps, than they are in reading, although SES still seems to be more important than race in explaining the achievement gap.[156] **Figure 3A** shows a 23 percentile racial gap in mathematics skills upon kindergarten entry, but, as **Figure 3B** shows, the gap is narrower for blacks and whites of similar socioeconomic status, except for those from the highest SES families.

FIGURE 2A   Reading skills at start of kindergarten

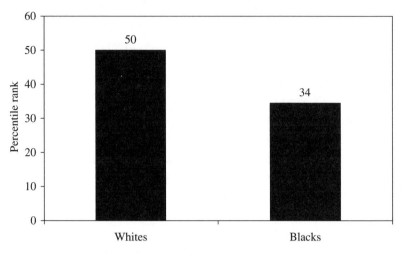

Note: The reading performance of black students has been normalized to the reading performance of white students.

Source: Lee and Burkam (2002).

FIGURE 2B   Reading skills on entering kindergarten by race and socioeconomic status

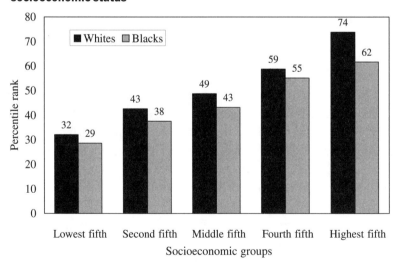

Source: Lee and Burkam 2002, unpublished data.

FIGURE 3A   Mathematics skills at start of kindergarten

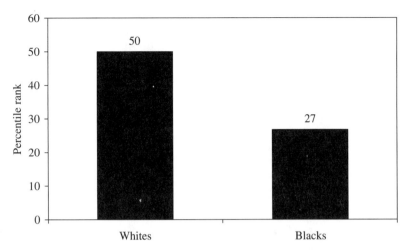

Note: The mathematics performance of black students has been normalized to the mathematics performance of white students.

Source: Lee and Burkam (2002).

FIGURE 3B   Mathematics skills on entering kindergarten by race and socioeconomic status

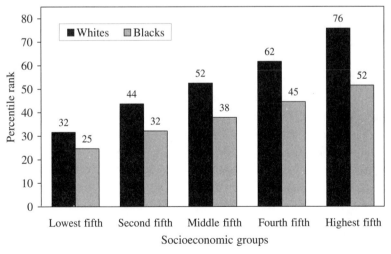

Source: Lee and Burkam 2002, unpublished data.

In math, black children in the top quintile score as well as middle-class whites (both are at the 52nd percentile), and upper-middle-class black children (in the fourth quintile) score about the same as lower-middle-class whites (in the second quintile). Lower-middle-class black children score about the same as bottom quintile whites (both are at about the 32nd percentile).

These race gaps, for both math and reading, might well be further diminished if additional social and economic characteristics could be controlled; for example, longer-term income and asset data, not only current family income. But, as noted above, even these more sophisticated social class measures would still be entangled by some cultural factors. All it is reasonable to say is that most of the racial test score gap probably results from social class factors, but a small part may also result from a culture of underachievement. It is possible, indeed likely, that cultural factors play a larger role for older children, but it is also likely that if social and economic conditions were equal for black and white kindergartners, and black children were then as successful in the early years of school as whites, cultural values that are hostile to education might be less attractive to black students when they were older.

Regardless of the historic origins of underachievement, if some black students aim too low in school for reasons that do not apply to whites, average achievement of blacks will fall below that of whites. The culture of low achievement should not be exaggerated in importance, above social class characteristics that apply equally to blacks and whites. But neither should we deny that aspects of black culture contribute to the gap.

Conservatives, both black and white, conclude from all this that community-based motivational campaigns can play a role in narrowing the gap. It seems plausible, but there is yet no evidence that such campaigns actually would have an effect. Because cultural and socioeconomic characteristics are so intertwined, it would be foolish to expect motivational efforts alone to succeed, but equally foolish to deny their potential contribution.

Summer and after-school learning

Earlier in this chapter, it was noted that scholars have never been able to attribute more than about a third of student achievement variation to school effects. Those scholars may even be overstating the school effect – analyses of data from summer learning have often seemed to show that the entire growth in the gap during the years children are in school develops during summer vacations, and so is probably attributable to out-of-school experiences. In these analyses, typical children from lower-class families seem to progress as rapidly during the school year as typical children from middle-class families, but the lower-class children fall behind in the summer, either because middle-class children learn more or forget less in the summer months.

Earlier, it was discussed how differences in home literacy support can cause a big gap when children first enter kindergarten. If children entered school with similar readiness, and if all subsequent learning then took place in school, there would be no achievement gap between lower- and middle-class children.[157]

Although some studies show that the widening of the gap takes place only during the summers, other studies go further: they find that the initial gap persists, but does not widen. In these analyses, on 12th grade reading tests the black–white gap is not much different than it was at the beginning of school.[158]

These data are not without controversy, and some recent studies do show the gap growing during school years, with only about half the 12th grade gap already existing in kindergarten.[159] But even this pattern could not be held to mean that unequal school or teacher quality widens the gap if the widening takes place almost entirely during summer months, when middle-class children's intellectual growth continues and lower-class children's growth stagnates.[160]

This effect of summer learning has been confirmed by testing children at both the beginning and the end of the school year, making it possible to distinguish gains from formal schooling and those from less formal summer experiences. Such testing confirms that lower- and middle-class children actually show similar growth during elementary school. But each summer, the gap expands. A survey of New York City schoolchildren 40 years ago found that black children learned only one-sixteenth as fast during the summer as during the school year, while white children learned one-fourth as fast.[161] Other studies since have confirmed these results.

The reasons for these summer learning gaps are not hard to fathom. Any skill takes practice to develop; reading is no different. Children who read for pleasure in the summer will be better readers, on average, than children who do not. As was shown earlier, middle-class children are more likely to come from homes where recreational reading has high status; as a result, this is the sort of activity to which children are more likely to turn in their leisure time. Middle-class children are more likely to have books purchased for them by parents and to get books from public libraries.[162] One survey of Philadelphia-area communities found that in neighborhoods where almost all adults were college-educated, retailers stocked 1,300 children's books per 100 children. In a blue-collar Irish and Eastern European middle-income area, there were 30 children's books per 100 children. In a multi-ethnic area there were 10 books per 100 children. And in a predominantly black area, retailers stocked fewer than one book per 100 children. The public library disparity was also huge, with six times as many juvenile library books in upper-income neighborhoods as in black neighborhoods.[163] These data do not mean that all middle-class children spend their summers accumulating books and going to libraries, or that no poor children do so; rather, because more middle-class than poor children read during the summer, the average proficiency of middle-class children will be higher no matter how effective school instruction may be.

During the summer, middle-class children are more likely to attend camp, take family vacations that expose them to new and different environments, go to zoos and museums, or take sports, dance, or music lessons. Each of these experiences for middle-class children, or lack of them for lower-class children, may contribute to growth in the achievement gap during the summer.[164]

Even during months that students are in school, they typically attend for only six hours each weekday. In afternoons, evenings, and weekends, middle-class children have more intellectually stimulating experiences, are exposed to more sophisticated adult language, and benefit from more economic security. If the gap really does not grow during the regular school year, schools are probably doing a great deal to narrow it during the regular school day, but these efforts are offset by gap-widening experiences in the after-school hours.[165]

We can't construct tests that separate learning during the school day from that in the afternoon or on weekends, but summer learning data are consistent with the achievement gap being entirely due to children's experiences before they enter kindergarten, in afternoons and on weekends, and during the summer. A strategy to close the achievement gap between lower-class and middle-class children cannot ignore these non-school hours.

Each black and each white school child, each poor and rich child, has a different combination of home literacy experiences, health conditions, family resources, and out-of-school opportunities. No single condition leads any particular lower-class child to achieve less than average middle-class children. Some lower-class children overcome these disadvantages and excel. But the accumulation of all them, for typical lower-class and middle-class children, for blacks and whites who are average for their races, makes an achievement gap between these groups nearly inevitable.

This chapter began by noting that, to most Americans, the notion is counter-intuitive that poverty should retard achievement. Subsequent pages have aimed to offer an insight into why the opposite is truly counter-intuitive: how can it be other than that children with such inferior preparations for learning, with such health, housing, and economic disadvantages, could do anything but perform less well, on average, in school?

Yet federal law today demands that, in 10 years, every school must wipe out the achievement gap by race and social class. Many educators and policy makers support this demand of the "No Child Left Behind" act, contending that higher-quality teachers and schools can overcome average social class differences. This claim may defy probability, but is not illogical. After all, the data from summer learning shows that schools do narrow the gap only to have their efforts undermined by out-of-school forces. If schools can narrow the gap in this way, perhaps schools can do even more. Although the achievement gap is not created by poor school quality, conceivably it could be erased by extraordinarily effective schools. The next chapter will argue, however, that some of the most commonly repeated claims that effective schools can close the gap are either fraudulent or misguided.

CHAPTER 2

Schools that 'beat the demographic odds'

The success of some poor children doesn't mean that poverty doesn't matter

The previous chapter described the many ways in which social class differences prepare children differently to learn. These differences appear not only in how families can support children from current income, but also in how families support children from other economic resources like savings for college, home equity, or access to stable rental housing; in their varied childrearing philosophies, conversational styles, literacy practices, role modeling, and parental social networks; in children's health that impacts learning, with differences in vision, hearing, dental care, lead poisoning, asthma, immunizations, birth weight and maternal smoking and alcohol use; in the ethnically and racially patterned cultural expectations about the payoff to education; and in the athletic and other enriching experiences that children enjoy in the after-school hours and in the summer.

Each of these contributes only a tiny bit to the learning gap between lower-class and middle-class children, but combined, the effects could be huge, and it is hard to see how even the greatest schools could overcome them.

These social class differences are not determinative; in the fashionable phrase, "demography is not destiny." The achievement gap is only an average of the performances of all children within large social class groupings. Some children from lower social classes do out-perform typical middle-class children, but differences in school readiness are so pervasive that an enduring average gap is almost inevitable. On average, lower-class children will achieve less.

But while class differences make the gap almost inevitable, it is not logically inevitable. Many commentators today claim that some schools and teachers already provide adequate educations for lower-class children. These schools and teachers are said to get middle-class scores from such children by maintaining high standards, consistent discipline, clear expectations, a focus on basic skills, and regular testing that holds everyone accountable. It makes sense that if some schools can succeed in these ways, then all schools should be able do so by using similar strategies.

The idea seems plausible because many lower-class youths have achieved academic and career success. As one prominent researcher recently put it:

> "[W]e know that income itself does not determine whether any individual child will achieve in the educational system; all around us we see children from families with low income who excel...."[166]

While this idea that "if some children can defy demographic odds, all can" seems plausible, it reflects a reasoning whose naiveté we easily recognize in other policy areas. In human affairs where multiple causation pertains, causes are not disproved by exceptions. Tobacco firms once claimed that smoking does not cause cancer, because we all know people who smoked without getting cancer. This now seems specious, but it was advanced for years without shame. Today, gun control opponents use similar reasoning when they assert that "guns don't kill, people do," simply because there are many guns whose owners don't use them to murder anyone. We don't insist that speeding does not cause highway deaths because we all know speeders who did not crash. We do not suggest that alcoholism does not cause child or spousal abuse because alcoholics are not all abusers. We understand that because no single cause is rigidly deterministic, some people can smoke, keep handguns, speed, or drink to excess without harm, but we also understand that, on average, these behaviors are dangerous. Yet despite such understanding, quite sophisticated people often proclaim that the success of some poor children proves that poverty or other social disadvantage does not cause low achievement.

One way to illustrate the flimsiness of such reasoning is to consider how multiple causality could be abused in the opposite way – although we rarely do so. Those who insist that poverty does not cause low achievement usually say that failure is caused instead by low standards and expectations, or inadequate testing and accountability. Yet we all know schools with high standards where some children fail, and we all know inadequate schools from which some students nonetheless emerge successful. These exceptions do not make it fashionable to conclude that standards and accountability must not matter. We recognize that, on average, students will do better in schools with high standards, even though not every student will do so.

Dr. William Sanders and the Tennessee value-added assessment system

Many educators have been convinced by William Sanders, an agricultural statistician, that better schools can themselves close the gap. With Tennessee test data, Dr. Sanders has created a "value-added" assessment system that purports to show how much learning can be attributed to teachers and schools independent of students' socioeconomic and personal characteristics.

The value-added system is complex, and it is fitting that an agricultural statistician designed it. For it turns out that separating the influence on crop yields of agricultural methods (like how much fertilizer to apply) from the influence of environmental features (like the amount of sunshine) is conceptually similar to separating the influence on student achievement of teachers from that of children's family circumstances, health, and inherited potential.

To simplify (or perhaps, for purposes of clarity, slightly to oversimplify) Dr. Sanders' method, he reasons that students' underlying patterns of performance reflect their own socioeconomic and personal characteristics. When students' performance departs from their underlying patterns, the change must be due to the influence of their teachers. For example, if a group of students consistently gets average scores at the 45th percentile on tests in grades 3 to 5, and then in sixth grade their rank jumps to the 50th percentile, Dr. Sanders infers that a 45th percentile performance was predictable from their backgrounds, but the jump in sixth grade must have been due to unusually effective teaching. Dr. Sanders calls this five-point jump the teacher's "value-added."

Most education analysts who investigate the performance of minority or low-income children do so by separating out the scores of these children by their race or economic status. That way, they can compare the scores of black students with other black students, or of low-income students with other low-income students. If some black students perform better than other black students, the analysts conclude that the first group must have had better teachers or schools, because the analysts believe they have removed the influence of race.

If Dr. Sanders' method is valid, however, separating students by race and social class is unnecessary, because he compares each child's performance in any year only to his or her own patterns established in other years. These patterns are assumed to reflect children's stable socioeconomic and personal characteristics, whatever those characteristics may be.[167]

To calculate teacher value-added, Dr. Sanders assembled years of data for every student and teacher in Tennessee. Computing teacher value-added requires knowing not only student scores in the teacher's class this year but identifying each student's underlying pattern, the students' scores for as many previous and subsequent years for which there are data. The more years of data that are available, the more certain we can be that a particular year's scores either fall within or are exceptions to students' underlying patterns. Calculations for each teacher and student must also use the scores of all other students in the teacher's classes in all these years. This requires computing power and skill that is beyond the capacity of most public agencies, making it impossible for independent researchers to validate Dr. Sanders' methods. Nonetheless, his value-added idea makes sense: with enough data, you should be able to predict students' performance due to their backgrounds and innate abilities. Deviations from this prediction can be chalked up to more or less effective teaching.

From this, Dr. Sanders has shown that, compared to students who had three years of teachers who were average in effectiveness, students gain about 25 percentile points if they had three consecutive years of teachers who were in the top quintile of effectiveness – that is, more effective, on average, than about 90% of all teachers.[168] (Teachers in the top quintile of effectiveness are those who are more effective than 80% of all teachers; in other words, the top quintile includes all those from the 80th to the 99th percentile in effectiveness, or an average of about the 90th percentile.) Thus, Dr. Sanders says, he has shown how to raise lower-class children's achievement to middle-class levels – if the most disadvantaged children can gain 25 points, on average, simply from switching to the best teachers, the performance of these students would approach that of the middle class. Dr. Sanders calls this effect of good teaching "awesome"; he is widely cited by those who say that good teaching can fully overcome the achievement gap.[169]

But this claim is too good to be true. Value-added assessment can probably identify more or less effective teaching with considerable accuracy. But improving teacher quality so that all teachers rise to the top quintile of effectiveness is a fanciful goal. Policy makers who cite Dr. Sanders do not appreciate how unattainable is a 40 percentile gain – moving teachers from about the 50th percentile in effectiveness to about the 90th. This is more than what researchers call a full standard deviation. In no field can a policy reform reasonably aim for such an enormous gain.[170]

Over long periods of time, of course, and with revolutionary advances in technology, average effectiveness can certainly improve by more than a standard deviation. The effectiveness of physicians rose by many standard deviations between 1900 and the present because we now know a lot more about disease and have better tools for dealing with it. A revolution in educational technology could occur some day, resulting in a similar transformation of teacher effectiveness. But given the pedagogies currently available, a feat comparable to the century-long transformation in medicine is not a reasonable education reform goal.

Many people don't have an intuitive sense of distributions, so here are two analogies to help think about whether we can possibly recruit or train average teachers to be as good as the 90th percentile group:

•   In 2000, real median household income in the U.S. was $42,000 a year. The 90th percentile household income was $112,000 a year, nearly three times as much.[171] We could imagine radical labor market or macroeconomic policies that might raise typical household incomes up to, say, $45,000 or even $50,000 in a few years. But policies to move the median to $112,000 are unimaginable. Improvement of 40 percentile points up a distribution is not a real world aspiration.

•   Here is a second illustration, for baseball fans. In the 2003 season, the Phillies were an average team, finishing in the middle of the National League East; the Phillies' median team batting average of

.263 was equal to the batting average of the median individual hitter in the Eastern division.

Imagine that the Phillies, in the winter of 2004, acquired a brilliant batting coach, resolved to lead the division in the following season. The coach would be silly, and doomed to fail, if his goal were to improve the Phillies' batting so much that every player on the team hit in the division's top quintile – or a team average of .305 and a minimum player average of nearly .300, a full 20 points higher than the median performance of the best hitting team in 2003. (That team, the league-leading Atlanta Braves, had only four players who hit in the division's top quintile.) Nothing like this has ever happened in baseball and, it is safe to say, it never will.[172]

Improving teaching faces the same statistical challenges as raising household incomes or batting averages. A more reasonable goal might be to improve teacher quality by five or 10 percentile points; in other words, by re-training teachers who are now in the middle of the distribution of effectiveness, so that they could become as good as teachers who are now better than 55-60% of all teachers. Or teacher quality could be improved by hiring only new teachers who are better than 55-60% of the current teacher workforce. This would be a substantial improvement, but unlike a wholesale gain of 40 points, it will not by itself overcome the deficits of home environment for lower-class children.

Even if we could improve teaching for lower-class children, it is not as easy as Dr. Sanders' acolytes think to identify high value-adding teachers. Dr. Sanders' data provide no guidance for the task. Value-added analysis does not claim to identify the characteristics of good teachers other than by a circular description – good teachers can raise student achievement but teachers are defined as good if they raise student achievement. Not only does the value-added system not pinpoint what the characteristics of good teachers are; the system cannot easily identify who the good teachers are in a timely fashion. More effective teachers cannot be identified in this system simply if their students score well in any year, or make big score gains in that year. Rather, high value-adding teachers can only be identified retrospectively, after statisticians have accumulated years of data on students who moved through their and other teachers' classrooms. It is hard to imagine that school principals and district offices could become so brilliantly insightful in their evaluation of teacher candidates to be able to identify and hire only those who, after such a complex statistical analysis, will prove to be as effective as the top 20% of the current pool.

Making the identification of the best teachers even more daunting, value-added analysis shows that there is apparently imperfect inter-subject correlation in teaching skill. Dr. Sanders' finding that a string of 90th percentile teachers can boost lower-class children to middle-class levels refers only to math. Teachers with high value-added in math do not do as well in reading. Or in social studies. Or in art, music, or social skills.

It is no accident that Dr. Sanders' dramatic results appear for math but not for reading. The socioeconomic test score gap is typically greater in reading than in math, because literacy is so much more a product of a child's home environment.[173] Proficiency in math is more a result of effective instruction in school. Thus, it is easier to show that 90th percentile teachers have a big impact on math scores than it is to make a similar showing for reading.[174] This is confirmed in Dr. Sanders' data. True, teachers who do better with math also tend to do better with reading. But the claim that great teaching can wipe out the test score gap requires not merely that math and reading effectiveness be related. Rather, it requires almost perfect correlation, something far from reality.

An analysis of New Jersey test scores, using 12 years of data on teachers, confirms this conclusion. Teachers who were more effective in math also tended to be more effective in reading, but the correlation was not nearly great enough to ensure that most teachers in the top quintile of effectiveness in math would also be that high in reading, or vice-versa. Only about half of teachers who were in the top quintile of effectiveness in teaching math were also in the top quintile of effectiveness in teaching reading. And one-quarter of those in the top quintile of effectiveness for math were below average in effectiveness for reading.[175]

Good school principals will usually seek teachers who can impart a balanced curriculum. Even if good quantitative evidence on teacher effectiveness were available, principals would still have to determine if a candidate at the 90th percentile of skill with math and the 55th with reading was superior to a candidate at the 60th percentile with both. Yet if such teachers could be found, Dr. Sanders' data suggest that even consecutive years of 60th percentile teachers can't come close to wiping out the achievement gap. Teachers identified in Dr. Sanders' value-added calculations need to be all the way up at the 90th percentile to close the gap.

Even if raising all teachers to the 90 percentile of effectiveness is not feasible, could the achievement gap be closed if the most effective teachers could be reassigned to the most needy students – in other words, if teachers in the top quintile of effectiveness were assigned to students in the bottom quintile of achievement? The idea makes theoretical sense but is politically and financially fanciful. Middle-class parents would never consent to removing the most effective teachers from their schools and re-assigning them to schools with lower-class children, while assigning less-effective teachers to middle-class schools. Nor would most teachers who were identified as being the most effective likely consent to such re-assignment.

Indeed, if Dr. Sanders' work leads to better ways to identify and retain more effective teachers, it could widen the achievement gap. The most effective teachers, in his value-added analysis, were most effective with children of all social classes. If the best teachers could be identified more easily, school districts with middle-class students would be able disproportionately to recruit such teachers because these districts have more money to spend and because their working conditions – the opportunity to work with easier-to-instruct students – are more attractive.

Some policy makers have proposed paying the best teachers an incentive bonus to accept re-assignment to schools serving lower-class students, but experience thus far suggests its impracticality as a way to eliminate the achievement gap. New York City has offered a 15% salary bonus to lure fully certified teachers to its most difficult schools, and this amount has not been sufficient.[176] The New York official responsible for the program speculated that it would probably take a bonus of more than three times that much, or at least $20,000, to fill these schools with fully certified teachers;[177] note that these were not necessarily the most effective, but only those with full certification. If this estimate were reasonable, luring the best teachers would require higher bonuses. Paying even $30,000 more to the most effective quintile of teachers would cost over $20 billion annually.[178] And, of course, the proposal wouldn't work unless there was agreement on how to identify the most effective teachers and which subject specialties were most important.

What kinds of teachers are likely to be more than a full standard deviation above the mean in effectiveness?[179] Teaching is both art and science. Pedagogical skills and content knowledge can be taught, but beyond these, the greatest teaching requires an instinctive affinity for the role. The greater the teachers, the more art and less science is involved. This is true in all fields. Most people achieve excellence by perspiration, but greatness – consistent performance in the top quintile – requires inspiration and innate skill as well. Much can be done to improve 50th percentile teachers, but the inspiration that gets them all the way up to the 90th percentile can probably not be taught. You have it, or you don't; if you don't, you can still improve your teaching, but incrementally.

Our discussion thus far of Dr. Sanders' conclusions regarding the relationship between effective teaching and the achievement gap has been conservative, in this sense: claims made for the value-added assessment system, by Dr. Sanders and then widely repeated, are even more extravagant than those described here. Usually, he talks not about a 25-percentile-point student achievement gain from substituting three years of the best teachers for three years of average teachers; rather, he describes a 50-percentile-point gain by substituting three years of top quintile teachers for three years of bottom quintile teachers (those who are less effective, on average, than 90% of all teachers).[180] But if improving teacher quality from the 50th to the 90th percentile is unfeasible, it is absurd to base a school reform program on the possibility of improving teacher quality from the 10th to the 90th percentile.

Nonetheless, despite its unreality, the attraction of this quick-fix for the achievement gap – simply improving the quality of teachers without having to worry about the social and economic causes of low achievement – has led other respected analysts, in addition to William Sanders, to make similar claims. Eric Hanushek and his colleagues, using test score data from Texas, suggest that the gap between black and white children in that state could also be eliminated by having consecutive years (five years, in their analysis) of teachers who are a full standard deviation above the mean in effectiveness, better than 85% of all teachers.[181] This suggestion is also not a practical one for raising the achievement of disadvantaged students, for reasons similar to those that apply to the Tennessee system.

In addition to the methodological problems already discussed, there are other possible flaws in the value-added assessment approach if it is used as a way to identify teachers who can get achievement from lower-class children that is comparable to typical middle-class achievement. The system assumes, for example, that teachers of comparable effectiveness can be equally effective with lower-class and middle-class students, and this assumption may be invalid.[182] The system also requires that tests used each year for each grade are properly scaled (in other words, that the tests are identical in their relative difficulty for that grade level); otherwise, teachers in some grades may seem to generate more value-added than others due solely to inconsistency in the tests. Yet tests are rarely so perfectly aligned with the curriculum. Problems like this have recently caused the Tennessee legislature to reconsider whether the value-added assessment system is a fair way to evaluate teacher effectiveness, and the legislature may cease using this type of analysis.[183]

The previous discussion has mostly granted that value-added assessment does what it claims – identify the relative contribution of better or worse teachers, independent of student characteristics – and has focused mostly on whether it is reasonable for policy makers to try to close the achievement gap by assigning only top quintile teachers to lower-class students. Yet the discussion may have been too generous. Widespread scholarly concern about the lack of independent verification of Dr. Sanders' claims led the Carnegie Corporation to commission a team of statisticians and psychometricians at RAND to conduct a technical analysis of value-added methodology. The RAND team considered the calculations of both Dr. Sanders and of Dr. Hanushek, and "identified numerous possible sources of error in teacher effects." It concluded that the value-added methodology should not be used for high-stakes decisions, like rewarding teachers for superior performance. RAND found that value-added analysis could reasonably identify teachers who were consistently more or less effective than average teachers, but was not sufficiently precise to distinguish top quintile teachers from others who were above-average in effectiveness.[184] If used appropriately, value-added techniques can help assess teachers, but they cannot accomplish what is too often claimed – identifying teachers who are so good that students' social class differences no longer affect learning.

Certainly, policy changes can improve the quality of teachers. Monetary incentives for better performance, changing the structure of teacher compensation, creating new roles for teachers who demonstrate superior skills, or any of the other common proposals to improve teacher quality may be effective. These proposals may well raise student achievement, and may well succeed in narrowing the social class achievement gap, if they were targeted only to lower-class students. However, based largely on the work of William Sanders, many educators have come to believe that improvement in teacher quality can be so dramatic that it can fully close the achievement gap. Yet if improvement of average teaching all the way up to the top quintile of present-day effectiveness is chimerical, then closing the achievement gap will have to rely on policies outside the classroom as well.

The Heritage Foundation's 'no excuses' schools

Some education commentators contend that there are examples of effective schools with high proportions of minority and low-income children who achieve at typical middle-class levels. These commentators conclude, therefore, that children's poverty must not be a bar to high achievement. Proponents of this view that poverty doesn't matter, because some high poverty schools succeed, can be either conservatives or liberals. Conservatives are attracted to the idea that some schools can eliminate the gap with present levels of funding because, if these schools can do so, more money spent on educating lower-class children is not needed; schools that do not eliminate the gap are probably wasting the funds they receive. The idea that only a few schools eliminate the gap while most do not helps to support conservative claims that most public schools do such a poor job that privatization is needed. For liberals, claims that some schools eliminate the gap are attractive because, if educators can be convinced that success is possible if only teachers try hard enough, perhaps teachers will then devote more attention to minority and low-income students.

Yet neither conservative nor liberal examples hold up.

The conservative Heritage Foundation identified 21 high poverty schools with high achievement and concluded that such schools owe their success to accepting "no excuses" for failure – their principals defy district bureaucracies, substitute "basics" for progressive fads, test students frequently, fire uninspiring teachers, and refuse to blame poverty for low scores. Heritage has published a list of such schools that, it claims, escape a destructive "cult of public education."[185]

But on closer examination, this list is less impressive than it appears. Some schools on the Heritage list were not neighborhood schools but schools where children could attend only if parents applied. Some were private schools. Only six of the 21 schools were fully non-selective neighborhood schools.[186] Selective schools can't be models for educating typical lower-class children because the distributions of lower- and middle-class test scores overlap; thus a selective school for lower-class students can find plenty of children who score near the middle of the national distribution. As Chapter 1 stressed, some low-income children always score above the middle-class average. On a test in which lower-class children score, on average, at about the 23rd percentile, about one-quarter of the lower-class children will score above the 50th percentile.[187] Schools to which low-income parents apply almost certainly have a disproportionate share of such unusually able children. Parents who go to the effort to apply to a particular school are more likely to provide literacy support at home and to monitor children's school efforts. The outcomes of schools whose children come with above-average family circumstances cannot be a standard for other schools that seem demographically similar but that draw on more representative populations of lower-class children.

For example, Heritage cites as a "no excuses" school one in Queens that houses a "gifted and talented" program for its entire district. To be eligible for this program, students must have I.Q. scores that are far above average, even though they come from low-income families. With its anomalous composition, we should expect such a school to have above-average test scores, but its practices can tell us little about how to improve the typical lower-class student's achievement.

The Heritage Foundation's *No Excuses* report assumes that the poverty of enrolled students, defined by their families' current incomes, is a sufficient way to identify schools that serve disadvantaged students. But as the previous chapter described, schools with low scores typically serve families for whom currently low income is only one problem. These families also suffer from poor parental education, high levels of stress, inadequate housing, poor health, and income that is permanently low, not just episodically so.

Data on school demography, however, usually disclose only those pupils who are racial minorities or who receive subsidized lunches. Their eligibility for the lunch program is based on their families' income for the most recent year; it can be as high as about $30,000 for a family of four. Children from families at the upper end of this lunch-subsidy eligibility are more likely to have stable homes and regularly employed parents. The Heritage report, however, falsely suggests that because schools with such children produce high scores, schools whose children have more serious problems can do so as well. In this respect, the Heritage Foundation's approach is no different from that of federal law – all children who get lunch aid, and the schools they attend, are deemed comparably challenged.

This kind of analysis yields some ludicrous results. One Heritage no excuses school, with high poverty and high scores, enrolled children of Harvard and M.I.T. graduate students. Graduate stipends may be low enough for subsidized lunches, but these children are not those whose scores are a cause of national concern, nor is their performance a model for truly disadvantaged children.

In another case, the Heritage report highlighted a school where many children got lunch subsidies, but 30% had parents with college degrees and 12% had parents with graduate degrees. This may be a good school, but its average scores provide no guide for closing the achievement gap for children of less-educated parents.

One school featured in the Heritage report, located in Houston, Texas, taught reading in the early grades with a near-exclusive emphasis on phonics. Training in basic skills like phonics is important for reading instruction, but as noted in the first chapter, too much reliance on the basics can result in a curious pattern, with higher scores in early grades but lower scores later. Social class differences show up more starkly in upper-grade tests that require conceptual thinking – not merely decoding words but interpreting what the words mean and reasoning about them – for which highly educated parents are more likely to train their children. The decline from lower to upper grades is likely to be most pronounced in schools that over-emphasize phonics in the early grades in order to get an artificial bump in early test scores. This apparently is what happened in the Heritage Foundation's Houston example; Heritage highlighted only the primary grade scores, not the declining scores in upper grades.

This pattern is not unique to the Heritage list. It also seems to characterize the most widely hailed school reform model, "Success for All," that drills students in basic skills and succeeds in teaching lower-class children to pass reading tests in the primary grades. But many children taught with this method then fall behind again by middle school.[188]

Two of the model schools featured by the Heritage Foundation were KIPP Academies ('KIPP' stands for the Knowledge Is Power Program) in low-income urban areas, one in Houston, the other in the Bronx. These schools emphasize good discipline, high standards, and college aspirations. They are "schools of choice"; parents must sign contracts to monitor children's homework and behavior and limit their television watching.

KIPP achievement is high. The Heritage report showed that the Bronx KIPP school had average reading scores at the 69th percentile.[189] But these are not typical lower-class students. That their parents chose to enroll them in this highly academic school sets them apart. KIPP's strategy works well for them but there is no evidence that it would be as successful for students whose parents are not motivated to choose such a school and to help enforce its academic rules.

In the Bronx KIPP school, 41% of students entered at or above grade level in reading, and 48% entered at or above grade level in math, not much different from the 50% you'd expect in a representative population.[190] If these schools are unusually effective (as they probably are), they can post even higher achievement. This is admirable, but it does not indicate that KIPP has shown how to get middle-class results from typical lower-class students without addressing the social and economic causes of failure.

In some ways, KIPP's unusual design itself proves this. Students attend until 5 p.m. each weekday, three hours on Saturdays, and three weeks in the summer – about 67% more time than students who are enrolled in regular schools.[191] This extra time allows KIPP to provide enrichment similar to what middle-class children often get – ballet, sports, musical instruments, art, and photography.[192] KIPP teachers also visit parents at home, to ensure they remain supportive of academic work.[193]

For its charters, KIPP typically gets the same funding per pupil as regular schools. It provides these extra services with foundation grants, by some admirable efficiencies, and by hiring only very young and energetic teachers, paid more than new teachers in regular public schools but less than experienced ones. No educational model, however, can assume that all teachers will be forever young, working extraordinary hours and never expecting salary growth that typically comes with years of experience and that enables teachers to support a middle-class family life. At present, KIPP teachers typically remain at KIPP no more than five years.[194] As KIPP schools mature, they will either have to force teachers to leave once they accumulate more experience, or find new financing sources to pay for salary growth. Such new financing will likely push KIPP's per-pupil costs above those of comparable regular schools.

KIPP and other Heritage no excuses schools may do a better job than most and utilize techniques that other schools should imitate. But this is different from the Heritage claim that nothing these schools do is "beyond the reach of every school in the country, period."[195]

The Education Trust's 'high-flying' schools

A liberal group, the Education Trust, also highlights schools where lower-class children get high scores. It, too, argues that these schools prove that any school can succeed with such children by enforcing higher standards. The Education Trust lists what it calls "high-flying" schools: 1,320 schools, at least half of whose students were both poor and minority, and whose test scores in math or reading were in the top third of their states.[196] The list includes about 10% of all schools that have majority poor or minority student bodies.

This is impressive. Ten percent is a lot; in business, a practice that succeeds 10% of the time is considered a benchmark, and competitors try to imitate it. If 10% of schools with typical lower-class children can raise achievement to middle-class standards, we should concede that poverty is no bar to high academic achievement.

But on examination, the Education Trust claim withers. The 1,320 schools do indeed have high scores – but in only one grade, in only one subject (either reading or math), and for only one year.[197] Such isolated results were mostly statistical flukes: all annual scores typically bounce around an underlying trend (as Chapter 3 discusses in more detail).

Because schools could qualify as Education Trust high-flying schools with up to half of their students from middle-class families, some of these schools likely had episodes of high average scores because their middle-class students did well, not because of those who were disadvantaged.

Like the Heritage Foundation's no excuses schools, some Education Trust high-flying schools had select student bodies –- magnet schools, for instance, that attract more highly motivated students from all across an urban area, not only from the school's immediate neighborhood. Some high-flying schools also had "gifted and talented" programs for children with high I.Q.'s; like schools of this type cited by the Heritage Foundation, such schools offer no clues about how to raise the achievement of typical lower-class children.

Even so, only a third of the high-flying schools had high scores in *both* reading and math. Only a 10th were high in reading and math in *more than one grade*. Only 3% were high in reading and math in at least two grades for *two years running*. Less than half of one percent of these high poverty and high minority schools were truly high flying, scoring well consistently. Such a tiny number is no benchmark.

'90/90/90' schools, and Boston's Mather School

The Heritage Foundation and the Education Trust are not the only ones claiming that some schools ignore social class to get high achievement and that therefore any school with lower-class students can do so. Another prominent advocate of this notion is Douglas Reeves, an author and educational consultant who travels the country lecturing to educators about how they can raise standards, get more accountability from teachers and schools, and improve their curricula. Many school leaders benefit from his insightful proposals, but Dr. Reeves doesn't stop with giving sensible advice. He also preaches that socioeconomic handicaps need be no bar to high achievement.

Dr. Reeves caricatures discussions of these handicaps by saying that they attribute low achievement simply to students' melanin, or skin color. Charges like Dr. Reeves', that it is racist to explain the average achievement of lower-class children by identifying the childrearing, health, economic, and cultural assumptions that make it harder for them to succeed, are common among advocates of the idea that any school can get high achievement from lower-class children. Many of those who make this accusation are conservative political activists, and they use the charge of "racism" in an attempt to confuse debate by casting those who advocate improving the social and economic status of minorities as opponents of the very minorities who would benefit from such policies.[198]

Dr. Reeves attempts to prove his claim by identifying a group of what he calls "90/90/90" schools in Milwaukee – where 90% of students are eligible for subsidized lunches, 90% are minority, and 90% meet "high academic standards."[199] Data from the group of schools he names, however, show that the claim is false. Students in Dr. Reeves' 90/90/90 schools score only above the "basic" level on standardized tests, below what the state of Wisconsin terms proficiency and even farther below what any knowledgeable observer would call "high academic standards."[200] No middle-class school would accept scores only at the basic level, but without examining Dr. Reeves' data, his audiences would never know that this is all his 90/90/90 schools can do.

Dr. Reeves' claims about these 90/90/90 schools were given added prominence by Kim Marshall, until recently the principal of Mather School in Boston, where 85% of students come from families with incomes low enough to qualify for the federal lunch program. In October 2003, Mr. Marshall authored the cover article in *Phi Delta Kappan*, an education policy magazine that is widely read by educators. Called "Standards Matter," Mr. Marshall's article attempted to show how the 90/90/90 schools were not unique, and that the Mather School too had delivered a "first-rate education" to all children, irrespective of their poverty or other socioeconomic problems. This was accomplished, Mr. Marshall wrote, with a combination of rigorous testing, high academic expectations, teachers working in teams, a high-quality consistent curriculum, and his own strong and visionary leadership. His success, Mr. Marshall said, proved there was no excuse for any urban school to be ineffective.[201]

Mr. Marshall was probably a fine principal, and he may have helped Mather School to be among the best. But Mr. Marshall omitted from his account that Mather was a school (one of those mentioned in Chapter 1) where a team of optometrists conducted a six-year demonstration, identifying and treating low-income children's vision problems of the sort that are typically uncorrected in low-income schools. The optometrists collected test scores and grades as well, and reported that children who received glasses gained 4.5 percentile points a year on reading tests, compared to children without vision problems who gained 0.6 percentile points a year.[202] Children who did not need lenses, but who had tracking or focusing deficiencies, got vision therapy, which also enhanced their reading skill. Mr. Marshall's article in *Phi Delta Kappan* suggested to other school leaders that if only they too improved their leadership and curriculum and intensified their testing, their schools would also overcome problems of poverty. The article may have made these other school leaders feel inadequate (that was perhaps the article's intention), for they were not likely to have been familiar with a report in a medical journal, *The Journal of Optometric Vision Development*, where the results of Mather School's eye project were described. In truth, if Mather was more successful than other high poverty schools, it was likely because of a combination of better leadership, curriculum, and accountability, as well as of programs like the optometrists' to address students' socioeconomic and health handicaps.

Pentagon schools

It has become commonplace to claim that the United States military has found a solution to the achievement gap, because of relatively high scores by minority and low-income students at Army base schools. As a headline in *The Wall Street Journal* proclaimed, "Pentagon-Run Schools Excel in Academics, Defying Demographics."[203]

No doubt, the Pentagon operates good schools. And one-half of its students qualify for subsidized lunches – with armed forces pay almost as low as that of graduate students, many children qualify for the federal subsidized lunch program.[204] But these students are not disadvantaged like the civilian poor. Soldiers get subsidized housing and medical care;[205] the military won't accept recruits without minimum attributes of self-discipline and educational attainment that are considerably higher than what exist in low-income civilian communities. Many parents of low-achieving civilian students are high school dropouts, but military personnel must have high school diplomas or their equivalent.[206]

Children of officers and enlistees are taught together, so Pentagon schools are integrated by social class and race in a way rarely found among civilians.[207] As a result, Army children whose parents came from lower-class backgrounds benefit from middle-class role models, a benefit that lower-class civilians don't often have.

Students at Pentagon schools have a full array of health and social services that are unavailable to most lower-class children. The military offers subsidized high quality early childhood and preschool services,[208] so military base children come to elementary school ready to learn to a degree rarely found in lower-class civilian neighborhoods. The military offers after-school enrichment and remediation, much like the KIPP Academies.[209] Army base children don't often lack vaccinations, vision care, or dental care, or suffer from untreated asthma.

Parents on Army bases cannot choose to be uninvolved at their children's schools. Soldiers get released time to volunteer in classrooms. Commanding officers can, and do, order soldiers to attend parent-teacher conferences, properly discipline children, and make sure homework is done. If children don't behave, their families may be evicted from base housing or, if the families are stationed overseas, shipped back home.[210] As *The Wall Street Journal* article acknowledged, after headlining that these schools defy demographics, "of course, it doesn't hurt that parents can be ordered to get involved."

Compared to national average spending of civilian school districts, Pentagon schools spend about 25% more per pupil, not including the housing allowances the Pentagon also gives teachers at its overseas schools.[211] The extra per pupil revenue enables the military to be selective about hiring teachers, and Pentagon school officials believe that this enables them to attract more highly qualified teachers than typical teachers at the nation's schools.[212] In addition, the Pentagon schools benefit from in-kind revenue: Army base schools can call on military units' unpaid labor for everything from maintenance to tutoring.[213] As with other oft-cited examples of schools that allegedly defy demographics, Pentagon schools are unusually well run. Their curricula are coherent and consistent, they have strong and committed leadership, and they provide well-designed teacher training based on the specific needs of students in each school.[214] It is not necessary to deny that the Pentagon operates good schools in order to conclude this is no proof that equally well-run civilian schools serving children whose parents are less stable and disciplined can close the achievement gap without directly attacking the social and economic causes of low achievement.

Rafe Esquith, KIPP, and affirmative action programs like AVID

The popular and educational press frequently offer accounts of particularly inspiring teachers. The articles usually conclude that if only schools had more teachers like them, lower-class children's achievement would soar. Fifteen years ago, the favored example was Jaime Escalante, a Los Angeles teacher whose high expectations of immigrant children inspired them to pass advanced placement exams in calculus. The film, *Stand and Deliver*, portrayed his achievements.

Yet Mr. Escalante could not duplicate his own feat. After publicity about his students' scores, a Sacramento, Calif., school district asked him to move to that city to create a similar program there, and Mr. Escalante accepted the challenge. Surely, if there are 90th percentile teachers, Mr. Escalante was one, but he could not stimulate immigrant children in his new school to similarly excel.[215] Whatever were the unusual circumstances of Mr. Escalante's achievements in Los Angeles, they did not provide a formula, for Mr. Escalante or others, to overcome demographic factors that predict low achievement for immigrant Latinos.

Recently, another Los Angeles teacher, Rafe Esquith, has won similar accolades. He is featured as a model in Abigail and Stephen Thernstrom's recent book, also titled *No Excuses*. And Mr. Esquith boasted of his achievements in his own book, *There Are No Shortcuts*, which is also the KIPP Academies' motto. The Esquith book describes how his fifth-grade students in a school with immigrant children from low-income families (a school he calls "The Jungle") produce full Shakespearean plays and classical music concerts, master good literature, and rank at the top of the nation in math. For sure, Mr. Esquith is a great teacher (in 1992, he won the Disney Teacher of the Year Award and was knighted by Queen Elizabeth), but he is being misused as an emblem for how schools can close the achievement gap.

The Thernstroms' book concerns the persistent low achievement of black students. The authors devote careful attention to social and economic conditions faced by black youth which, as Chapter 1 described, are more severe than those faced by other children whose low income makes them seem superficially similar. The Thernstroms also emphasize cultural factors that may lead blacks to make less effort in school than that made by others with similar economic and social problems. But the Thernstroms claim that Mr. Esquith's success (along with that of KIPP Academies, which he inspired) proves that these factors should be "no excuse" for low performance.

The book's use of Mr. Esquith shows how ideological and undisciplined this discussion has become. For although the Thernstroms' concern is purportedly black students' achievement (the subtitle of their book is "Closing the Racial Gap in Learning"), Mr. Esquith's so-called "jungle" school had virtually no black students; enrollment at his school was almost entirely children of Korean and Central American immigrants.[216] Although in low-wage jobs here, many of the parents were well-educated in their homelands. Some of the Central American parents, for example, were professionals who fled civil wars in the 1980s.[217] Children of such immigrants may have school difficulties, but their family and community support for education is different from that of black children whose parents are both poor and poorly educated. It takes nothing from Mr. Esquith's achievement to say that he is a questionable guide for closing the black–white academic achievement gap.

Mr. Esquith's high-achieving students are also not representative even of their own ethnic groups. In his book, he tells that he taught children with unusually high I.Q.'s, assigned to him because his classroom was specially designated as being for the "gifted and talented." There is no reason to think that similar techniques would suffice with typical immigrant students.

Most important, Mr. Esquith's experience does not show how high standards and expectations alone can raise achievement. He can be no model for regular teachers, as he tried single-handedly to provide all of the out-of-school experiences that middle-class children enjoy, and which help to promote their success. He expected students to arrive at his classroom every morning at 6:30 a.m., not 8 a.m. when regular school starts, and to stay with him until 6 p.m., although school is out for all other students at 3 p.m. Not even all of Mr. Esquith's students volunteered for this; the widely repeated accounts (including that of the Thernstroms) of his students' unusual accomplishments are based on the volunteers, not on an average of all his students. It is when these volunteers show up on Saturdays and during the summer that Mr. Esquith found time for Shakespeare and music lessons, math team and fine arts, and whatever extra drill in math and literacy was required. Mr. Esquith took students on camping trips in the mountains, on tours through the Midwest to retrace the Crazy Horse route, and on visits to Washington, D.C.

Mr. Esquith's extra time with students was unpaid. When he began teaching, he raised money for books, airfares, musical instruments, and theatrical productions by working extra jobs at night and on Sundays, and barely sleeping. He delivered take-out meals, worked as a messenger, and ushered at rock concerts to earn extra funds for class activities.

As he gained in renown, wealthy benefactors made contributions. This is no formula for how teachers can spur high outcomes for lower-class children. Rather, what Rafe Esquith's book really shows is how expensive are after-school, weekend, and summer activities for children who don't get them at home, and how impossible it is to duplicate the benefits middle-class children receive without finding a way of duplicating similar activities.

This discussion is not meant to minimize what people like Jaime Escalante, Rafe Esquith, or the KIPP Academies have done, or what they continue to do. Although the Thernstroms insist that such teaching contrasts with public school incompetence, these exemplary teachers and schools are actually engaged in something like affirmative action. They select from the top of the ability distribution those lower-class children with innate intelligence, well-motivated parents, or their own personal drives, and give these children educations they can use to succeed in life.

What is disturbing is only their supporters' insistence that these schools accomplish more than that, raising the average academic level of lower-class children up to that of the middle-class. KIPP's annual report cites President Bush's endorsement, "KIPP has the absolute right attitude for education. It says every child can learn." The report claims that KIPP's success will trigger "the widespread expectation that public schools everywhere can help students overcome disadvantages to succeed academically and in life."[218] In truth, all children can learn, but how much they learn depends on socioeconomic conditions as well as school effectiveness. Schools can help students overcome disadvantages, but not all students will do so.

In more candid moments, KIPP's own leaders acknowledge this. According to David Levin, KIPP's co-founder and superintendent of its Bronx school, KIPP narrows the achievement gap but can never eliminate it, even for its specially selected students, because the gap is fixed by differences in home literacy years before students enter school.[219] This makes it impossible, Mr. Levin agrees, for KIPP to accomplish what the "no excuses" pundits claim it can do. Although KIPP students doubtlessly do better than they would in a regular school, indeed much better, they still can't do well enough to pass tests that would gain them admission to New York City's most academically selective high schools like Bronx High School of Science or Stuyvesant High School.[220] Of course, few middle-class students can pass these exams either. But that no KIPP students have done so suggests that the distributions of KIPP and middle-class children are still not congruent.

Other efforts like KIPP also help raise the share of minority students who succeed. A national program called AVID (Advancement Via Individual Determination) invites minority and low-income children with above-average ability, who would be first in their families to attend college, to prepare in school, after school, and on weekends for SAT exams.[221] AVID propels students into the middle class, where they might not otherwise land. But AVID's work with the most talented minority students provides no formula for closing the achievement gap, which depends on learning by typical blacks that is comparable to that of typical whites.

With the nation unwilling to address its vast social class inequalities so that typical lower- and middle-class children have the same chance to succeed or fail, such affirmative action programs are essential. But their success does not mean that equivalent achievement for all children can be produced by better schools or teachers.

As this chapter noted at the start, there is nothing illogical about a belief that schools, if well operated, can raise lower-class achievement without investing in health, social, early childhood, after-school, and summer programs. But while the belief is not illogical, it is implausible, and the many claims made about instructional heroes or methods that close the gap are, upon examination, unfounded. The only prudent conclusion is that raising achievement of lower-class students will be very expensive, requiring more than high standards, testing, and tough accountability.

CHAPTER 3

Standardized testing and cognitive skills

Standardized tests' imperfect description of the gap

This book has described in very general terms the gap in achievement between lower-class and middle-class students, and between black and white students. The discussion has been vague about how big this gap might be, and how much specific policies might be expected to narrow it, simply because too little is known about the academic achievement gap to describe it with any certainty. The size of the gap differs on tests published by different companies; it differs for pupils of different ages; and it differs in different subjects, like math or reading. In approximate terms, however, standardized tests generally show that average academic achievement of black students is about one-half to a full standard deviation below average white achievement – in other words, if white students score, on average, at the 50th percentile on standardized tests, black students score, on average, somewhere around the 23rd percentile.[222] But these test score differences tell an incomplete and often inaccurate story about black–white differences in school outcomes.

There are two reasons for this. First, standardized tests themselves can give inaccurate and sometimes even misleading information about the performance of students in the academic areas that tests are supposed to measure; as a result, the information that standardized tests give about the academic achievement gap is also not fully reliable. Second, standardized tests do not measure many non-academic, or non-cognitive, skills that we want young people to gain from education. If, for example, we want schools to develop habits of good citizenship, standardized tests of academic knowledge tell little about whether students have learned these habits, and what the gap in these habits might be between students of different social classes.

This chapter discusses the first of these problems, the limited ability of standardized tests to provide accurate information about academic skills. The next chapter will describe how little we know about gaps in non-cognitive skills.

Defining proficiency

State and federal law now assume that the achievement gap can be gauged by the number of students who reach the "proficiency" mark on one standardized test or another. The federal No Child Left Behind law provides serious penalties for schools that fail to make sufficient annual gains in these numbers and that fail to narrow the gap in the percentage of black and white, lower- and middle-class students who are proficient. Indeed, the law now requires that all students in each major racial and economic sub-group be proficient in math, reading, and science by 2014. The policy is both harmful and unworkable.

The problem is not that tests of academic performance are invalid. Standardized tests can do a good job of indicating, though not with perfect certainty, whether students have mastered basic skills, can identify facts they should know, can apply formulas they have learned, or can choose the most reasonable inference from alternatives based on passages they have read. Such tests have a place in evaluating schools, as they do in evaluating students. However, they are of little use in assessing other important academic skills, like creativity, insight, reasoning, and the application of knowledge to unrehearsed situations – each a part of what a high-quality school should teach. Such skills can be assessed, but not easily in a standardized fashion.

To judge schools exclusively by their test results is, therefore, to miss much of what matters in education. Relying on proficiency benchmarks makes things even worse. Federal law requires that every public school child in grades 3 through 8 be tested annually in reading and math (and within a few years, periodically in science). The law requires every school to report the percentage at each grade level who achieve proficiency and, separately, the percentage of each racial and ethnic minority group and the percentage of low-income children who achieve it. If every grade and sub-group does not make steady progress toward the national goal – the proficiency of all students in each subject by 2014 – then serious penalties kick in.

But what exactly is "proficiency"? In the past, test scores were reported with scale numbers that had little meaning to non-educators, or by percentile ranks – for example, that a particular school (or student) scored at the 45th percentile in relation to a national average of the 50th percentile. Percentile ranks are actually a quite useful way to think about test scores, and they effectively indicate where efforts for improvement should be concentrated. Yet they became an easy target for unsophisticated politicians (and education policy makers) who demanded to know not how students or schools performed compared to others, but whether they met absolute standards of proficiency.

What is most curious about this abandonment of test scores reported in percentile rank terms (called, by educators, "norm-referenced" scores) is that policy makers often say that schools should imitate the ways of big business. But in this way, at least, education is moving away from established business practice. As Chapter 2 noted, private sector manufacturers often establish performance standards by "benchmarking," comparing their own performance to that of their competitors. If corporate quality control departments want to know how many defects are acceptable, or how many hours it should take to assemble a product, or how many customer complaints the company should consider tolerable, they don't pull standards out of thin air; rather, they set targets by looking to see how many defects, manufacturing hours, or customer complaints have been achieved by their most successful competitors. "Benchmarking" is simply the corporate term for "norm-referencing" in education.

The recent shift in how educators report test scores, from percentile ranks to the percent of students who have achieved an absolute standard of proficiency, has done as much damage to schools as over-reliance on testing itself. The new testing law models its definition on the one used by the National Assessment of Educational Progress (NAEP), a set of federal exams in a variety of subjects given to a sample of students nationwide. The NAEP tests such a broad span of skills that each test-taker can be asked only a small share of its questions, and the test results must be aggregated to generate average performance numbers. The NAEP then describes these group averages as either "below basic," "basic," "proficient" or "advanced." Panels of citizens decide where the lines between those categories should be drawn. It is natural for adults to exaggerate what young people, if only they were properly taught, should be able to do with consistency.

Proficiency, in other words, is not an objective fact but a subjective judgment. And the NAEP judgments have not been very credible. The NAEP finds, for example, that only 32% of eighth-graders are proficient in reading and only 29% are proficient in math – seemingly a national calamity.[223] But international tests show that most students in other nations are also not close to proficiency as defined by the NAEP.[224] If most students in the United States or elsewhere in the world have never been proficient in this sense, how meaningful is it that less than a third of American students are now meeting this target?

In 1993, shortly after the federal government first began reporting scores in terms of proficiency, the General Accounting Office charged that the government had adopted this method for political reasons – to send a dire message about school achievement – notwithstanding its questionable technical validity.[225] Confirming the General Accounting Office's conclusions, a National Academy of Education report found that the NAEP's definitions of achievement levels were "fundamentally flawed" and "subject to large biases," and that U.S. students had been condemned as deficient using "unreasonably high" standards.[226] A National Academy of Sciences panel summarized this broad expert consensus as follows:

> This committee, as well as the U.S. General Accounting Office, the National Academy of Education, and other evaluators, have judged the current achievement-level-setting model and results to be flawed. It is clear that the current processes are too cognitively complex for the raters, and there are notable inconsistencies in the judgment data by item type. Furthermore, NAEP achievement-level results do not appear to be reasonable compared with other external information about students' achievement.[227]

Today, NAEP "report cards" include disclaimers, urging the public not to take proficiency levels too seriously and acknowledging that scientific panels have concluded that NAEP results should "be interpreted with caution."[228] But ignoring their own warnings, the reports continue to announce, without further qualification, scandalously low levels of student "proficiency."[229] These "facts," not their unscientific basis, become part of our folk wisdom about student performance.

Under the new federal law, each state must now set its own proficiency standards, and the states are using methodologies, like citizen panels, similar to the NAEP's. The consequences have often been ludicrous. New York State had to cancel the results of its high school math exam when only 37% of test-takers passed, down from 61% in the previous year when the curriculum and instructional methods were similar and proficiency was supposed to be defined in the same way.[230] On Massachusetts' state science exam in 1998, only 28% of eighth-graders passed the proficiency point; yet on an exam administered internationally, Massachusetts students did as well as or better than students anywhere in the world except Singapore.[231] On Texas' reading exam, 85% of fourth-graders passed the state-set proficiency point while the NAEP found that only 27% were proficient.[232] In each of these cases, low-income and racial minority students were proficient at much lower rates than white middle-class students. This is a serious problem. But because the setting of proficiency levels by different groups of panelists is open to almost unlimited variation, it is impossible to know how serious the problem really is.

There is a further absurdity, if the goal is to evaluate how much the gap between lower- and middle-class (or black and white) students is being narrowed: a state's proficiency definitions can be – and given the penalties in federal law, they increasingly will be – watered down to the point that all children can achieve them with little improvement in instruction. Some states have already begun this process, deciding that what they previously had defined as failing will now be considered proficient.[233]

Defining the black–white test score gap as the difference in the percentage of students who are proficient opens education policy to almost endless political manipulation. As Chapter 1 observed, states can make their test score gaps disappear by defining proficiency as either a very low standard or a very high one. Critics can make the test score gap seem extraordinarily large if they define proficiency about halfway between the average score for blacks and the average score for whites. The only way to get a truly informative picture of the gap in test scores between black and white students is to study the difference in the relative scores of students from the two groups and the extent to which these score distributions overlap – in other words, norm-referencing the performance.

While some states try to escape federal penalties by defining proficiency too low, other states have bet that the new federal law is so unworkable that it will be repealed. For although education officials nowadays frequently mouth the rhetoric that all children can achieve to the same high standards if only schools hold all children accountable for great performance, almost all of these officials also know in their hearts (but don't publicly admit) that such a goal will be unrealizable so long as children come to school from vastly different social and economic backgrounds. Knowing that a law requiring them to do the impossible must, at some point, be unenforceable, some state officials have decided not to do anything for now about schools that make very slow progress toward proficiency for every sub-group – and have decided not to worry about the inconceivably spectacular improvements those schools would have to make just before 2014, by which date all students must be proficient, if the law were to remain in effect.[234]

The federal law was intended to raise student achievement to high standards. But for those states that choose to comply by lowering their proficiency definitions, the law's incentives are functioning instead to reduce state standards toward the existing levels of student achievement for the lowest-performing groups.

Alignment of tests, standards, and instruction

The incentives of the No Child Left Behind law are distorting teaching as well. Rational teachers in many states have begun to focus most of their attention on those students who are just below the proficiency point, because only their improvement is rewarded in the accountability system. Because students below the proficiency point are more likely to be minority or low income, this approach probably does some good. But it still distorts instruction in ways in which longer-term effects are incalculable. Imagine a class with some students who score well below the proficiency point, some close to it, and some well above. It makes no sense to waste instructional time on the high-scoring students, and little sense to waste much of it on the low scorers, who are even more likely to be minority or low-income students. The most surefire way to show annual progress and avoid serious penalties is to aim for a small improvement, which is all that's necessary, from the nearly proficient group.

Teachers who organize their instruction in this way are not being irresponsible; rather, the federal incentives are accomplishing what they were designed to do. Framers of the law – both Republicans and Democrats – relied on the fact that school leaders, from superintendents to teachers, are more likely to achieve a goal if there are serious penalties for not doing so. But when planners try to manage complex systems that have multiple goals by setting quotas only for the most easily quantifiable of those goals, the incentives distort the output.

It is not the states' official intentions that get watered down. States have mostly complied with the law's requirement that they promulgate high standards for all students. But their tests, which state education officials claim are "aligned" with these standards, point teachers in quite another direction.

True alignment of tests and standards has two parts. First, every test question must assess a skill that is actually included in the standards. This kind of alignment mostly does exist. But just as important, every skill included in the standard must be assessed – either by tests, student work samples, or other evaluations – and each skill should have the same relative weight in the assessment system as in the standards. This is not happening.[235]

Consider a typical elementary school reading standard, common in many states, that expects children to be able to identify both the main idea and the supporting details in a passage. There is nothing wrong with such a standard. If state tests actually assessed this ability, there would be nothing wrong with teachers "teaching to the test." But in actuality, students are more likely to find questions on state tests that simply require identification of details, not the main idea. For example, a passage about Christopher Columbus might ask pupils to identify his ships' names without asking if they understood that, by sailing west, he planned to confirm that the world was spherical. In math, a typical middle-school geometry standard expects students to be able to calculate the area, perimeter, or volume of various figures and shapes, like triangles, squares, prisms, and cones. Again, that is an appropriate standard, and teachers should prepare students for a test that assessed it. But, in actuality, students are more likely to find questions on state tests that ask only for measurement of the simpler forms, like triangles and squares. It is not unusual to find states claiming that they have "aligned" such tests with their high standards when they have done nothing of the kind.

At first glance, it may seem that such fudging is harmless. Until students are proficient on a basic skills test, some people think, there is no point in wasting time on higher skills. But effective teaching requires that basic and higher skills not be taught sequentially but simultaneously, so they can reinforce each other. With the Columbus passage, a child need not be able to recall every detail before he or she is taught how to summarize the theme of the passage. In math, students who are learning to add, subtract, multiply, and divide may still make errors when they perform these operations. But while continuing to practice these basic skills, they should also be learning more difficult topics. If students are given tests that ask for little but basic arithmetic skills, their teachers are unlikely to spend much time introducing them to algebra. State policy makers may conclude from rising test scores that students are closer to meeting high standards, but those policy makers would be wrong.

It is possible to have standardized tests where the proportion of questions assessing higher skills (creative writing, for example) is high. Then teachers would have incentives to emphasize these skills in their instruction. But including many questions of this kind is expensive. Tests requiring non-standardized written answers take a lot of time to administer, and either instruction or other test items must be sacrificed to make that time. Independent readers must be also hired and undergo training to ensure that they use consistent standards of judgment when reading student work. Because assessing more complex skills is so time consuming and costly, the NAEP, which does a better job than other tests of including more complex items, does so only by giving each test taker but a small part of a total test. Students' answers are then statistically combined to generate broad average scores, but not individual results. If we wanted to align tests and standards, so that teaching to the test really did teach what we want students to know, we'd have to invest a lot more in test development and scoring than we do now.

At higher grade levels, standardized tests include a few more questions that require conceptual skills to answer, although not as many as would be included in tests that were truly aligned with high standards. As Chapter 1 described, older students' unpreparedness for these more complex questions may help to explain why the current school-reform movement has had some success in narrowing the achievement gap between lower-class and middle-class children at the lower grades, only to see the gap widen again as children grow older. The pattern may simply reflect the fact that testing (and, therefore, instruction) in the lower grades is increasingly concentrated on basic skills, which are relatively easy – with enough drill – to impart. But such instruction may leave students, especially those from homes where intellectual inquiry is not modeled, unprepared for curricula in the upper grades, where tests cannot continue to exclude more advanced skills without looking ridiculous.

The inaccuracy of tests that hold schools accountable for closing the gap

One further problem makes a folly of the new system, and that is its inaccuracy. Tests, considered by themselves, are not reliably precise even as indicators of the skills they do assess. Yet if schools are to be held accountable for their test results, precision is what's needed. A school either meets its required mark or it does not.

Most people understand that a single annual test should not be the exclusive means of evaluating a student because a student's performance can vary – even if only a little – from day to day; students have their good days and their bad.

School-wide tests should be somewhat more reliable, because when some students have bad days, others have good ones. If these average out, test-based accountability should work. But statisticians can show that for test scores to average out accurately enough for us to know what proportion of a grade's students have passed a precise proficiency point, very large populations are required, much larger than the grade cohorts in typical schools. In reality, school averages, like student scores, wobble around their true values. Year-to-year changes in school averages are even less reliable.

By sheer happenstance, there might be higher-ability students in the fourth grade one year than the next. Consider how teachers think of their classes as "good" or "bad" in any year. A less able teacher could produce greater score gains in a class with better pupils than a more able teacher could produce with worse students – even if the classes are demographically identical. Much of the variance in school reading gains is a result of this "luck of the draw," that is, whether this year's students are easier to teach than last year's, notwithstanding their similar family backgrounds. The smaller the school, the less reliable is a single test as a measure of achievement because a few extreme scores can more easily distort an average.

Other statistical problems of small populations also make test results inaccurate indicators of the quality of instruction or the size of the test score gap. A rainy day could affect student dispositions. Test-takers might be distracted by a barking dog or a car alarm going off one year and not the next. The effects of such events could be tiny, yet in the new federal system, schools are sanctioned based on incremental changes in their annual performance scores. A tiny effect is enough to trigger penalties.

The statistical difficulties of pinpointing precise performance are exacerbated because of the federal law's laudable intent of holding schools accountable for the learning of minority groups within a school. Because sub-groups have fewer students than the school as a whole, minority scores are even more inaccurate. A perverse consequence is that the more integrated a school, the more likely it is to be deemed failing.

In the summer of 2001, when the Bush administration and Congress were designing the new federal requirements, two econometricians – Thomas Kane and Douglas Staiger – circulated a paper showing that the proposed system would result in many of the wrong schools being rewarded or punished solely because of these statistical sampling problems.[236] The paper was so persuasive that the introduction of the bill was held up for several months while administration and congressional experts tried to solve the problem. They couldn't. But they introduced the bill anyway, and the result has been some remarkable anomalies: schools rewarded one year and punished the next with no underlying change in teaching effectiveness; schools rewarded under a state's system and simultaneously punished under the federal one. Such arbitrariness undermines the incentive system itself.

Can all this be fixed? Not if we insist on a mechanistic system that allows federal administrators to judge whether schools are successful or failing simply by examining data reports from annual tests. Not if we redefine the achievement gap as differences in the rates at which racial minorities and lower-class students approach politically manipulated definitions of proficiency. And not if the purpose of these tests is to assess whether schools are reaching an impossible goal – equalizing achievement between children of different social classes while we fail to reform the economic and social institutions that ensure unequal achievement, on average, for children of different social classes.

CHAPTER 4

The social class gap
in non-cognitive skills

The goals of education, including non-cognitive goals

Although standardized tests do not provide a complete picture of the academic achievement gaps between lower-class and middle-class students, they do show that black students are less skilled than white students in the cognitive areas that tests measure. If black children's experiences – social, economic, cultural, and educational – make them less ready to develop skill in these areas, and if strong cognitive skill leads to economic and civic achievement, then black children's test performance predicts less success for them as economic, social, and political actors.

Yet even if standardized tests were precise in their definition of the academic achievement gap, the story would still be incomplete. There may also be non-cognitive gaps between children of different social classes that are just as important. It is not the intent of standardized tests to measure these.[237] Obsessed with test scores, educators have devoted almost no effort to identifying or measuring non-cognitive skills. It is especially necessary to call attention to this issue now, because efforts to close the black–white test score gap may inadvertently widen the non-cognitive skill gap. Even if schools' efforts to raise test scores of lower-class students were well-designed (as the last chapter showed, they may not be), if these efforts result in less attention paid to other school outcomes, they could exacerbate adult social and economic inequalities that, policy makers seem to think, better test scores could prevent.

There is, after all, little disagreement that Americans want outcomes besides literacy and numeracy from schools. Public opinion, state courts, governors, and Congress all seek a broad array of outcomes and processes from public education, not cognitive skills alone.

While public opinion surveys consistently include higher test scores as a school goal, they are not the only goal and apparently not the most crucial. In one such survey, conducted in 1994, over two-thirds of Americans said that teaching values was a more important role of public schools than teaching academic subjects; the top rated "value" was teaching students to solve problems without violence.[238] In another recent survey, Americans were asked to rank school purposes; respondents gave their highest rank to preparing responsible citizens; helping students to become economically self-sufficient was second.[239] In yet another poll conducted recently, 80% of respondents said that whether graduates practice good citizenship was a "very important" way to measure schools, but only 50% said test scores were a "very important" way.[240] When asked whether the primary function of schools should be to teach basic subjects like English, math, and science, or to provide a balanced education in which the basics were only one factor, fewer than one-third of Americans said the basics should be primary.[241] A few years ago, several national education organizations conducted joint focus groups in Illinois of school board members, clergy, businesspeople, mayors, law enforcement officers, college faculty, reporters, and others. All agreed that preparing good citizens, not academic achievement, was the most important goal of public schools.[242] They were, in fact, only restating what Thomas Jefferson called upon public schools to accomplish – not only academic proficiency, but to "understand duties to neighbors and country, and to observe with intelligence and faithfulness all social relations...."[243]

In 30 years of lawsuits in the various states, plaintiffs representing minority students (or their school systems) have demanded increased state funds to guarantee adequate educations to these students. These claims require a definition of "adequacy" before we can say how much money schools need to generate it. Most courts have proclaimed broad definitions of adequacy. In a typical case that provided a model followed subsequently by courts elsewhere, the West Virginia Supreme Court in 1979 ordered the state to provide sufficient funds to ensure that all children have, in addition to literacy, numeracy, and civic knowledge, the self-knowledge to "choose life work and to know their options," the capacity as adults for "recreational pursuits, interests in all creative arts, such as music, theater, literature, and the visual arts," and a sense of "social ethics... to facilitate compatibility with others."[244]

Several state courts have adopted similar language, but their decisions have been ignored by state and federal policy that now judges schools exclusively by gains on cognitive tests. A conflict between what we say we want from schools and the near-exclusive focus on academic tests has been growing for decades. A National Academy of Education report in 1987 put it this way:

> At root here is a fundamental dilemma. Those personal qualities that we hold dear – resilience and courage in the face of stress, a sense of craft in our work, a commitment to justice and caring in our social relationships, a dedication to advancing the public good in our communal life – are exceedingly difficult to assess. And so...we are apt to measure what we can, and eventually come to value what is measured over what is...unmeasured. The shift ...occurs gradually....In neither academic nor popular discourse about schools does one find nowadays much reference to the important human qualities....The language of academic...tests has become the primary rhetoric of schooling.

In response, a panel convened by the U.S. Department of Education urged that instead of relying only on the academic National Assessment of Educational Progress to measure how well schools were doing, the nation should develop a new indicator system that balanced all skills students should have. The panel urged the government to measure "learner outcomes" like tolerance, comprehension of pluralism, self-direction, responsibility, and commitment to craft, among others. But the panel's recommendation went entirely unheeded.[245]

Taking these objectives seriously requires developing a better definition than we presently have of the achievement gap between lower-class and middle-class students. Describing the gap in literacy and numeracy, despite how imprecise we must be, is easy compared to the challenge of describing the gap in non-cognitive skills. Is there a gap in graduates' participation as democratic citizens? Is there a gap in their resilience and courage in the face of stress? In their interests in creative arts? In their social ethics? Can American policy be faithful to Jefferson's proposal for public education without asking if there are racial or social class gaps in understanding duties to neighbors and country, or in the faithfulness with which we carry out all social relations?

We don't know much about such gaps, if they exist, partly because they are difficult, though not impossible, to measure. An even greater problem is that there is so little interest in measuring them. Yet if gaps exist in these areas, closing the test-score gap alone, even if possible, would not close the racial or social class gaps in economic and social status that, after all, are the ultimate reasons to equalize education.

There was once more interest in this topic than there is now. In the wake of the Coleman report, whose findings were discussed in Chapter 1, there was great enthusiasm for analyzing large datasets to identify the causes of inequality. In 1979, a team led by Christopher Jencks synthesized many such studies and found that the strongest predictor of adult economic success was family background. How much young people knew, measured by test scores, played a small role. Young people's non-cognitive traits, like leadership ability, mattered more. How many years of school young people had completed played an even greater role.[246]

In considering these distinct influences on adult success, do not confuse years of schooling, usually called "attainment," with test scores, called "achievement." If a group of students with more completed schooling is more successful than another group with less schooling, even though both groups have the same average test scores, then it is plausible that the first group may have gained some unmeasured benefit from school attendance other than academic knowledge.

Also, do not confuse attainment itself with earned degrees. The Jencks team found that adult success could be predicted by years of school completed, considered separately not only from test scores but from degrees students received. In other words, not only are high school graduates more successful than young adults who drop out but who have the same test scores; students who finish the 11th grade are more successful than those who finish the 10th, even if their test scores are the same. Also, students who finish three years of college are more successful than those who finish two; this is the case even if the first group gained no added cognitive skills by staying in college an extra year, demonstrated by their having test scores that were no higher than the scores of the students who dropped out of college earlier.

The anti-social score gap

The Jencks team reported that non-cognitive skills (perhaps they should be called character traits) play an important role in adult success, perhaps more than test scores, but the team did not analyze black–white differences in these non-cognitive skills, or ask whether such differences might play a role in subsequent racial inequality.

Since the Jencks' report was published, researchers have mostly failed to examine the subject. One prominent exception has been the Nobel prize–winning economist James Heckman. From a national longitudinal survey of children and youth, Dr. Heckman and his colleagues calculated "anti-social" scores from the frequency of children's dishonest, cruel, non-cooperative, violent, or disobedient behavior.[247] **Figure 4A** shows the percentile ranks of 12-year-olds from families in each income quartile. Children with higher percentile ranks on the anti-social scale exhibit more anti-social behavior. Twelve-year-olds from families at the bottom of the income distribution have the worst anti-social scores, on average. Those from middle-income families have better behavior, on average; and those from the highest-income families are, on average, the best behaved.

The bars on the left side of **Figure 4B** show that the anti-social score gap is nearly as great by race as by income. Black 12-year-olds rank worse than white 12-year-olds on the anti-social scale. However, as with cognitive scores, these differences narrow when more sophisticated definitions of socioeconomic status are used to define similar groups of students. The two bars on the right side of Figure 4B show that, for 12-year-olds whose mothers have similar test scores and educational attainment, and whose families have similar incomes and structure (for example, whether mothers are married), black students have only slightly more anti-social behavior, on average, than white students. So the anti-social score gap results mostly from socioeconomic differences and partly from cultural differences or from unidentified socioeconomic gaps. In this way, black–white behavioral gaps are very similar to the black–white academic gaps that were described in Chapter 1. A similar policy conclusion is also suggested by this finding: social and economic policies to narrow inequality might be as important as school reforms, if not more so, in efforts to narrow the behavioral gaps between black and white children – just as academic test score gaps could

FIGURE 4A Anti-social scores of 12-year-olds, by family income quartile

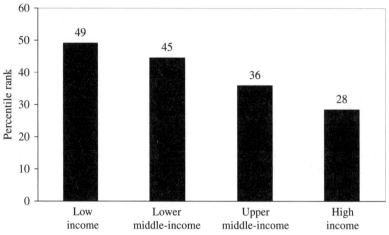

Source: Carneiro and Heckman (2002); Masterov (2004).

FIGURE 4B Anti-social scores of 12-year-olds, by race

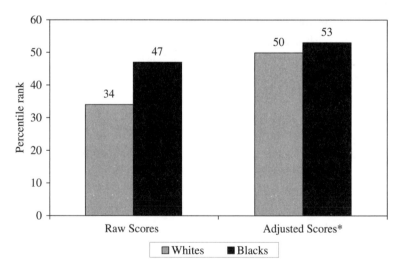

* Anti-social scores of black and white 12-year-olds whose family income, family structure, and mother's education are similar.

Source: Carneiro and Heckman (2002); Masterov (2004).

be narrowed more effectively if policies aimed to improve the economic, health, and social circumstances of black families.

Also like academic gaps, these behavioral differences are nearly as great when measured at four years of age as at 12. This pattern is evident in **Figures 4C** and **4D**, which display changes in the anti-social score percentile rankings from age 4 to age 12, for all white students, for all black students, and for students of all races in each family income quartile. Figures 4C and 4D are adjusted to compare students from families with similar income, structure, mothers' test scores, and mothers' educational attainment. Although the relationships between the anti-social scale scores of students by race and income bounce around a bit at different ages, on the whole black students and low-income students exhibit more anti-social behavior at both preschool and end of high school. Because there has been so little inquiry into these non-cognitive skills, it can't be known if anti-social test score gaps from preschool to high school are attributable to regular school or to family, preschool, after-school, and summer experiences. But it is plausible that providing early childhood, health, after-school, and summer programs for lower-class black children would narrow the black–white anti-social score gap, as it would the academic gap.

This outcome might be even more likely if these programs focused on social skills, not only on academics. That focus was the original intent of Head Start, although the current administration now wants to convert it more exclusively to a literacy program. After-school and summer programs, too, as Chapter 1 emphasized with respect to laying the foundation for academic success, should concentrate on activities that build social skills, like leadership, conflict resolution, and teamwork.

Schools that truly narrow the black–white gap are those where students of both races gain academic proficiency as well as productive and socially responsible behavior. If these outcomes were highly correlated, that is, if students with high math and reading scores were also more likely to become productive workers and good citizens, it might make sense to judge schools by tests alone. But these outcomes will likely be correlated only if schools teach them successfully in a balanced way. When schools are judged exclusively by academic test scores, the correlation diminishes because such strong incentives exist to overemphasize basic skills that dominate the tests and ignore activities that tests can't or don't cover.

FIGURE 4C   Anti-social scores, by race, from 4 years old to 12 years old*

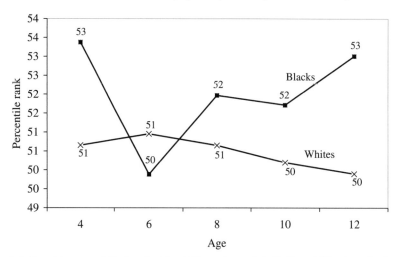

* Anti-social scores of black and white children, at ages 4, 6, 8, 10, and 12, whose family income, family structure, and mother's education are similar.

Source: Carneiro and Heckman (2002), Masterov (2004).

FIGURE 4D   Anti-social scores, by family income quartile, from 4 years old to 12 years old*

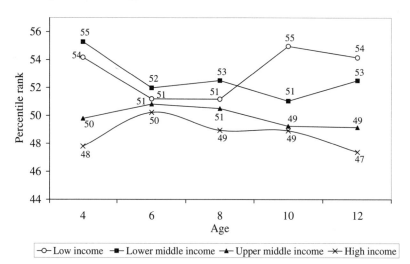

* Anti-social scores of black and white children, at ages 4, 6, 8, 10, and 12, whose family income, family structure, and mother's education are similar.

Source: Carneiro and Heckman (2002), Masterov (2004).

Affirmative action's evidence of leadership: Bowen-Bok, and the 'four percenters'

Some evidence suggests that test scores don't always correlate with other behavioral outcomes that Americans seek from adequate schools. And although the anti-social score gaps between black and white children seem to parallel the cognitive test score gaps, there are also some behaviors where the performance of black students seem to outshine the performance of similar white students. When these behaviors are considered, it is apparent that a too-exclusive focus on academic test scores may blind us to the relative benefits that black students gain from education.

Some of this evidence comes from debates about affirmative action – whether minority students with lower cognitive scores (usually, on the College Board's SAT) should sometimes be admitted to colleges in preference to whites with higher scores. The debate is usually framed as whether diversity's benefits are important enough to justify admitting minority applicants who are less qualified than white applicants. Some affirmative action proponents say that the education of all students improves when students are exposed to others from different backgrounds. Proponents of affirmative action also argue that social stability requires business and the military to recruit diverse college-educated leaders, even if the diverse group had been less qualified for college admission than a more homogenous class of higher-scoring white high school graduates.

Diversity and social stability are valid goals, but the reasoning used by affirmative action proponents to support them is at least partly flawed. The affirmative action argument assumes that applicants with high SAT scores are more qualified than those with lower ones.

The flaw in the argument does not stem from an implicit accusation that standardized tests like the SAT are racially biased. We can accept that students with high SAT scores do have greater cognitive skills. And for this discussion, we can stipulate that colleges should accept only the best qualified. Rather, the flaw stems from the assumption that cognitive skills (reflected by SAT scores) alone, or even mostly, make up college qualifications. What colleges should seek are young people with the best potential to develop leadership, self-discipline, ambition, a strong work ethic and moral code, as well as academic proficiency. The SAT measures only progress toward the last of these, and measures it only in part. If the other behavior and character traits are not highly correlated with cognitive skills, then heavy reliance on tests to judge college applicants can distort the admission process. Reducing this reliance can yield a more, not less, qualified pool. If this more qualified pool of applicants is also more diverse, that is an incidental benefit.

The College Board's own research confirms that academic proficiency is not the only index of qualification for college. The board has always shown that SAT scores of entering students, along with another measure of academic skill, their high school grades, can predict whether these students get good grades in their freshmen year of college. But the College Board also acknowledges that, if colleges define success not only by freshman grade point average but also by receipt of honors, election or appointment to leadership positions, or organizational accomplishment in college, then prediction of success is improved when admission decisions rely not only on SAT scores but on students' extracurricular activities as well as on application essays that include autobiographical narratives and statements describing their ambitions.[248]

In a 1998 book, *The Shape of the River*, former Princeton University president William Bowen and former Harvard University president Derek Bok defended affirmative action while granting that SAT scores may predict college success, if that success is defined simply as higher college grades. Bowen and Bok went on to ask, "what are we trying to predict? Much more, surely, than first-year grades or even [college] graduation....It is the contributions that individuals make throughout their lives and the broader impact of higher education on the society that are finally most relevant."[249]

Bowen and Bok found that black students with lower SAT scores, admitted to Ivy League and similarly selective universities, had somewhat lower college completion rates and grade point averages than students who had higher SAT scores. But the lower-scoring affirmative action admittees also went on to be more active than higher-scoring white students in community, social service, youth, educational, cultural, alumni, religious, and political groups.[250] The lower-scoring affirmative action admittees were more likely to be organizational leaders as well. They were more likely later to graduate from law and medical school (and less likely to graduate from business school or to get a Ph.D.). Black students who graduated from these highly selective colleges in the bottom third of their classes were as likely later to earn professional or doctoral degrees as white students who graduated in the middle third.

The Bowen-Bok data suggest that the affirmative action debate has been poorly framed. College students who proceeded to medical school were, in this respect at least, more qualified for admission to elite universities than students who did not choose to serve the community in this way, even if the first group had lower SAT scores. Students who used their college experiences to lead civic groups were, in this respect at least, more qualified to attend elite universities than students who were less likely to be civic leaders, even if the first group had lower SAT scores. Lower-scoring students who are more likely to make such contributions to society should not be thought less qualified for college and admitted under affirmative action programs; rather, if university admission committees could have made a proper evaluation of these students' qualifications, the students should have been admitted on the basis of merit alone. Those with high scores but less leadership potential may be less qualified overall. Merit and test scores are not identical. And if high schools are to properly prepare their students for admission to college, high schools should learn how to assess students' potential for leadership and civic responsibility as well as their cognitive skills.

It is, however, harder to have standardized measures of leadership than of mathematical or literacy skill. Indeed, it may prove to be impossible to develop standardized non-cognitive measures. But not enough effort has yet been devoted to identifying reasonable ways of evaluating such qualities. Most high schools and college admission committees have simply reacted to the difficulty by ignoring what they truly know are education's broad purposes, and instead conflate college qualification with cognitive test scores.

Difficult though it may be, however, schools and colleges can try harder to devise ways to predict leadership potential. One such attempt also stems from affirmative action controversies. Three state universities, those of Texas, Florida, and California, have evaded affirmative action prohibitions by giving an edge to students who rank higher in their high school classes, even if these students have low test scores relative to applicants statewide. These university admission policies aim to find students with hidden academic potential. But inadvertently, the policies may also identify students with non-cognitive skills that colleges should seek.

California, for example, banned formal affirmative action but created a second group of admittees in an attempt to reduce the number of minority students who would be disqualified for admission if SAT scores remained an important qualification. Traditional applicants continue to be judged mostly by their SAT scores and high school grade point averages. Students in the new category can qualify if their grade point averages in high school academic courses are in the top 4% of their graduating classes, regardless of the absolute value of their grade point averages or of their SAT scores. Some, though not all, students in the new "four percent" category may have lower SAT scores than the minimum to qualify for traditional admission.

The university has now examined how students from these two groups fared in college. The four percenters actually have higher college grades, on average, than students in the traditional group, although some four percenters may have had lower high school grades and lower SAT scores than traditional admittees. So the four-percent plan probably did identify students with hidden academic potential, as the plan intended to do. But the plan succeeded in other unintended ways as well. Irrespective of their college grades, the four percenters turned out to be more active in the civic and cultural affairs of their universities and university towns than traditional admittees, and the four percenters are more likely to aim for graduate school after getting bachelor's degrees. They study more and get intoxicated less than traditional admittees. Four percenters in the lower half of the university's SAT distribution are more serious about responsibilities like attending class regularly, studying outside class, and turning in assignments than are traditional admittees in the upper half. The traditionals are more likely to be binge drinkers and to neglect their studies than are the four percenters. [251]

California four percenters are more likely to be Latino immigrants or children of immigrants, and their families have lower incomes than the families of traditional admittees. Four percenters are more likely to work part time while in college to help pay their tuition – yet the four percenters still find more time for study because they spend less time socializing. More motivated than traditional students, they may succeed in college even if their SAT scores were lower. As Bowen and Bok showed for students at more elite universities, test scores are not the only measure of student ability when it is defined as the capacity to make the most of a university experience.

Possibly, the California high schools from which successful four percenters graduate are doing something right that test scores don't measure. Four percenters seem to have learned self-discipline and study skills that all high schools should teach. Perhaps they gained a sense of responsibility to the broader community from activities provided by their high schools. These are possibilities that education researchers should investigate. Narrowing the achievement gap, defined broadly as the gap between lower- and middle-class students' cognitive *and* non-cognitive skills, requires identifying which school practices enhance the chances for such achievement and measuring how effectively schools carry out these techniques.

In California, the four percent plan has mostly benefited Mexican-origin youths, not black students. Possibly, black students in the top 4% of their high school graduating classes are more heavily recruited by the affirmative action programs of out-of-state private universities. Possibly, black students in the top 4% of their high school classes have not yet been sufficiently motivated to apply for admission to the University of California, even though they are now eligible, or possibly black students who could qualify for the four percent group have not yet understood that they must take a college preparatory schedule of courses in high school. But whatever the reasons, these findings suggest that policy makers should do more to examine enhancing the potential for student engagement, responsibility, and community contribution, as well as test scores, when they craft policies to narrow the black–white gap in secondary school accomplishment.

Persistence in school, self-confidence, and adult earnings

The effect of schooling on adult earnings also exposes an imperfect correlation between cognitive test scores and other school outcomes. Adults apparently earn more if they attended higher-spending elementary and secondary schools, even if their test scores were not higher.[252] That higher school spending raises students' later earnings, independent of their test scores, may result from spending on academic learning that contributes to economic productivity but that is not well-measured by standardized tests; it may result from spending on non-academic activities that develop economically valuable character traits; it may result from higher adult–student ratios that help children mature more responsibly; or it may result from other yet-unidentified causes. At this point, we simply don't know.

Recent studies confirm Professor Jencks' finding that students with more years of completed school earn more than those with similar test scores and less attainment. Test scores explain only about a fifth of the relationship between more schooling and higher earnings, leaving about four-fifths to non-tested qualities that students gain in school.[253] One study found that a one-standard-deviation test score jump, that is, from the 50th to about the 84th percentile, corresponds to only 4% higher earnings.[254] Other studies have found somewhat larger gains.[255] We don't have enough information to interpret these properly; possibly, schools teach cognitive skills that enhance adult success but are not correlated with test scores, because tests do better at assessing basics than more complex cognitive skills like reasoning, analytic, and conceptual ability. Yet it may also be that students gain labor market skills by staying in school longer, independent of their academic gains. The balance of returns to education could be, at least in part, attributable to non-academic learning in schools.

Among semi-skilled production workers, those who stayed in school longer, again comparing those with similar test scores, are less likely to quit their jobs, and so are more valuable to employers. Little is known about why students with more years of school are more reliable workers; perhaps young people with perseverance are more likely to stay in school and also more likely to stay on the job, so schooling itself may not entirely cause their reliability.[256] But in this, perseverance is no different from literacy. Although reading skill stems from a combination of innate ability, home environment, and schooling, we nonetheless think it appropriate to hold schools accountable for literacy achievement. If perseverance is also due to these combined factors, schools should expect to develop student perseverance to a similar extent, even though we acknowledge that perseverance is also partly an innate trait and partly one that is learned from parents.

Other evidence that attainment matters more than achievement to economic success comes from high school dropouts who get equivalency diplomas by taking tests in academic subjects typically studied in high school. The equivalency diplomas are called "GEDs" because they are based on tests of General Educational Development. If employers valued cognitive skills alone, adult earnings should be the same for high school graduates and for GED-holders who had similar scores on a common test. But in fact, comparing GED-holders who have less than 12 years of schooling with high school graduates who received no further education after high school, graduates earn more than GED-holders whose test scores are the same. Completing the last year of high school and getting a diploma is worth an increase in earnings that is 10 times as great as increasing test scores by a full year's worth of learning.[257] Employers value high school diplomas for reasons that go beyond the academic skills that graduates have gained.

This is not simply because of a "credential effect" – employers mistakenly thinking that a high school diploma means that graduates know more than dropouts. The induction practices of the U.S. Army provide good evidence that earning a high school diploma reflects actual traits that are superior to those of dropouts with similar test scores.

Because of its poor experience with GED-holders, the Army accepted them prior to 1991 only if their minimum test scores were much higher than those the Army required of high school graduates. Still, although GED-holders may have had better cognitive skills, GED-holders' attrition from the Army was nearly twice that of high school graduates. So beginning in 1991, the Army took only recruits with regular diplomas; it would not accept GED-holders no matter how high their test scores.[258] In 2000, the Army reversed its policy again, but with even higher qualifications for GED-holders than before.[259] Now, the Army accepts GED-holders, but only if they score much higher than graduates on a cognitive test, as well as even higher still on a test the Army administers to assess motivation and reliability. Like employers, the Army also seems to value skills that are not captured by academic tests.

The credential rate for black and white students is similar when both diplomas and GEDs are counted.[260] But a much larger share of black than white students get GEDs, and a much smaller share of blacks than whites earn regular diplomas – only about 50% of black students get regular diplomas, vs. about 75% of whites.[261] This important aspect of the black–white gap seems to be getting worse, not better.

These findings do not deny that a GED is useful for some purposes. Although it is less valuable in the workforce than a high school diploma, even when GED-holders have comparable cognitive skills, many dropouts get a GED because they come later to recognize education's value, and they use the GED to become college-eligible. This is a legitimate purpose for the GED, and it is not undermined by data on the unsatisfactory labor market experience of adults who have only a GED. The data illustrate only that high school apparently provides skills or characteristics not measured by academic scores, and that dropouts lose the chance to acquire valuable traits, besides the testable cognitive skills they fail to gain, by not staying in school.

Even for students who fail the new and tougher academic exit exams that states are now beginning to require of high school graduates, more school would probably have led to higher earnings, [262] both because students learn more by staying in school (even if not enough to pass graduation exams) and because the discipline of school attendance apparently has labor market value. Although the evidence is still controversial, it seems that dropout rates, particularly for lower-class students, are increasing because of new test-based graduation requirements. If this is the case, schools today may be preparing students less well for productive work than schools of the recent past that had lower test standards but higher graduation rates. Certainly, test scores should not drop too low, but narrowing the black–white gap requires balancing these competing goals.

Self-confidence is apparently one non-cognitive trait that predicts labor market success. A survey conducted 35 years ago asked young men questions designed to determine whether they liked to be challenged and whether they felt they could control their destinies. Twenty years later, those who scored higher on the challenge and control measures earned more than those who scored lower. For young men of similar social class characteristics, scores on these challenge and control scales were better predictors of future wages than the number of years of school they completed or their literacy test scores. [263]

A similar study used a high school student questionnaire from 1980 to determine whether students felt they could do things as well as most other people or if they felt proud of themselves. A decade later, those who had high self-esteem in high school were earning more than those with similar academic scores but less self-esteem, perhaps because members of the first group were more self-confident about working collaboratively, or perhaps because they persevered with greater confidence that they would eventually succeed. [264]

Perhaps self-confidence is enhanced by outshining one's peers. Recall that high school class rank can predict college success, independent of cognitive skill. Class rank also predicts earnings; students with similar test scores who rank higher in their high school classes earn more as adults. There is similar evidence from higher education about the importance of class rank for future earnings. When students with similar SAT scores attend more selective colleges, they are likely to rank lower in their classes than when they attend less selective colleges where they are likely to rank higher. Students who rank higher at less selective schools earn more as adults than those with similar cognitive skills (SAT scores) who rank lower at more selective schools.[265] It could be that workers' economic productivity is increased if they developed the competitive traits that lead to higher class rank, or perhaps if they have enhanced self-confidence from outperforming their classmates.

Findings like these don't tell us if schools did or could have done something to increase young people's acceptance of challenges, belief that they can control their own futures, or pride in their accomplishments. But if legislators and school boards expected schools to develop higher scores on assessments that measured these traits, and if they expected schools to narrow any corresponding black–white gaps, schools might do more to enhance these traits.

Some education critics mock schools for trying to teach self-esteem rather than concentrating exclusively on academics. Certainly, some programs to teach self-esteem have been silly and were excuses to avoid challenging students, especially lower-class students, to do their academic best. Children should not be encouraged to take pride in unworthy accomplishment, but neither should they be permitted to feel that their worthy accomplishment is not of value.[266] Doing well on standardized tests is, as critics of self-esteem programs insist, one way to increase self-esteem. Higher test scores, however, are not the only way. Schools should be expected to enhance student beliefs that they have enough control over their environments that their actions have real consequences. Schools, in their academic programs, counseling, and non-academic activities, should be expected to help children learn to take an appropriate pride in their own contributions. If, in an obsessive drive to raise test scores, schools drop concerns about self-esteem and stress only academic learning, students' later success may well be impeded.

There is other limited information about character traits that contribute to adult economic success and that schools might enhance. One finding has been that workers with similar cognitive test scores, years of schooling, and socioeconomic characteristics earn more if their homes are neater. Before becoming concerned about this finding, remember the caution about averages that this book has emphasized so often: many highly productive and high-earning workers are sloppier than those who are less productive and earn less. But on average, workers with neater homes earn more, when these workers' other characteristics are similar.[267] Certainly, schools will not make a big impact on the black–white gap in labor market outcomes by urging students to keep neater homes. But neatness can be taught – the military certainly knows how to teach such habits. If neatness of homes is a proxy for a broader set of attributes, and if this finding suggests that organizational skill contributes to adult success, there is much schools can do to design activities that improve such skill.

One curious phenomenon, long familiar to economists, is that taller men earn more. Every extra inch of male adult height produces a wage gain of about 2%. At first glance, this could have either of two explanations. Either employers discriminate in favor of tall workers, or tall people have other characteristics that make them better employees. Apparently, only the latter explanation is true – employers don't discriminate in favor of tall people because they are tall, but only because tall people happen to have other traits, aside from height, that employers value.[268]

How do workers develop such traits? One clever analysis took account of the fact that young people grow at different rates, spurting at different ages, so while most tall adults were tall adolescents, not all were. Researchers compared the earnings of tall workers whose growth had come at different points in their development; these were workers who had similar adult heights, but different heights when they were 16-year-olds. They found little wage advantage for tall adults who were not tall as teenagers. This finding makes it less likely that employers discriminate in favor of tall men, because employers are typically unaware of their workers' heights as teenagers. The earnings advantage apparently stems from the fact that tall teenagers acquired other characteristics that shorter teenagers did not. If schools could do better at developing these traits in all young people, graduates would probably be more productive in the labor market.

Self-confidence is again a likely explanation. Taller boys are more popular (among both male and female peers); they are also more likely to participate in athletics than shorter boys, and sports contribute to confidence, teamwork ability, and discipline. Adults who were high school athletes earn more than non-athletes who had similar test scores.[269] There's not much that schools can do to make short boys more popular with the girls, but they can encourage all children to take part in team activities and ensure that participation is acknowledged and rewarded. After-school programs like debate teams, drama clubs, school newspapers, band, and orchestra can build similar confidence and discipline for students who don't participate in sports.

Woody Allen knew something about what we want from young people when he said that 80% of success is showing up. Thomas Edison said that genius is 99% perspiration. Americans read an Aesop's fable to their children about tortoises and hares, and a more modern story about a "little engine that could," both of which stress the value of character and perseverance.[270] If we truly believe these morals, we should want to know not only about schools' test scores but about the character traits of their graduates.

Complementing school curricula with civil rights enforcement

We need not rely on sophisticated data analyses to know that employers agree with Woody Allen. They are anxious to tell us. Surveys conducted by business groups like the National Association of Manufacturers, by government agencies like the Census Bureau and Labor Department, and by education policy groups have consistently shown that employers complain far more about job applicants' communication skills, punctuality, responsibility, attitude, teamwork ability, and conflict resolution skills than about their verbal and mathematical abilities. Indeed, employers report so reliably their concern with non-cognitive skills, it is remarkable that schools are held accountable mainly for better test scores, purportedly because these are needed to prepare graduates for the workforce.[271]

Many employers complain that black high school graduates, compared to whites, have less of a work ethic and interact more poorly with customers, co-workers, and supervisors. These employers say that black job applicants and employees, particularly males, have poorer communication skills, are less friendly, are less likely to be properly groomed and attired, are less able to work in teams, and are less enthusiastic, dependable, and willing to learn. The employers claim that black high school graduates are overly defensive and resentful of supervision.[272]

These employer beliefs could reflect racist attitudes that have little or no relationship to black graduates' actual workplace performance. Or, because black high school graduates have these deficiencies more often than whites, and because it is difficult to test individual applicants for these qualities, employers may reject black applicants without having any reason to believe that the rejection was deserved in any particular case. Or, employer attitudes could reflect accurate judgments about skills that black high school graduates lack.

The reality is probably a combination of these. Schools should be expected to remedy only the last of these conditions, the actual behavioral traits that make some students poor employees. Schools cannot change employer attitudes that are not based on the actual qualifications of applicants. Therefore, school reforms to improve black graduates' personal skills and to narrow this aspect of the black–white gap will not be fully effective (or perceived as legitimate by many black high school students and adults) unless these reforms are complemented by more aggressive enforcement of employment discrimination laws, and perhaps by the strengthening of these civil rights laws as well. As Chapter 1 described, at least part of the reason for the poor performance of black students is their belief that efforts in school will not pay off in labor market success. Educational policy that aims to provide black high school and college graduates with better cognitive skills and non-cognitive traits will be frustrated to the extent that the realities do not change on which this belief is based.

Because policy is now so exclusively focused on math and reading scores, educators have devoted too little attention to developing curricula that strengthen economically valuable character traits or to developing ways to measure whether schools implement such curricula successfully. And just as academic curricula can be corrupted by tracking minority and lower-class children into less demanding courses, if schools were expected to adjust character traits to employer demands, they may also run the danger of tracking students by social-class-related behavioral characteristics. For students with similar socioeconomic backgrounds and cognitive skills, some character traits may be productive in some jobs and unproductive in others. Habits such as the taking of initiative may be more rewarded in high status jobs while passive obedience may be more rewarded in lower status jobs. Aggressive behavior may be rewarded for men in high status jobs but not for women.[273] Employers may overlook behaviors in young white workers – tardiness or disrespect, for example – that they do not tolerate in young black workers.

Educators may properly refuse to accommodate to these practices with curricula that reinforce such differences by gender and race. Instead, along with school emphases on non-cognitive skills, legal challenges to employment practices (equal opportunity lawsuits, for example) may have to consider not only discrimination in hiring but also the preference of firms for different behaviors in female and male, black and white employees. Such problems, however, cannot be addressed if policy makers continue to pretend that schools' only role is to teach academic subjects and that school reform can ignore other outcomes.

Testing integrity, personality, and employability

Some school reformers believe that if employers were persuaded to pay more attention to high school transcripts, achievement would rise because students would know that grades pay off later in the labor market. These reformers are undoubtedly correct, but employers ignore transcripts for a good reason – they don't tell the most important things employers need to know about what students learned. That's why the best employers often give their own tests, covering more than academics, to potential hires.

In the late 1980s and early 1990s, school reformers cited Japanese manufacturing success to show why better math, science, and verbal achievement was necessary to improve economic performance. These reformers believed that Japanese manufacturers outperformed U.S. manufacturers because Japanese workers had higher test scores. The concern turned out to be misplaced because, by the mid- to late 1990s the U.S. economy, including its manufacturing sector, was outperforming Japan's, without any reversal in relative test scores between the two countries. But what showed the concern to be even more unwarranted was the behavior of Japanese manufacturers that established operations in the United States. When Toyota set up a factory in Kentucky, for example, it had a reputation for demanding a highly skilled high school educated workforce. U.S. policy makers expected this to mean that Toyota would demand good scores on math and verbal tests from job applicants. In fact, Toyota tested applicants for 26 hours, but only three were on cognitive skills; the other 23 were on communication, teamwork, and other non-cognitive traits.[274]

There are many types of tests for non-cognitive abilities. Among them, for example, are tests for integrity, that ask applicants questions like whether they think taking small items home from work constitutes theft; or personality tests, that ask applicants about themselves, like how often they enjoy taking chances.[275] To those of us who are not psychologists, it seems that applicants might give what they expect is the right answer rather than a truthful one, and so the tests would be invalid. Yet it turns out that such tests predict future job performance fairly well. And scores on such integrity and personality tests are not at all correlated with scores on tests of literacy and math.[276] Other employer non-cognitive tests, such as those for teamwork ability or work habits, also don't correlate highly with tests of cognitive skill.[277] And while there is a big difference between mean black and white student scores on cognitive tests, there seems to be no black–white gap on job applicants' integrity test scores.[278]

This does not mean there are not big black–white gaps on other non-cognitive measures. The contrast between a big racial test score gap on children's anti-social scores and the lack of a racial gap in adults' integrity scores begs for further examination. It is shocking that educators have done so little to investigate the non-cognitive traits that schools may enhance. Because we know so little about how much responsibility innate dispositions, families, or schools bear for non-cognitive traits, this chapter is largely speculative.

Employers must decide what balance of cognitive and non-cognitive skills they seek. If employers have test instruments that can assess both kinds of characteristics, schools can and should develop them as well. This does not necessarily mean they should be used to evaluate individuals. But schools should expect satisfactory group performance on non-cognitive as well as cognitive traits.

Many high school educators across the country have been influenced by the work of Theodore Sizer, and some have attempted to evaluate students' academic skills by "performances" rather than by standardized tests.[279] In these performances, students give oral as well as written presentations of artistic and academic projects, and answer questions from adult experts. In New York State, for example, controversy has arisen over whether some alternative urban high schools serving mostly lower-class students should be permitted to substitute such academic performances for standardized academic exams as graduation requirements.[280]

As with affirmative action debates, discussion of these performances has been poorly framed. It is not simply a question of whether performances do as good a job as standardized academic exams in assessing academic knowledge. Rather, it is whether such performances can assess communication skills, confidence, discipline, and the ability to adapt to unforeseen situations, because these skills are as important, if not more so, than academic knowledge per se.

Because education policy is now so exclusively focused on tests of math and reading, too little attention has been given to developing curricular programs that strengthen economically valuable character traits, or to developing ways to measure if schools implement such curricula successfully. This failure does disproportionate harm to black and minority students.

The Toronto (Ontario) school board recently announced that it would issue "employability" certificates to eligible high school students who did not pass high-stakes academic exit exams.[281] To earn certificates, students will need passing evaluations in practical problem solving, response to criticism, teamwork, time management, and other non-academic skills.[282] This is a big step forward and, if the scheme succeeds, the Toronto schools will be the first to attempt such non-cognitive assessments. But it is too bad that the Toronto board sees this as an alternative to a regular diploma. All students should meet an appropriate balance of academic and non-cognitive requirements for graduation.

Civic and democratic participation

As noted above, public opinion, state supreme courts, governors, and Congress all say that an important outcome of schools should be graduates' democratic participation. In New York State, this is a criterion of an adequate education: the court defined well-educated students as those who function intelligently as voters and jurors, engaging in and contributing to public life. Policy makers today assume that this goal can be accomplished by teaching math, literacy, history, and civics, and that students who know these are more likely to be effective democratic participants.

While students should certainly gain an understanding of history and world and civic affairs, democratic activity also requires organizational skill like proficiency in decision making and cooperative behavior. It requires the motivation to participate in public life and a belief that an individual's action can be effective. If there are black–white differences in these traits, then simply narrowing the history test score gap would be a misleading indicator of whether, in fact, students were equally prepared to be democratic participants.

As with other non-cognitive skills, it is not easy to measure the gap in the skills and attitudes that permit effective civic participation, but it is possible. What matters is not how students perform on history or civics tests, or even whether their schools operate community service programs. What matters is how former students behave when they are adults. We now have only fragmentary evidence about the effect of high school programs on civic participation, and some of it is contradictory.

Only one-third of 18- to 24-year-olds voted in the last presidential election. Barely half of those who were citizens even registered. Slightly more white than black young adults voted, and eligible white young adults registered at a rate only a tiny bit higher than eligible blacks.[283] The voting participation gap is apparently smaller than the gap in history and civics test scores.[284] So schools' biggest challenge here is not how to close a gap, but how to increase the capacity and motivation for political participation for both blacks and whites equally.

History and social studies instruction, at least as they have been conducted for the last 150 years, seem to have little impact on the quality of citizenship. Students who are actually taking a civics course, or took one recently, do better on tests of civic knowledge, have more tolerant attitudes toward dissent and minorities, and express greater intentions to participate in politics as adults. But the effects are weak and may fade rapidly, certainly in the cognitive area. Students who previously took civics but are not currently enrolled in a civics class do no better on civics exams than students who never studied the subject.[285]

Community service programs also produce better civic attitudes, but here too, the positive effects of these programs may fade quickly. Some studies find longer-term impacts but cannot detect independent effects: students who volunteer for community service may also be those who would be more likely to participate as adults, even without a school program. No research has been able to tie any curricular program directly to subsequent voting participation.[286]

Students whose teachers encourage them to express opinions in class have more positive attitudes toward participation in politics than students whose teachers mostly lecture. But whether students whose classrooms were participatory actually do participate more as adults is unknown.[287]

Extra-curricular activities – student government, for example – are also associated with greater political knowledge and confidence in the ability to influence public life. Adults are more likely to participate in civic, service, church, and professional groups if they belonged to service clubs in high school. And if adults participate in voluntary organizations, they are more likely to vote. So there is at least an indirect link between participation in extra-curricular activities and voting behavior. But adolescent club participation may not have influenced later voting activity. Attributes that dispose students to be club members may also be those that lead to greater adult engagement.[288]

Although there is no evidence that history knowledge leads to better or more loyal citizenship, the relationship seems plausible. But there are reasons to be cautious. Consider that white students get higher scores on tests of history than black students. But black students are more than four times as likely to discuss the national news with their parents as are white students.[289] Which is a better measure of the effectiveness of instruction: test scores or an inclination to discuss public affairs outside the classroom?

Because it is impossible to assign causality in these relationships, the only sure way to answer questions about the efficacy of school programs would be to conduct experiments, and education policy makers and researchers have not done so. Schools could be randomly assigned to receive funds for community service programs. Researchers could then track graduates to see if they participated differentially in public life as adults. Similar randomized experiments could be performed with alternative history curricula and pedagogies. Careful experiments would take a decade or more to track the adult effects of high school treatments. Yet we have wondered about the behavioral results of history instruction, community service, and civic education for a long time – if we had undertaken such experiments 20 or 30 years ago, we would have much better information by now about the value of these alternative approaches.

In 1992, the federal government surveyed a national sample of 12th graders and has followed them since. As the left bar of each pair in **Figure 5A** shows, when they were high school seniors 44% of these students participated in some form of unpaid community service. As with other outcomes, there is both a socioeconomic and a racial gap. Of seniors from high-income families, 60% engaged in community service; of those from middle-income families, 41% did so; and from the lowest-income families, 28% served. White students participated in these activities at a 47% rate, and black students at a 36% rate.[290]

But this school service activity did not necessarily translate into adult civic involvement. As the right bar of each pair of Figure 5A shows, when these students were young adults (eight years after high school graduation), participation rates of those from the wealthiest families had fallen off by more than the rates of those from middle- or lower-class families. And the racial patterns in participation were reversed. Black students were less likely to engage in service as high school seniors, but they were more likely to volunteer in their mid-20s. Indeed, the share of blacks who volunteered as adults was higher than the share of those who engaged in high school service activities, while the share of whites who volunteered as adults was much smaller than that of those who served in high school.[291]

Partly, this pattern seems to result from the ineffectiveness of mandatory community service programs. As **Figure 5B** shows, 11% of high school seniors from the wealthiest families were required to engage in so-called "volunteer" activities for a class, while many fewer middle- and low-income students were similarly required to "volunteer."[292]

Figure 5C shows that young adults who had a community service requirement in high school volunteered as adults barely any more than those who performed no service whatsoever in high school. Only those who truly volunteered in high school, without being required to do so, made greater contributions as young adults.[293] This may tell us something about the importance of encouraging but not requiring high school service.

Yet high school curricula cannot entirely explain these trends. Black and white high school seniors were required to participate in commu-

FIGURE 5A   Comparing the percent of students who engaged in high school community service activity with their volunteerism as young adults

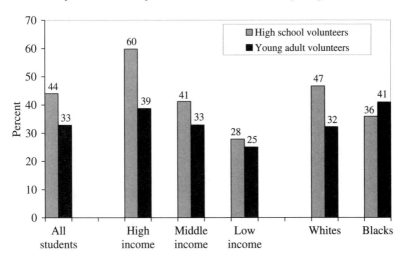

Source: Planty and Regnier (2004).

FIGURE 5B   Percent of students required by school to enlist in service activities

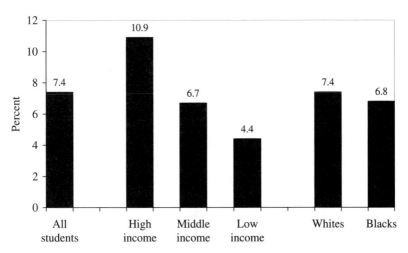

Source: Planty and Regnier (2004).

FIGURE 5C   Percent of adults volunteering in service activities by whether their high school service was mandatory or voluntary

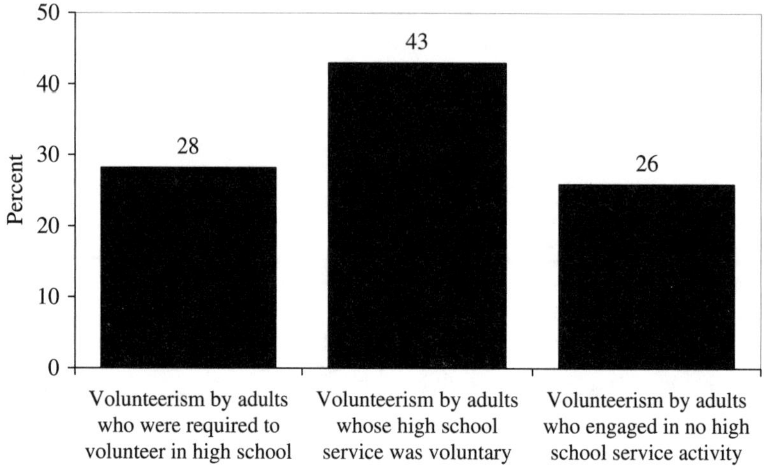

Source: Planty and Regnier (2004).

nity service at roughly the same rate, yet black volunteerism increased in young adulthood, while white volunteerism declined.[294]

If, instead of focusing so much on test scores, educators investigated whether students from particular schools were more active in community work as adults, and whether this related to high school programs in which these young adults participated, we would have information about which programs were successful and which were not, both for all students and for black and white students separately.

Few high schools today follow their former students in any systematic way, and high schools that do follow them don't do so for very long. Some school districts have hired commercial firms to survey former students at periodic intervals after graduation, but the data collected are usually minimal. Collecting data on the broad group of outcomes that schools claim to want to produce, however, would become a higher priority if educators felt responsible for these outcomes.

Regular surveys of high school graduates' civic activities, leisure pursuits, and employment are expensive, but affordable if we really wanted to hold schools accountable for the civic, workplace, and behavioral outcomes of students, not only their test scores. As with the assessment of more complex cognitive skills (writing, for example), if these outcomes are not assessed, teachers cannot be expected to devote much time or energy to improving them.

Like academic proficiency, all school outcomes, civic participation included, result from efforts of schools as well as the efforts of other family and community institutions that influence youth. For example, black young adults who participate in volunteer activities at greater rates than whites may partly owe this greater participation to church-sponsored activities. If so, schools cannot properly be held accountable for this aspect of differences in participation. Similarly, voting participation of all young adults reacts not only to school influences but to national and local events. If adults are more apathetic, perhaps because of economic or social conditions, perhaps because of disillusion with political leaders, better instruction when they were students might not immunize these adults from such cynicism. It would be useful, however, to know whether graduates of some schools were more apathetic than graduates of others. Data could be gathered to elucidate this.

Perry Preschool, Head Start, and Project STAR

Early childhood programs offer added evidence about the importance of measuring race and social class gaps in non-cognitive as well as in academic achievement. Black children gain in academic skills from Head Start. But their test score advantages seem to disappear by third grade, while the non-cognitive benefits of Head Start, like avoidance of criminal activity, apparently last for years.[295] This is not an anomalous result of Head Start. Studies of other early childhood programs find similar outcomes.

One experiment was begun in 1962 by the Ypsilanti, Mich. school district. It created a preschool for three- and four-year-olds in a neighborhood whose school-age children attended the Perry Elementary School. That school served unusually disadvantaged black children; over half had been held back at least once by age 10, and fewer than half eventually graduated from high school. Toddlers were identified for the district's preschool experiment and were randomly assigned either to attend a model preschool or to receive no benefit. The population had low I.Q.'s; most of the children's mothers and fathers had dropped out of high school; only half of the fathers were employed; and, among those who were employed, virtually all held unskilled or semiskilled jobs.[296]

In the experimental group, three- and four-year-olds attended the preschool for two-and-a-half hours each weekday. Teachers also visited mothers at home to train them to supplement the curriculum. The teacher–child ratio was about 1-to-6. The curriculum emphasized exploratory and inquiry learning. Mothers, for example, were taught not to ask children direct factual questions to identify letters or colors but rather to ask open-ended questions, like "what happened?" or "how did you do that?" These are questions similar to those described in Chapter 1 as being more typical of upper-middle-class childrearing.[297]

The initial experimental results were, like Head Start results, discouraging. After the first year, the preschool group's average I.Q. gained 13 points over the no-program group. But then, the advantage began to fade. By age 7, it fell by more than half, and by age 10 there was no longer any I.Q. advantage for those in the experimental group. The fade-out was similar on tests of arithmetic, reading, and language.[298]

But the researchers who conducted the Perry experiment have continued to publish data on test scores and on other outcomes until the participants were 27 years old. Academic scores rebounded after elementary school; at age 14, the preschoolers again had a significant advantage. During their school careers, fewer former preschoolers than those from the no-program group were thought to be mentally impaired and placed in special education.[299] More of the former preschoolers than of the control group eventually graduated from high school.[300]

At age 27, those who attended preschool had higher earnings, on average, than those in the no-program group. Former preschoolers had been arrested only half as often as those in the no-program group. Fewer preschoolers than those from the no-program group had been on welfare or received other government support, like public housing. The former preschoolers had half as many out-of-wedlock children as those in the no-program group.[301]

The experiment was carefully designed, so these big behavioral differences probably did result from educational experiences at ages 3 and 4. Especially because test scores rebounded in high school, we can't be certain that the behavioral outcomes were not a consequence of greater cognitive ability. Nor can we know if the rebound in high school test scores was a consequence of self-discipline, self-confidence, greater attachment to school and enthusiasm for learning, or other non-cognitive traits whose origins lie in early childhood training.[302] Or whether cognitive and non-cognitive skills were independent results of preschool. But the data are consistent with the view that preschoolers gained non-cognitive traits that led to better behavior as far out as 24 years later. The children are now 40 years old, information on their skills and behavior is again being collected, and the data are again being analyzed. These data will tell us whether the cognitive or non-cognitive effects of a high-quality early childhood program persist even into middle age.

Nonetheless, we have to be hesitant about these Perry results because there has been so little interest in this kind of experimental research, or in the variety of outcomes that the Perry investigators have tracked, that the experiment has not been replicated. We should have been doing dozens of such experiments, not only one. The Perry sample is small (123 children) and so there is a chance that the results would not be confirmed in other studies. For now, however, the Perry results are almost all we have to go on in measuring the non-cognitive outcomes of early childhood programs.

And the Perry results are consistent with non-experimental evidence. Studies of Head Start find a similar pattern. Academic gains do fade out in elementary school. Yet although Head Start centers vary widely in quality and none are sufficiently well funded to have a design like Perry's, Head Start children have less need for special education and less grade retention than children who were not in the Head Start program.[303] Adolescents and young adults who attended Head Start centers as children have better health (they are more likely to have been immunized), higher earnings, lower rates of delinquency, and higher high school graduation and college attendance rates than comparable youths who were not in Head Start. Some of these benefits seem even to apply to Head Start participants' younger siblings who themselves did not have a Head Start experience – the younger children apparently benefit from having better-behaved older brothers and sisters.[304]

Studies of other preschool programs produce similar, if not identical results – a fadeout of academic gains in elementary school but lower rates of high school dropout, special education placements, criminal arrests, and other adolescent and adult problems.[305]

Considering all this, it would be shortsighted to evaluate preschool by its immediate effect on participants' academic scores. Early childhood services seem to have lasting benefits, not only in academic achievement but in behavioral, employment, and other non-cognitive outcomes. These long-term non-cognitive benefits may be more important outcomes of early childhood education than of elementary and secondary schools. But the same is true of cognitive outcomes. The foundation for both is laid in early childhood. Even in regular school, the most powerful school years are likely the primary grades.

All this received added confirmation from a class size experiment in the late 1980s, when the State of Tennessee randomly assigned children to small or regular-sized classes from kindergarten through third grade. The cognitive benefits of the experimental treatment, smaller classes, have been widely publicized, and several other states have initiated class size reduction policies as a result. One important finding was that black pupils' test scores benefited more from small classes than white pupils'. Researchers are now able to compare these students' outcomes as they moved through their school careers. Children who were in small classes in kindergarten through third grade had fewer disciplinary problems after they returned to regular classes in the fourth grade, compared to their fourth grade classmates who had not been in small classes in the previous years. When they got to high school, children who had been in small classes in kindergarten through third grade were more likely to take college entrance exams than comparable students who had not been in small classes but whose school experiences were similar after the third grade. Small classes in the primary grades had a bigger impact on college entrance exam-taking by black than by white students. Small classes cut the black–white college admission test-taking gap in half.[306]

Is this because youths in the experimental group had better cognitive skills and so felt more qualified to succeed in college? Or is it because small classes helped them develop self-confidence and ambition that may influence both test scores and college applications independently, and to different extents? It is plausible that at least some of the college-application effect is attributable to non-cognitive skills that emerge from more intensive teacher–pupil relationships in small classes earlier in children's school careers.[307]

Comparing school and social reform to improve cognitive and non-cognitive skills

As it would be unwise to hold preschool and primary grade programs accountable only for narrowing the race and social class test score gap, ignoring non-cognitive outcomes, so it would be unwise to hold regular schools after the primary grades accountable only for test scores. A serious effort to narrow the black–white gap should find ways to help schools narrow the gap in non-cognitive as well as cognitive skills.

If policy makers did try to hold schools accountable for non-cognitive skills, they would probably find that, as with academic gaps, schools are only partly responsible for behavioral and attitudinal differences between black and white pupils. Policy makers would probably find that, as with academic gaps, schools are less important creators of these differences than are the social and economic inequalities that children experience outside school. But educators should still explore whether schools can make a difference, and how much, in careful experiments that assess the long-term impacts on behavioral characteristics of instructional styles, curricula, and disciplinary and dress codes.

Policy makers might find that if schools attempted to overcome non-cognitive skill gaps that arise from socioeconomic conditions, schools would have some success by providing opportunities for lower-class children to develop organizational skills in after-school clubs and non-academic pursuits, and by implementing curricular reforms that provide more opportunity for student collaboration, voice, and inquiry. These may, because time in school is scarce, result in slightly larger test score gaps. Or, if cognitive and non-cognitive skills are mutually reinforcing, there may be less of a conflict in narrowing these two kinds of gaps, especially over the long run. As the evidence of delayed test score benefits from early childhood programs seems to suggest, paying attention to both cognitive and non-cognitive development (including social and affective traits) in the early years may not pay off as much in higher test scores in the primary grades as they do when children are older. But until educators actually try some new approaches, and conduct some experiments, it can't be known which of these speculations about the interactions between cognitive and non-cognitive skills is correct.[308]

CHAPTER 5

Reforms that could help narrow the achievement gap

School integration, and
Sen. Moynihan's call for making choices

Public discourse about education pays great attention to the stubborn persistence of a black–white test score gap, and public schools come under great criticism for their apparent inability to do much to close it. Some of this criticism may be entirely justified. But what this book has tried to suggest is that there is more to the story than school reform. No society can realistically expect schools alone to abolish inequality. If students come to school in unequal circumstances, they will largely, though not entirely, leave schools with unequal skills and abilities, in both cognitive and non-cognitive domains. This is not a reason for educators to throw up their hands. Rather, along with efforts to improve school practices, educators, like students they try to prepare, should exercise their own rights and responsibilities of citizenship to participate in redressing the inequalities with which children come to school.

Income is more unequal and lower-class families have less access to medical care here than in any other industrial nation. The gap in average achievement can probably not be narrowed substantially as long as the United States maintains such vast differences in socioeconomic conditions. Although some lower-class children can overcome these handicaps, and although more effective schools can help narrow the gap a little, it is fanciful to think that, no matter how much schools improve, children from such different social classes can emerge at age 18 with comparable academic abilities, on average.

It is also fanciful to think that, 50 years after the Supreme Court's school desegregation decision, the country can ignore growing segregation by race and social class. It has become fashionable to claim that if children attend good schools, they can succeed no matter who sits next to whom. Yet anyone with children knows that peers are influential. A striking finding of the Coleman report was that who sits next to whom does matter. Ambitions are contagious; if children sit next to others from higher social classes, their ambitions grow. This finding has been reconfirmed often.[309] Lower-class children achieve less if the share of low-income children in their schools is higher. The drop is most severe when the subsidized lunch population exceeds 40%.[310] This truth has not changed since *Brown vs. Board of Education,* but we Americans are apparently unwilling to consider the housing, transportation, zoning, and other urban policies that would permit families of different classes to live in close proximity so their children can attend the same neighborhood schools.

One of the great impediments to effective policies that might enhance more equal outcomes between children of different social class backgrounds is the tendency of educators to think only about school reforms. In reality, however, for lower-class families, low wages for working parents with children, poor health care, inadequate housing, and lack of opportunity for high-quality early childhood, after-school and summer activities are all educational problems. When a parent's earned income falls, or a parent loses a job, there are educational consequences for their children. Educators who are concerned about the educational consequences should not fail to take notice of the economic and social conditions that cause poor school performance. As citizens who are more informed about these matters than most others, educators should not hesitate to call attention to the consequences for children's achievement of the social and economic hardships their families may suffer.

One of the most insightful 20th century analysts of education and social policy was the late Senator Daniel P. Moynihan. A few years after the Coleman report was issued in 1966, Mr. Moynihan was President Richard Nixon's domestic policy advisor. Marshall Smith (who many years later served as under-secretary of education in the Clinton administration) recalls getting a telephone call from the White House in 1969 or 1970. Having considered the implications of the Coleman report, Mr. Moynihan "asked me whether I would rather put $1,000 into a family to cover one year of [an educational program like] Head Start for one of its children or put $1,000 into that family to buy food, clothing, and shelter by means of a negative income tax. I conveniently ducked the question by saying I would do both."[311]

Yet public budgets are not unlimited, and smart policy requires making choices and setting priorities. Americans have continued to duck the Moynihan question since he posed it to Marshall Smith 35 years ago. We should stop doing so. We can make big strides in narrowing the student achievement gap, but only by directing greater attention to economic and social reforms that narrow the differences in background characteristics with which children come to school.

After serving in the White House, Mr. Moynihan went to Harvard where, together with Professor Frederick Mosteller, he convened a seminar to consider the Coleman report and its implications. In their summary of that seminar, Moynihan and Mosteller wrote that the Coleman report had been widely misinterpreted as a conservative document by those who noticed only its finding that differences between schools had relatively little impact on the variation of student achievement, and who concluded that, therefore, there was little to be done. But Moynihan and Mosteller countered that the report was actually quite radical, because it directed attention toward the social and economic policy initiatives that could make a big difference in raising the academic achievement of lower-class children.[312] It is this radical conclusion that educators should embrace if they truly hope to narrow the achievement gap.

If the nation can't close the gaps in income, health, and housing, there is little prospect of equalizing achievement. Yet there are policies that could help, if not to close the achievement gap fully, then to narrow it. If the achievement distributions of blacks and whites could be pushed closer together, more black students could use education to climb above their parents' stations. More black students could be recruited by affirmative action teachers and programs like Rafe Esquith, KIPP, and AVID, and the elites of our society might become more diverse.

Without more experiments where we compare, for example, the relative effects of reducing class size or establishing a vision clinic, spending money on recruiting better teachers or investing in housing, allowing children to transfer to "better" schools or supporting their parents' incomes so they can move to "better" neighborhoods, it is inevitable that we will continue to duck the Moynihan question.

In the absence of good experiments, citizens and policy makers have to make judgments based on a review of the literature, their own experience, and their good judgment. Although I remain open to contrary evidence, this book argues that efforts to truly enhance lower-class children's opportunities do not seem to be primarily regular school reforms, although those, too, can help. The discussion in Chapter 2 showed why it is false to claim that higher standards, more testing and accountability, and better school leadership can close the achievement gap. However, although these school reforms cannot close the gap, they may be able to narrow it some; by how much remains to be determined. This book does not discuss the importance of these school reforms in detail, only because most education writing nowadays focuses exclusively on such reforms within the regular elementary and secondary school system. This book has nothing to add to these recommendations, some of which are excellent. Rather, the goal here is to direct attention to reforms that are less-often promoted but that are at least as important, if not more so, than reforms in the organization and conduct of regular schools.

Although there is little practical hope that Americans will make a realistic commitment to close the achievement gap between lower- and middle-class children in the present political environment, incremental steps can certainly be taken in that direction. The most important steps, however, are probably not those that are currently most fashionable, among either liberal or conservative school reform advocates. More money to raise teacher salaries and smaller class sizes may be good ideas, but they are unlikely, by themselves, to make a big dent in the achievement gap. And they will especially not make a dent if they are implemented for all students and not targeted only for lower-class students.[313] Yet, as discussed above, it is politically unrealistic to expect middle-class voters to support reforms that transfer good teachers from schools serving middle-class children to those serving lower-class children, or that reduce class sizes in lower-class schools so that they are substantially smaller than those in middle-class schools.

There is no certain way to decide, if incremental reform is on the agenda, what changes would be more important than others. But, after considering the causes of low achievement that were described in this book, educators and policy makers may reconsider what reforms to begin with, if a choice were offered. While careful to insist that the achievement gap will not be closed without all the necessary reforms being implemented, what follows are some ways that the process might begin and how the gap might be narrowed.

Income inequality

Low-income families have seen their incomes grow far less than those of middle- and upper-income families in recent years. As a result, there are too many families with inadequate incomes to provide security for their children. Doing something about the wide income gap between lower- and middle-class parents could be one of the most important educational reforms we could consider.

In terms of national income distribution, the lowest fifth of families with children saw their after-tax incomes decline by 1.2% per year from 1979 to 1989. These families had gains in the early 1990s (up 2.5% annually from 1989 to 1995), largely because of improvements in the earned income tax credit in those years. But after-tax income growth for these low-income families was just 1.1% per year in the boom of the late 1990s. Then the recession hit, and it reduced their incomes by 5.8% from 2000 to 2002.[314] Consequently, over the entire 1979-2002 period, the after-tax incomes of the lowest fifth of families with children rose by just 2.3%, and, during much of this period, these families' already-low incomes were declining, placing them (including their children) under extraordinary stress.

In contrast, comparable middle-income families saw their after-tax incomes rise by 17% during this period, even after considering a 3% decline in the recent recession.[315] Thus, the last few decades have seen a widening income gap between those in the bottom and those in the middle.

A more positive development is that the ratio of black to white median family income increased from 57% a quarter century ago to about 64% today. This still leaves black family incomes far behind those of whites. The ratio of black to white median family wealth has improved at an even greater rate, from 7% to 12%. Yet these trends still leave a far greater disparity in wealth than in income.

Many families with children in the bottom of the income distribution, especially minority families, have incomes that are too low to adequately support children. In 2000, at the end of the 1990s boom, 11% of Americans had incomes below the poverty line, no different from the poverty rate of over 30 years ago, in 1973.[316] The racial disparity in poverty rates has diminished, as black poverty has dropped from 31% in 1973 to 23% in 2000, while the white poverty rate has risen from 8%

to 10%. This still leaves the black poverty rate more than twice as great as the rate for whites. Moreover, a third (33%) of black children under the age of 6 were poor in 2000, as compared to 13% of young white children.[317]

According to many researchers, the official poverty line (roughly $18,000 for a family of four in 2001) sets too low a threshold to describe the income families need to assure minimal stability. A more realistic basic family budget is probably about twice the poverty line. Using such a standard, half of all black families and one-fifth of all white families had inadequate incomes in the late 1990s.[318]

If Americans truly want to narrow the black–white achievement gap and to narrow the gap between all lower- and middle-class children, supporting the incomes of low-wage parents can make an important contribution. In real dollars, the value of the minimum wage has plummeted by 25 percent since 1979.[319] While few parents of schoolchildren work for the minimum wage, many work in industries whose wage structure is affected by the level of the minimum wage.[320] An increase in the minimum wage could well have an impact on student performance, comparable to the impact of within-school educational reforms. Other reforms to labor market institutions, such as rules making it more possible for workers to seek and obtain collective bargaining rights (as the law was intended to facilitate), would also lift the wages of low-income workers who are trying to support children.

In the 1990s, the federal government moved to offset trends toward growing income inequality, primarily by the expansion of the earned income tax credit, a subsidy to low-income working parents with children. It had an impact. In 2000, low-income single mothers earned, on average, about $8,000, but after the tax credit and other public assistance their average income nearly doubled, to about $16,000.[321] However, as discussed above, this income, at about the poverty line, is still not high enough to enable their children to have a reasonable chance to achieve, on average, at the level of middle-class children.

A commitment to attaining low unemployment would be particularly helpful to low-income families and to minorities, groups who are disproportionately hurt by recessions. The 4% rate of unemployment achieved in 2000, if it had been sustained, could have done much to increase the security of low-income families and their children.

Stable housing

Also important are reforms, not typically thought of as educational, that help lower-class families afford stable and adequate housing. Chapter 1 described high mobility rates in lower-class neighborhoods that inevitably result in lower student achievement. When children move in and out of schools, not only does their own achievement suffer but so too does the achievement of their classmates whose learning is also disrupted. There are many reasons for the high mobility of low-income families, but one of them is the lack of affordable housing in many urban areas today, a lack that is growing worse from the gentrification of urban cores and the acceleration of housing prices faster than wages and inflation. A serious commitment to narrowing the academic achievement gap should include a plan to stabilize the housing of working families with children who cannot afford adequate shelter. A national housing policy that reduced the mobility of low-income working families with children might also do more to boost test scores of their children than many commonly advocated instructional reforms.

One federal program to subsidize the rents of such families is the "Section 8" voucher program. It is under constant political attack, and is never fully funded.[322] The average cost of a Section 8 voucher is now about $6,700 per family per year.[323] The federal government spends about $14 billion annually on Section 8 vouchers and provides these subsidies to about two million families, only about one-fourth of those who are eligible.[324] If vouchers were provided to all eligible families, the cost could rise to $56 billion. If this investment were considered solely as an expenditure that contributes to an adequate education, it would be equivalent to about $1,000 on a per pupil nationwide basis.[325] Even with a commitment to undertake such spending, the money could be appropriated only very gradually, because there is presently not available sufficient housing stock to accommodate the families who need it.

An experiment to test whether housing policy could affect student achievement (as well as other outcomes) was stimulated initially by a housing desegregation suit in Chicago. A settlement required the Chicago Housing Authority to provide federal housing vouchers that would help public housing residents (mostly black) to move to rental units in desegregated neighborhoods. This "Gautreaux" program (the name is that of the plaintiff in the original lawsuit) seemed to show that families who moved to the suburbs had better employment outcomes than comparable families who utilized their vouchers for rental units in the city. Adolescent children of the suburban movers also apparently fared better than their urban counterparts, having lower high school dropout rates and better academic achievement. Although grade point averages of suburban and city movers were nearly identical, similar grades probably represented higher achievement in the suburban than in the urban high schools, because suburban high schools had higher standardized test scores.[326]

These results whet the appetites of housing experts for a true experiment, and in 1994 Congress appropriated funds for the Department of Housing and Urban Development to implement a "Moving to Opportunity" (MTO) experiment, designed to determine whether low-income families benefit from living in communities where fewer families were poor.[327] Such experimentation is rarely possible in social science, because it necessarily requires granting a benefit widely believed to be beneficial (i.e., better housing) to some participants and not to others. It also usually requires a degree of social engineering with which policy makers justifiably feel discomfort.[328] The denial of a benefit to a control group presents the most difficult ethical problems, but these problems are mitigated if the benefit is scarce due to no fault of the experimenters, and the experimental pool from which both treatment and control groups are drawn can comprise volunteers entirely. The benefit can then be allocated in some random fashion lending itself to observation of an experiment.

These conditions were met in the MTO experiment, because in all major cities there are long waiting lists for Section 8 vouchers, and demand for private apartments whose owners are willing to participate in the program far exceed the supply.[329] So establishing a control group whose members do not receive subsidies does not withhold a benefit from those who otherwise might receive it.[330]

The MTO experiment established lists in five cities (Baltimore, Boston, Chicago, Los Angeles, and New York) of families with children who presently live in public housing or who live in subsidized privately owned low-income housing projects that are located in high-poverty neighborhoods, i.e., Census tracts whose poverty rate exceeded 40% in 1989. To get on the lists, families had to express an interest in utilizing vouchers to move to private apartments in low-poverty communities,

defined as Census tracts where poverty was less than 10%. MTO officials then randomly selected families from these waiting lists for three
groups: the main treatment group that received vouchers for subsidies
to rent private apartments in low-poverty communities (the families were
given counseling and assistance in locating such apartments); a comparison group that received vouchers for subsidies to rent private apartments in any Census tract where they could find them without counseling and assistance; and a third group, the controls, that received no
vouchers for private housing. Scholars were invited to track the experiment over a 10-year period and report on the results in each of the five
cities.

Although it was generally expected that the mover families and their
children would benefit, this was not certain. As noted earlier, evidence
suggests that the effects on children of associating with higher-achiev-
ing peers is positive. But there is also some evidence that placing lower-
class children in middle-class communities can lead these children to
withdraw from academic competition due to feelings of inadequacy.[331]

At this point, the MTO evidence is mixed. One study found that
younger children in mover families had higher elementary school test
scores than the controls, but the outcomes for adolescents were more
ambiguous. Teenagers from mover families were more likely to be disciplined in school and were more likely to drop out than those in the
control group. This might not be because the behavior of the movers
deteriorated; it could be because the disciplinary and academic standards in the suburban high schools were higher than the standards in the
neighborhoods where the controls resided.[332] It also may be the case
that by adolescence, children's behavior and achievement patterns are
already well established, and that moving to a more mixed neighborhood would therefore be beneficial mainly to young children.

A recent study of adolescent outcomes from the experiment, com-
bining data from all five sites, found that adolescent girls in mover families were less likely to drop out of high school, had better test scores,
and were less likely to use marijuana than girls in the control group. For
adolescent boys, there were no significant educational differences between the movers and the controls, but the movers were more likely to
smoke or use alcohol than the controls.[333] Further study will be necessary to understand better these surprising differences between males
and females.

The MTO experiment was exceptional, because there is little interest these days in conducting more experiments of this kind. So while the results of this experiment are more encouraging than not, especially for younger children, we can still only speculate about how important such efforts might be in narrowing the achievement gap. It seems reasonable, though not certain, that if funds spent to stabilize housing were included in a broader program that facilitated the movement of low-income families to mixed neighborhoods, the achievement gap might be further narrowed as children benefited from the positive peer influences that characterize more integrated educations. Along with rental subsidies and assistance to families in finding rental units in mixed neighborhoods, such a broader program, to be effective, should also include changes in local zoning laws that now prevent low- and moderate-income rental units from being located in many middle-class neighborhoods, and better enforcement of fair housing laws that prohibit racial discrimination by realtors and landlords. These should all be considered educational, not only housing, programs.

School–community clinics

Without fully adequate health care for lower-class children and their parents, there is little hope of fully closing the achievement gap. So a high priority should be establishing health clinics associated with schools that serve disadvantaged children. Because, as Chapter 1 described, many lower-class children have health problems that impede learning, an adequate education cannot be delivered to these children unless they have adequate medical care. Because parents in poor health cannot properly nurture children, an adequate education also requires that lower-class parents get the means to achieve good health for themselves.[334] These goals require the establishment in lower-class neighborhoods of school clinics that serve children through their high school years, and their parents as well.

To narrow the achievement gap, a school-community clinic should include services that middle-class families take for granted and that ensure children can thrive in school. Clinics associated with schools in lower-class communities should include obstetric and gynecological services for pregnant and postpartum women, pediatric services for children through their high school years, physicians to serve parents of all school-age children, nurses to support these medical services, dentists and hygienists to see both parents and children semi-annually, optometrists and vision therapists to serve those who require treatment for their sight, social workers to refer families to other services, community health educators, and psychologists or therapists to assist families and children who are experiencing excessive stress and other emotional difficulties.

For elementary and secondary schools, the nation currently spends over $8,000 per pupil, on average.[335] Health clinics that provided a full array of services, associated with schools serving lower-class children, would add another $2,500 per pupil to the annual cost of education of the children in these schools.[336] Some of this money is not entirely new public spending. The costs for some of these services are eligible for Medicaid or other public reimbursement. However, because, as Chapter 1 described, some children and their parents who should get Medicaid and other public health services do not presently receive them, either because the application is cumbersome or because parents fear or do not know to apply, only guaranteed access through a school-based clinic can ensure that children will be healthy enough to learn to their full capacities.

Several small programs could be implemented relatively cheaply. For example, putting dental and vision clinics in schools serving low-income children would cost only about $400 per pupil in those schools. This is a lot less money than is often proposed for school reforms like teacher professional development or class size reduction. Schools might get a bigger test score jump, for less money, from dental and vision clinics than from more expensive instructional reforms. Designing experiments to evaluate this possibility would not be difficult.

Early childhood education

Low-income and minority children can benefit fully from good schools only if they enter these schools ready to learn. So narrowing the achievement gap requires early childhood education programs, staffed with professional teachers and nurses, and with curricula that emphasize not only literacy but appropriate social and emotional growth. As the discussion in Chapter 1 about social class differences in language development showed, gaps in vocabulary and conceptual ability develop before the age of 3.

Lower-class children's preschool and early childhood experiences should provide an intellectual environment comparable to what middle-class children experience – rich in language, where well-educated adults are companions, instructors, and role models. Lower-class children should hear more sophisticated language, be exposed to books at an early age, and experience the excitement of stories read, told, and discussed. They should be challenged to think and talk about these stories as children of educated parents are challenged – by considering counterfactuals and relations to other experience.

To achieve in school, toddlers and preschoolers who don't gain these experiences at home will have to gain them in formal programs. These programs differ from typical daycare settings in lower-class communities where low-income children may be parked before television sets and rarely taken on interesting excursions or guided in exploratory play. Typical daycare staff for lower-class children are poorly paid, and they often have educations that are no greater than the children's parents'. Probably because of the low wages paid to child care staff, the educational background and training of caregivers for low-income children declined in the 1990s.[337]

Adequate early childhood programs also differ from Head Start, which typically does not serve children until the age of 3 or 4, too late to fully compensate for their disadvantages.[338] But there are nonetheless exemplary aspects of Head Start. Although the Bush administration is attempting to shift the balance of Head Start instruction toward more academic activities – pre-literacy activities, for example – most Head Start programs have addressed not academic skills alone but also children's health, dental, nutritional, social, and emotional needs. Head Start also includes a role for parents, and staff members are required to visit parents to instruct them in "middle-class childrearing skills."[339]

To narrow the achievement gap later on in life, lower-class toddlers probably should begin early childhood programs at six months of age, and attend for a full day. Three- and four-year-olds should attend preschool, also for a full day. Centers and preschools should operate year-round.[340]

This attendance schedule for Head Start would be costly. Early childhood experts recommend that programs for infants from six months to one year of age should place teams of two caregivers with groups of no more than eight children, or an adult-to-child ratio of 1-to-4. As toddlers mature to two years of age, early childhood standards recommend increasing this group size to 10 children, a ratio of 1-to-5.[341]

To provide an intellectual environment that is similar to one that gives middle-class children a boost, preschool teachers (for four-year-olds) should have a bachelor's degree in early childhood education. Each should be assisted by a paraprofessional, in groups of 15, resulting in an adult-child ratio of 1-to-7.5. This permits adequate supervision of group work and play, individual and group reading aloud, and less formal instruction.[342]

These recommendations are neither new nor radical. British reformers established "infant schools" for toddlers of impoverished factory workers in the 1820s, arguing, as experts do today, that costs of infant schools would be recouped in reduced costs for crime and welfare.[343] These schools, and arguments, were widely imitated in the United States before the Civil War, until American experts decided that very young children should be socialized at home, not in school.[344]

Today, most experts again recognize that such services are needed, although they rarely say so publicly, regarding the expense as politically unrealistic. One recent exception has been Susan B. Neuman, assistant secretary for elementary and secondary education during the first half of the George W. Bush administration. Dr. Neuman resigned in 2003 and subsequently denounced the No Child Left Behind law for what she called its "troubling assumption" that all children's early childhood experiences prepare them for school success.[345]

On the contrary, Dr. Neuman said, "from the beginning, the playing field is...not equal." Early childhood education should start in "the toddler years," with high professional-to-child ratios, so adults can engage in what she described as "the rich language interactions that are necessary to allow children to explain, describe, inquire, hypothesize, and analyze." It is not low expectations that cause disadvantaged children to fail, Dr. Neuman concluded. Rather, she said, "our failure has been to adequately compensate for the gap when it can best be overcome – in the earliest years."

An adequately staffed early childhood center should also have professionals who help bridge the gap between lower-class parents and schools. For parents of young preschool and primary grade children, a home-school teacher can offer parent workshops on appropriate play activities and discipline. She can visit children's homes, observe regular classrooms, and consult with regular teachers, then make parents aware of children's skill levels and help parents, to the extent they are

able, support teachers to aid instruction. Such a professional can prepare parents to meet with teachers, help them to interpret school docu-
ments (like report cards), and connect parents with others who have
similar problems and concerns.

An adequate early childhood program for lower-class children would
also employ visiting nurses. Home nurse visits to pregnant women and
those with newborns should monitor mothers' and infants' health as
well as teach health-related parenting skills that affect children's ability
to learn. Nurses in an early childhood program should also conduct
community education programs. Educating pregnant women and new
mothers along with all young women of childbearing age about the
effects on children of smoking and alcohol would be one obvious role.

Where such programs have been tried, there is good evidence of their
value. In one randomized controlled experiment, nurses visited low-income unwed mothers during their pregnancies and continued these visits
during the first two years of the newborns' lives. The researchers then
continued to track the children through adolescence. The youngsters who,
along with their mothers, received the nurse services had less adolescent
crime, sexual activity, cigarette and alcohol use, and associated behavioral problems, compared to a control group that received no such services. The visiting nurses also affected the mothers' behavior: the mothers had less closely spaced subsequent unplanned pregnancies and less
alcohol and drug abuse themselves. Mothers' behavioral changes of this
kind are known to reduce anti-social behavior in children. In the experiment, children of mothers who were visited by nurses during pregnancy
had higher I.Q. scores at ages 3 and 4, and these scores were attributable
solely to nurses' success in getting mothers to reduce smoking.[346] Added
positive effects flowed from other behavioral changes.

Adding the cost of such early childhood programs to regular education finances would boost average annual costs of elementary and secondary schools for lower-class children by another $2,500 per pupil.[347]

After-school programs

After-school and summer programs are also necessary contributions,
organized to provide not only added opportunities for academic work
but also the non-academic activities that enhance students' personal skills
of the sort described in Chapter 4. When middle-class children leave

school in the afternoons, they may go to Girl or Boy Scouts, religious groups, Little League, or soccer practice, or take art, dance, or music lessons. Lower-class children are more likely to play informally or watch television.[348]

As Rafe Esquith and the designers of the KIPP model understand, structured after-school activities contribute to academic proficiency. Children with broader experiences can empathize with literary characters who share those experiences, and this enhances the incentive to read. It is also after school that privileged children are more likely to practice social responsibility in church or youth organizations and develop the organizational skills and discipline that make them more effective adults.

Every child has a somewhat different collection of skills, abilities, and interests. Children who may not excel in math may get a chance to do so in soccer, drama, or piano. Self-confidence gained may carry over to academics. It is unreasonable to think that lower-class children can achieve, on average, at middle-class levels without similar opportunities. Although some lower-class students have these opportunities at the YMCA, Boys and Girls Clubs, the Children's Aid Society, or publicly funded after-school programs, many do not.

Adolescents need such activities not only for what they provide but what they prevent. Students without supervision are at greater risk for truancy, stress, poor grades, and substance abuse. They are most likely to be perpetrators or victims of crime in the first few hours after school.[349] An adequate after-school and weekend program for lower-class children would add another $5,000 per pupil annually to the cost of these children's elementary and secondary schools.[350]

Summer programs

The first chapter reported that the achievement gap between black and white children grows the most during summer vacations from school, when middle-class children have experiences – reading books, going to camp, visiting museums, and traveling – that reinforce their school-year learning, while lower-class children fall behind. An education that hopes to narrow the achievement gap significantly, therefore, should provide comparable summer experiences – not only a summer school of extra drill in reading and math and not even a summer school only of more advanced academic skills. Art, music, drama, dance, and physical education teachers should be more numerous in summer than in the regular year.

A summer program that truly provides lower-class children with such "middle-class" experiences would add another $2,500 to annual per-pupil costs in the schools lower-class children attend.[351]

The dangers of false expectations, and adequacy suits

All told, adding the price of health, early childhood, after-school, and summer programs, this down payment on closing the achievement gap would probably increase the annual cost of education, for children who attend schools where at least 40% of the enrolled children have low incomes, by about $12,500 per pupil, over and above the $8,000 already being spent. In total, this means about a $156 billion added annual national cost to provide these programs to low-income children.[352] Even such expenditure will not fully close the gap, but it might increase the overlap in outcomes of black and white, lower- and middle-class children.

There would be some offsetting savings. If lower-class children had adequate health care and intellectually challenging experiences in an early childhood program, their later placement in special education programs would almost certainly decline. Some fragmentary evidence of this was cited above: experiments that tested high-quality preschool programs (like the Perry experiment) showed that children in these programs were less likely to require special education when they got to regular schools. Similarly, vision therapy, adequate prenatal care, reduction in adult smoking and alcohol use, and other health interventions have also proven to reduce the placement of children in special education programs. For the last 35 years, special education has been the fastest-growing category of education spending, consuming about 40% of all new money given to schools.[353] A significant part of this growth is attributable to the learning difficulties and mental retardation of lower-class children whose disabilities result disproportionately from inadequate health care and inappropriate early childhood experiences.

Education policy makers often say that higher salaries are needed for teachers in general, and even higher salaries than these are needed to attract the most qualified teachers to take jobs in schools where children are most in need. This is certainly the case today. Teaching lower-class children who come to school not ready to learn is difficult, and even if dedicated teachers volunteer for the task, they often wear down and leave for easier assignments after a few years. But if lower-class children came to school ready to learn, in good health, and with adequate early childhood experiences, teachers would find more success and fulfillment in working with them. Less of a salary increment would be needed to attract teachers to work with such children.

Another often recommended policy is smaller class sizes in the early elementary school years, especially in schools that mostly serve children from lower-class families. These smaller class sizes have had a demonstrable effect on life-long achievement, but they are expensive. In the Tennessee experiment, for example, class sizes in kindergarten through third grade were reduced from 24 to 15, a big decrease. If this reduction were implemented for lower-class children only, average per-pupil spending for these children would go up by about $500, not including the cost of building new classrooms to house the added classes.[354] But if teachers of lower-class children had the opportunity to build on the academic and social achievements of a fully adequate early childhood program, it is likely that higher achievement could be generated without so drastic a decrease in primary grade class size.

The $156 billion in new spending, suggested here to make a significant dent in the achievement gap, is not on the political agenda, nor will it be, no matter who is elected president in November 2004. But to say that this spending is not politically realistic is not the same as to say that it is unaffordable. An average annual spending increase of $156 billion is only about two-thirds of the average annual cost of federal tax cuts enacted since 2001.[355] So if Americans truly wanted to significantly narrow the social class differences that produce an educational achievement gap, we could do so.

Many lawsuits around the country involve plaintiffs, usually representing minority children or the school districts in which they are numerous, who demand something called "adequate school funding." At this writing, the most prominent case is one in New York State where the Court of Appeals has found that the state's school financing system is unconstitutional because it does not give lower-class children the opportunity to achieve at middle-class levels. Such lawsuits, if successful, can improve education for minority and low-income youth. But advocates of this litigation should take care not to raise expectations that even significantly more new dollars in schools alone will close the academic gap. In New York, the plaintiffs have proposed an added $4,000 per pupil for schools in New York City, a 24% increase in per-pupil spending. The plaintiffs say these new funds should mostly be used for smaller classes and higher teacher pay. Such new spending will certainly improve education for New York City youngsters. But advocates for the plaintiffs have gone further, and say that such an increase could close the achievement gap and enable all students to achieve at high enough levels that they qualify for admission to academic colleges.[356] This expectation is bound to be disappointed. If social class differences in readiness for learning are unaddressed, such a goal can only be met if high school graduation and college admissions standards are diluted to unrecognizability.

Funds sought in adequacy cases, while substantial, are tiny compared to what is truly needed for adequate outcomes. Schools, no matter how good, cannot carry the entire burden of narrowing our substantial social class differences.

While an additional $156 billion annually to make a significant dent in the black–white achievement gap is not politically realistic, it is important to consider it because, in the absence of such spending, talk of closing the achievement gap is unrealistic, perhaps even irresponsible.

Teacher morale

In American education today, policy makers and educators frequently invoke slogans like "no excuses," or "all students can learn to the same high standards," proclaiming what they say is their commitment to close the achievement gap between lower-class and middle-class children. Some say that these incantations are harmless, and, even if they are hyperbolic, serve the useful purpose of spurring teachers, principals, and other school officials to greater efforts to raise the achievement levels of minority and other disadvantaged students.

Such whips can serve this useful purpose. But they can also do great damage. They de-legitimize good and great teachers who dedicate themselves to raising minority student achievement in realistic increments. They drive out of the teaching profession decent teachers who feel inadequate to the task of reaching utopian goals, or who resent the cynicism of politicians and administrators who demand that such goals be attained. If this disconnect continues between what is realistically possible and the goals we establish for educators, the nation risks abandoning public education only to those willing to pander to political fashion by promising to achieve in schools what they know, in their hearts, is not possible. And in the polity, "no excuses" slogans provide ideological respectability for those wanting to hold schools accountable for inevitable failure.

Conclusion

If as a society we choose to preserve big social class differences, we must necessarily also accept substantial gaps between the achievement of lower-class and middle-class children. Closing those gaps requires not only better schools, although those are certainly needed, but also reform in the social and economic institutions that presently prepare children to learn in radically different ways. It will not be cheap.

Raising the achievement of lower-class children, and narrowing the gap in cognitive achievement and non-cognitive skills between these children and those from the middle class, are more ambitious undertakings than policy makers today acknowledge. What this book has tried to show is that eliminating the social class differences in student outcomes requires eliminating the impact of social class on children in American society. It requires abandoning the illusion that school reform alone can save us from having to make the difficult economic and political decisions that the goal of equality inevitably entails. School improvement does have an important role to play, but it cannot shoulder the entire burden, or even most of it, on its own.

Appendix: What employers say about graduates

Surveys conducted by business groups, government agencies, and education policy groups have consistently shown that employers complain far more about job applicants' communication skills, punctuality, responsibility, attitude, teamwork ability, and conflict resolution skills than about their verbal and mathematical abilities. Here is a sample of such conclusions over the last two decades.[357]

- A survey of employers conducted in 2003 found that the most important qualities sought in recent college graduates were communication skills, honesty and integrity, interpersonal skills, motivation and initiative, a strong work ethic, and teamwork skills, in that order. These employers (400 firms were surveyed, including firms in the service sector, manufacturing, and nonprofit and governmental sectors) cared about cognitive skills and generally said they sought candidates with a "B" average. But once candidates met this cutoff, their grade point averages were unimportant in comparison to the non-cognitive skills required.[358]

- In 2001, the National Association of Manufacturers surveyed executives of 600 member firms about skills shortages they encountered. It found that when firms rejected applicants for production jobs, it was because of problems with "employability skills" (timeliness and work ethic) in 69% of the cases, but because of poor math skills in only 21% and poor reading and writing skills in only 34%. When these firms rejected applicants for professional jobs, employability skills were the cause in 16% of the cases, poor math skills in 4%, and poor reading and writing in 6%.[359]

- A 1996 survey of 3,000 rural manufacturers, conducted by the U.S. Department of Agriculture, found that 31% of them complained of serious difficulty finding workers with a "reliable and acceptable work attitude," and 22% had serious difficulty finding workers who were good at problem solving. Only 12% had serious difficulty finding workers with basic math skills, and only 5% had major complaints about basic reading. The department also surveyed 1,000 urban manufacturers with similar results.[360]

- A 1994 survey conducted by the Census Bureau of over 3,000 representative manufacturing and non-manufacturing firms asked employers what factors they considered in deciding whether to hire an applicant for a nonsupervisory job. The most important was the applicant's attitude, followed by his or her communications skills. The least important were academic measures like teacher recommendations, the reputation of the school attended by the applicant, grades, test scores, and years of schooling.[361]

- In the late 1980s, a group headed by two former secretaries of labor, William E. Brock (a Republican) and Ray Marshall (a Democrat), surveyed hundreds of American employers about the deficiencies in skills that high school graduates bring to the workforce. Messrs. Brock and Marshall expected employers to complain that graduates couldn't read or do algebra well enough for the modern workplace. To their surprise they found very few employers who complained about inadequate cognitive skills of new hires. What employers (80% of them) did complain about was the work ethic and social skills of new hires – such as their ability to work in teams to solve problems, their ability to resolve interpersonal conflicts, their reliability and attitude, and their appearance.[362]

- In 1988, the federal departments of education and labor jointly surveyed small- and medium-sized employers who responded that schools should emphasize teaching self-discipline, reliability, perseverance, acceptance of responsibility, and respect for the rights of others.[363]

- A 1987 report of the National Alliance of Business urged that greater attention be paid to the "fourth 'R'" of schooling: readiness for work, which includes reasoning, problem solving skills, reliability, responsibility, and adaptability to change.[364]

- A 1984 survey of a random sample of Fortune 500 companies along with thousands of smaller firms found that "employers are looking for young people who demonstrate a set of attitudes, abilities, and behaviors associated with a sense of responsibility, self-discipline, pride, teamwork, and enthusiasm."[365]

- A 1983 survey of employers found that 48% gave first priority to "character" in making hiring decisions, while only 5% gave first priority to "education."[366]

- Observational studies of workplaces also confirm that many if not most workers, even in technologically sophisticated industries, require relatively low levels of academic proficiency but higher levels of non-academic skills. For example, a prevalent mode of workplace training in American industry appears to be "peer training," where experienced workers train new hires.[367] Observational studies find that successful workers are those with strong communication and even pedagogical skills, qualified to teach their peers how to be more productive.

Endnotes

1.   Clark argued that segregation created a feeling of inferiority, and that it was difficult for the achievement of black children to overcome this stigma.

2.   For discussions of the historical context of the Coleman report, see Moynihan 1968; Mosteller and Moynihan 1972; and Grant 1973.

3.   Mosteller and Moynihan 1972.

4.   Henceforth, for simplicity, I will say that, compared to white students who are on average at the 50th percentile, black students are on average at about the 23rd percentile.

5.   To be more precise, the achievement gap will disappear if the proficiency point is either excessively simple, or excessively difficult. If you ask fourth graders to take a test with questions like the addition of 2+2, almost all from every socioeconomic group will get it right, and so there will be no test score gap. If you ask fourth graders to take a test that requires solving differential equations, almost none will do so, and there also will be no test score gap. The biggest test score gap between students from two socioeconomic groups will appear if proficiency is defined as the midpoint between the average scores of students from those groups.

6.   If the average black student scores at about the 23rd percentile in a national normal distribution in which the average white student scores at the 50th percentile, about one-quarter of the black students are statistically likely to score higher than the average-scoring white student.

7.   Jencks, forthcoming.

8.   Gardner 1999.

9.   Shonkoff and Phillips 2000.

10.   Bianchi and Robinson 1997; Hoffereth and Sandberg 2001.

11.   Denton and Germino-Hauskens 2000, Table 20, p. 52. Of children whose mothers have at least a bachelor's degree, 59% are read to daily. Of children whose mothers have no more than a high school diploma or equivalent, 39% are read to daily. Of children whose mothers have less than a high school diploma, 36% are read to daily. Of white children, 49% are read to daily. Of black children, 35% are read to daily.
     Of children whose mothers have at least a bachelor's degree, 93% are read to at least three times a week. Of children whose mothers have no more than a high school diploma or equivalent, 75% are read to at least three times a week. Of children whose mothers have less than a high school diploma, 63% are read to at least three times a week. Of white children, 86% are read to at least three times a week. Of black children, 68% are read to at least three times a week.

12.   Denton and Germino-Hauskens 2000, Table 19, p. 51. Of children whose mothers have at least a bachelor's degree, 71% have more than 50 books in their homes; of

children whose mothers have only a high school diploma, 37% have this many books; of children whose mothers did not graduate from high school, only 14% have this many.

13.   Rathburn and West 2003, Table 4.

14.   Torney-Purta et al. 2001, p. 65.

15.   Other countries do not track their achievement gaps with as much precision as we do in the United States. In some countries, there is resistance to collecting data by income or ethnicity because of a feeling that this somehow legitimizes a non-assimilationist ideology (Rothstein 2000a). For descriptions of gaps in other nations, see Begag 1990; Castles et al. 1984; Garner 2004; Neuman and Peer 2002; OFSTED 1999; Ogbu 1992b; and Sciolino 2004. For a discussion of poor educational attainment of low-income children of all ethnicities in Great Britain, see Ermisch 2001.

16.   OECD 2001.

17.   Lemke 2002, p. 37; Figure 17, p. 44.

18.   Snow and Tabors 1996.

19.   Lareau 1989.

20.   Mikulecky 1996.

21.   See also Britto and Brooks-Gunn 2001, who report on a survey that included only poorly educated single African American mothers. Within this group, more expressive language use during book reading predicted children's achievement, but the survey does not lead to any reliable conclusions regarding whether the use of expressive language is related to social class.

22.   Mikulecky 1996.

23.   Mikulecky 1996

24.   Snow and Tabors 1996.

25.   See Lareau 2003 for a general discussion of these childrearing pattern differences.

26.   Tourangeau et al. 2002, Section 7.4.2, pp. 7-18.

27.   Portas 2004. Additional data analysis provided to the author by Carole A. Portas. In the lowest 20% of families by socioeconomic status, 79% of parents believed that their children should know the alphabet letters when they entered kindergarten. But only 55% of families from the highest 20% of families by socioeconomic status shared this belief. For believing that children should know how to count at kindergarten entry, the shares were 71% and 50%, respectively.

28.   Lareau 2002, 2003.

29.   Heath 1983.

30.   Heath 1983.

31.   Heath 1983.

32. The childrearing practices of upper-middle-class parents have come under se-vere criticism by developmental psychologists for placing too much decision-making responsibility on children and robbing them of their childhood innocence. However valid these criticisms may be, they do not negate the congruence of such childrearing practices with the skills required for high academic achievement.

33. Kohn 1969.

34. Comer 1988; Heath 1983; Lareau 2003.

35. Hofferth and Sandberg 2001; Lareau 2003.

36. Heath 1983.

37. Brooks 1916.

38. Gill and Schlossman 2000.

39. Lareau 2003.

40. Hart and Risley 1995; Hart and Risley 2003. The Hart-Risley findings have sometimes been mis-reported as meaning that children of professionals had larger vocabularies than the vocabularies of adults on welfare (not than the much smaller vocabularies that adults on welfare use when speaking to children). See Nunberg 2002; Bracey 2003.

41. Wilson 2002. Some historians disagree with this interpretation, but Wilson's summary of the controversy is persuasive.

42. Kalil, Pattillo, and Payne 2001; however, Geronimus 1997 argues that children born to poor black teenagers may have better outcomes than children born to poor black young adults, because health for the very poor deteriorates very early and so black teen mothers may be in better health than black young adult mothers.

43. Lareau 2002.

44. Sanderson 1996, Table 1, p. 4.

45. Hudson 2003, Figure 1; 72% vs. 82% figure from Kaufman and Naomi 2000, Table 4, p. 18.

46. Calculated from Hudson 2003.

47. NCES 2003a, Table 22-1.

48. Ogbu 2003.

49. Kahl 1953.

50. Horvat, Weininger, and Lareau 2003.

51. Horvat, Weininger, and Lareau 2003.

52. Rothstein, Carnoy, and Benveniste 1999.

53. See, for example, Bankston and Zhou 1995; Zhou and Bankston 1998.

54. Hofferth and Sandberg 2001.

55.   Kao, Tienda, and Schneider 1996.

56.   Covello 1936; Olneck and Lazerson 1974; Sowell 1994. This history is summarized in Rothstein 1998. Thernstrom and Thernstrom 2003 also review these differences.

57.   Ogbu 2003.

58.   See, for example, Thernstrom and Thernstrom 1997. The most prominent scholarly advocate of the claim that discrimination no longer plays a role is James J. Heckman who claims (1998) that "[a] careful reading of the entire body of available evidence confirms that most of the disparity in earnings between blacks and whites in the labor market of the 1990s is due to the differences in skills they bring to the market, and not to discrimination within the labor market."

59.   Black–white wage differences seem to be small for workers of similar cognitive skills when those skills are measured by the Armed Forces Qualifying Test, but not by other tests. And even on this test, when results are controlled for years of education, a black–white wage difference re-emerges for workers who have similar achievement and attainment. (White workers have more education, on average, than black workers of similar ages.) See Darity and Mason 1998.

60.   Race, not test scores, plays a bigger role in explaining differences between black and white earnings than between black and white hourly wages, because black workers, once hired, are likely to earn close to (but still less than) what white workers with similar test scores earn. But because black workers are unemployed for longer periods than white workers with similar test scores, and because, if employed, they work fewer hours, the annual earnings of black workers are lower. The more frequent unemployment and fewer hours of employment of black men than of white men with similar skills is probably the result of continued discrimination. See Johnson and Neal 1998.

61.   Darity and Mason 1998.

62.   Pager 2003. Thernstrom and Thernstrom 1997 acknowledge that in a highly credible audit study in Washington, D.C., white applicants were more successful than black applicants whose qualifications were similar. But the Thernstroms dismiss the significance of this study because it tested only private sector openings, whereas many job vacancies in Washington, D.C. are governmental, and in federal jobs black applicants might even have an advantage. This may be the case, but private sector employment in Washington, D.C. is more representative than government employment of all employment nationwide. If employment discrimination persists for black applicants in the private sector in Washington, D.C., it probably persists nationwide, in employment overall.

63.   Darity and Mason 1998.

64.   Darity and Mason 1998.

65.   Kluegel and Bobo 2001.

66.   Noguera 2001; also, Mickelson 1990; Ogbu 2003.

67.   Kao, Tienda, and Schneider 1996. Ogbu 1990 cites the relative success of black Caribbean immigrants to argue that the relative lack of success of native-born blacks stems from an experience of oppression, not biology. This may be true, although it is

difficult to know how much the superior performance of immigrants is attributable to the fact that the most highly motivated Caribbean blacks are those who choose to immigrate.

68.   Ogbu 2003.

69.   It has often been reported that black students accuse their more academically talented peers of "acting white" in order to pressure these better students to conform by reducing their achievement. Critics of this explanation have noted that a culture of underachievement is not the exclusive preserve of black students; white youths, too, who are good students are sometimes ridiculed by their peers for being "nerds" or "geeks." My discussion adopts the conclusion of Ronald F. Ferguson (Cook and Ludwig 1998) that black students come under more such pressure than white students whose social characteristics are similar, but Ferguson acknowledges that there are insufficient data to fully resolve this issue. The problem of anti-intellectual pressure felt by students of both races has been discussed and debated not only by John Ogbu 2003 (and see also Fordham and Ogbu 1986) but by Steinberg 1996, Bishop et al. 2003, and Cook and Ludwig 1998 (including the comment by Ronald F. Ferguson).

70.   Egbuonu and Starfield 1982; Starfield 1982.

71.   Orfield, Basa, and Yun 2001.

72.   Festinger and Duckman 2000.

73.   The normal incidence of vision problems in children is about 25%. Clinicians and researchers have found incidences of more than 50% in some communities, although there has been no systematic nationwide survey of vision problems by race or social class. See Gould and Gould 2003; Orfield 2003; Orfield, Basa, and Yun 2001; Duckman 2003; P. Harris 2003; Harris 2002.

74.   Harris 2002.

75.   There is surprisingly no experimental evidence on the relationship between prenatal care and vision, and little good research evidence generally on the relationship between socioeconomic conditions and children's vision. In the following discussions, I have been guided by personal correspondence and conversations with academic and clinical optometrists, including Professor Robert Duckman (State University of New York), Dr. Paul Harris, Dr. Antonia Orfield, and Professor Harold Solan (State University of New York). I also relied on the advice here of Dr. Barbara Starfield at Johns Hopkins University. Sara Mosle, a former teacher in a low-income school (and now a journalist and historian) stimulated this line of inquiry for me when she showed me her unpublished article, "They Can't Read Because They Can't See." See also Festinger and Duckman 2000; Harris 2002; Orfield, Basa, and Yun 2001; Solan et al. 2003.

76.   NCES 2003b, Table 117.

77.   Orfield 2003.

78.   Gould and Gould 2003.

79.   Orfield et al.2001; Orfield 2003.

80.   Egbuonu and Starfield 1982.

81.   Some medical authorities state that antibiotics have been overprescribed for young children's ear infections and that painkillers alone would sometimes suffice. However, without good access to personal pediatricians who know a child's history, parents cannot themselves determine whether antibiotics or painkillers are the proper treatment in any particular case. See Altman 2004.

82.   GAO 2000, Figure 1, p. 8.

83.   Egbuono and Starfield 1982; GAO 1999; Neisser, et al. 1996; Neisser 1997. There is scientific controversy regarding how much lead exposure is harmful to children.

84.   Brookes-Gunn and Duncan 1997.

85.   GAO 1999.

86.   Barton 2003; Blum 2004.

87.   Johnson 2003.

88.   Frieden 2003.

89.   Associated Press 2003b.

90.   Forrest et al. 1997; Halfon and Newacheck 1993.

91.   Associated Press 2003a. Vaughan 2003.

92.   Whitman, Williams, and Shah 2004; Ritter 2004.

93.   Halfon and Newacheck 1993.

94.   Whitman, Williams, and Shah 2004.

95.   Hilts 2000.

96.   Halfon and Newacheck 1993.

97.   Forrest et al. 1997.

98.   *Morbidity and Mortality Weekly Report* 2002, Table 2.

99.   The accuracy of these rates may be questioned because they are self-reported (by parents) and because there may now be more awareness of asthma, leading parents to categorize respiratory problems as asthmatic that they might not have categorized in this way in 1980. However, there seems to be a consensus among public health professionals that asthma has increased, even if the specific rate of increase reported here is open to question. Noguera 2003 found a chronic respiratory disease rate of 40% in an Oakland, Calif. school.

100.   Welfare Law Center 2000; Dubay, Haley, and Kenney 2000.

101.   Mills and Bhandari 2003, Figure 4. Note that the figures presented here are for "black alone or in combination," vs. "white alone, not Hispanic."

102.   Komaromy et al. 1996. From the 1990 Census, a neighborhood with high concentration of black and Hispanic residents was defined as one with more black and Hispanic residents than 85% of all neighborhoods. A high poverty neighborhood was defined as one where more than 25% of the residents had household incomes of less than $15,000.

103. Brown et al. 2003.

104. Hoffman et al. 2003, p. 17. Of white children between the ages of 19 and 35 months, 21% lack standard immunizations. Of black children this age, 28% lack them.

105. Starfield 1997.

106. Astley 2003; Simmons et al. 2002.

107. Richardson et al. 2002; Streissguth et al.1994.

108. Abel 1995.

109. CDC 2002b.

110. Abel and Hannigan 1995.

111. Astley 2003.

112. CDC 2001a.

113. CDC 2001b, Table 2.15.

114. Hack, Klein, and Taylor 1995.

115. Hoffman, Llagas, and Snyder 2003, p. 15.

116. Whyatt et al. 2004; Berkowitz et al. 2004; Whyatt et al. 2002. The researchers plan to follow the children born as the pesticide ban was being enforced, to determine whether those born to mothers with less exposure in fact have better academic performance and behavior.

117. Rich-Edwards et al. 2001; Wadhwa et al. 2001; Halfon 2002; Lu 2002; Lu and Halfon 2003.

118. Abel and Hannigan 1995.

119. Egbuonu and Starfield 1982.

120. Brown and Sherman 1995; Murphy et al. 1998b.

121. Karp et al. 1992.

122. CDC 2002c.

123. Brown and Sherman 1995.

124. America's Second Harvest 2003; Koch 2002.

125. Neisser et al. 1996.

126. Figlio and Winicki 2002. Whitney Allgood (personal correspondence) reports that the principal of her child's school this year assigned parents to deliver healthy breakfast foods for classes taking standardized tests, for each day of testing. At this school, most children are middle class, and the breakfasts were not served to alleviate real hunger but only to ensure that children were well-nourished on testing days, a condition that is less likely for low-income children.

127. That some lower-class children go hungry or are poorly nourished, and many fewer middle-class children have these characteristics, is not inconsistent with higher

rates of obesity for low-income children, attributable to poor dietary habits (CDC 2002a). Having excessive caloric intake does not boost children's academic achievement, but if some lower-class children have inadequate nutrition, the average achievement of lower-class children will be lower.

128. Nord, Andrews, and Carlson 2003, Table 6. "Low-income" here refers to children living in families whose income was below 130% of the poverty line. Table 4 shows that 11% of low-income children lived in households where someone was hungry. Parents report that, when there is insufficient food, adults go hungry before children do.

129. U.S. Conference of Mayors - Sodexho 2003; Zeller 2004.

130. Rosso and Fowler 2000, Table III.2

131. Kaufman 2003. New York City was found in violation of federal regulations for not ensuring that families were made aware of their eligibility.

132. Brown 2003.

133. O'Donnell 2001.

134. Meyers et al. 1989; Murphy et al. 1998a.

135. Kerbow 1996; Bruno and Isken 1996.

136. GAO 1994.

137. Bruno and Isken 1996.

138. For the effects of high mobility on non-mobile students and teacher practices, see Kerbow 1996; Wang, Haertel, and Walberg 1994. For the effects of mobility on the test score gap, see Hanushek, Kain, and Rivkin 2004a.

139. In one national database that tracked children for six years, of white children who were from families that were poor at some time during the period, only 22% were poor for at least five of the six years. For blacks, however, of those who were from families that were poor at some time during the period, 55% were poor for at least five of the years. See Brooks-Gunn et al. 2003.

140. Geronimus 2000. Causation can work both ways, for adults. Adults who are in poor health are able to earn less and are therefore more likely to be poor for extended periods. However, this would not explain why children would have more extended periods of living in families in poverty if their health was poor.

141. Duncan and Brooks-Gunn 1997.

142. Brooks-Gunn and Duncan 1997.

143. McLoyd 1990; McLoyd et al. 1994; Flanagan and Eccles 1994.

144. McKinnon and Humes 2000; U.S. Census Bureau 2002a. In 2002, black families of all ages included an average of 1.27 children; white families of all ages included an average of 0.91 children.

145. Zajonc 1976; Zajonc 1983.

146. Grissmer et al. 1994.

147. Grissmer 1999.

148. The data on income are from 1979 to 2000; see Mishel, Bernstein, and Boushey 2003, Table 1.4. The data on wealth are from 1983 to 1998; Mishel, Bernstein, and Boushey 2003, Table 4.6. These are the most recent comparable data.

149. Keister, forthcoming.

150. Brown et al. 2003.

151. Phillips et al. 1998.

152. Cameron and Heckman 2001; Fryer and Levitt 2002; Phillips et al. 1998.

153. Herrnstein and Murray 1994. Phillips et al. (1998, p. 138) conclude that "[e]ven though traditional measures of socioeconomic status account for no more than a third of the [black–white] test score gap, our results show that a broader index of family environment may explain up to two-thirds of it." There are other differences, for example health and housing, not considered by Phillips et al. that might explain even more of the gap.

154. Lee and Burkam 2002, Figure 1.2. Lee and Burkam express these data in standard deviation units, -0.62 for math, -0.4 for literacy. This figure compares blacks to whites, and assumes that whites have an average ranking on these tests at the 50th percentile. The figure converts Lee and Burkam's data from standard deviation units to percentile ranks. This requires an assumption that test scores are normally distributed.

155. Lee and Burkam Figure 1.5 illustrates a few race vs. SES differences. Other data cited here and in subsequent paragraphs were provided to the author by Lee and Burkam. In all cases, Lee and Burkam present their results in effect sizes, or standard deviation units. The percentile ranks used here were estimated assuming normal distributions.

156. The greater gap in math than in reading is unexpected, because most analysts would expect home influences to play a bigger role in reading than in math, but perhaps this is not the case, especially in early childhood. The difference in the math and reading gaps in this early childhood survey warrants further examination, and should be confirmed by other studies before being taken too seriously. Although it is hard to imagine how the absolute difficulty of a math and reading test could be compared, the difference in the math vs. reading gap could have something to do with the relative difficulty of the tests given to the entering kindergartners in the Early Childhood Longitudinal Study sample.

157. It is hard to be certain about how much of the gap is attributable to what schools do, and how much is attributable to home influences, partly because there is no single good way to measure the achievement gap. Here are some "back-of-the-envelope" calculations to illustrate the conceptual difficulty of measuring the achievement gap.

The most common way to measure it is in percentile ranks. On tests of math and reading, it seems that lower-class four-year-olds, on average, achieve at about the same level as middle-class four-year-olds who are at about the 34th percentile in a distribution of all middle-class four-year-olds' achievement. More precisely, average low-SES four-year-olds' achievement is 0.55 of a standard deviation below average middle-class four-year-old achievement in math, and 0.47 of a standard deviation below average middle-class four-year-old achievement in literacy skills. This social class gap is similar to the black–white skill gap at age 4. See Figures 2A, 2B, 3A, and 3B and Lee and Burkam, Figure 1.3.

At 9 years of age, the black–white achievement gap is a full standard deviation in reading and almost as great in math. (The average reading scale score for nine-year-olds on the National Assessment of Educational Progress in 1999 was 186 for black students and 221 for white students; the average math scale score for blacks was 211 and for whites it was 239; NCES 2003b, Tables 111 and 123). In percentile terms, this means that average black nine-year-olds had reading and math proficiency that was about 30 percentile points below average white proficiency.

So, measured by changes in percentile ranks, we would say that the black–white gap grew by about 14 percentile points from 4 to 9 years of age. Or we could say that the gap nearly doubled (an initial gap of 16 percentile points increased by an additional 14 percentile points).

But this gap would look different and have different rates of change if we measured it in "real" terms. For example, Hart and Risley 1995, Table 5 (p. 176) report that, at age 3, children of parents who are professionals have a vocabulary of about 1,100 words, children of working-class parents have a vocabulary of about 750 words, and children of parents receiving welfare have vocabularies of about 525 words. If we assume that an average of what Hart and Risley called "professional" and "working class" children are comparable to what Lee and Burkam describe as middle SES, and if we assume that an average of Hart and Risley's "working class" and "welfare" children are comparable to what Lee and Burkam describe as low SES, then the Hart and Risley finding can be interpreted as that middle SES children's vocabularies are 45% higher (925 words vs. 638 words) than low SES children's vocabularies at age 3.

Moats 2001 reports that at first grade, the difference between the vocabularies of "linguistically rich" and "linguistically poor" children is 20,000 vs. 5,000 words. If we assume that these categories are comparable to the professional and welfare categories used by Hart and Risley, and do a similar interpolation, we can interpret Moats' claim as one finding that middle SES children in first grade have vocabularies (roughly 16,000 words) that are nearly 80% higher than those of low SES children (roughly 9,000 words).

Thus, in percentile (or standard deviation) terms, the gap grew by nearly 100% from early childhood to the primary school years (comparing Lee-Burkam findings to NAEP nine-year-olds' scores). But from early childhood to primary school, the average middle-class student has learned 19,000 new words while the average low-income student has learned only 9,000 new words (comparing the Hart-Risley and Moat reports). Does this mean that the gap has more than doubled? Or, if there was a 45% gap in vocabulary words in early childhood and an 80% gap in primary school, does this mean that the gap didn't quite double?

In sum, in average percentile ranking, the achievement gap nearly doubled from early childhood to elementary school, or it grew by 14 percentile points. In absolute number of vocabulary words, the gap more than doubled. The gap in vocabulary words grew in percentage terms, but at a slightly slower rate – by about 75% (from a gap of 45% to a gap of 80%).

The numbers used here should not be taken seriously for any purpose except this illustration. Actually equating results from ECLS, NAEP, Hart and Risley, and Moats is not statistically possible. These are only "back-of-the-envelope" reflections for the sole purpose of illustrating that reports of the gap are a function of how the underlying data are measured and defined.

It becomes even harder (probably impossible) to measure the gap in real terms when describing subject matter that is not as easily quantifiable as "numbers of vocabulary words." There is no way to measure, in real terms, the gap between mean achievement in arithmetic and achievement that is half a standard deviation below the mean. Percentile ranks (or standard deviation units) are the only way such a gap can be measured.

158. Phillips 2000, Table 2 and p. 104. The Phillips data compare achievement in the 12th grade with achievement in the first grade, so they do not precisely explain changes in the gap since kindergarten.

159. Phillips 2000, pp. 108-109.

160. Phillips 2000; Allington and McGill-Franzen 2003; Entwisle and Alexander 1992. One recent study (Fryer and Levitt 2002) finds no growth of the achievement gap during the summer, but this claim is at odds with most of the research literature.

161. Hayes and Grether 1983.

162. Mikulecky 1996.

163. Neuman and Celano 2001, Tables 1, 3, 8.

164. Entwisle, Alexander, and Olson 2000.

165. Hauser 2000.

166. Gitomer 2003.

167. Sanders et al. 1997. For purposes of this discussion, I assume that value-added analysis does in fact have the capacity to separate students' personal and socioeconomic characteristics from teacher effects. However, the technique relies on an assumption that these characteristics are stable for students throughout their school careers, and so any deviation from a child's pattern of performance can be attributed to teaching. For individual children, this assumption is certainly invalid. Just as the quality of a child's teacher changes from year to year, so too do a child's background characteristics change over time. Parents' unemployment, divorce or remarriage, changing health conditions, or other personal or family economic crises can surely affect the underlying pattern of a child's performance, and so deviations from a previous or subsequent pattern may not reflect the influence of teachers alone. It is untested whether, aggregated to the level of all children of a given teacher, such changes in student background characteristics occur with enough magnitude and frequency to make the value-added assumption invalid.

168. Sanders and Rivers 1996, Figure 1. This 25-percentile-point gain is an average of a 16 percentile gain in Sanders' and Rivers' School System A and a 33 percentile gain in their School System B.

169. Sanders and Rivers 1996. See, for example, Fallon 2003. Although Dr. Sanders claims that he has identified teacher value-added, and many policy makers repeat this claim, actually he has identified the value-added of being in a particular classroom. Certainly, the effectiveness of a teacher is a very important ingredient of classroom effectiveness, but it is not the only one. For example, equally effective teachers may have different value-added because they teach classes of different sizes, have aides of different effectiveness, have textbook sets of different quality, are given different de-

grees of support from the school administration, have substitutes of different quality when they are ill, or experience a variety of other classroom differences. In reality, Dr. Sanders is attempting to identify classroom value-added, not teacher value-added. However, for purposes of this discussion, the distinction is not important because Dr. Sanders' work is cited to prove that student background characteristics can be overcome by more effective teaching. If he were cited to prove that student background characteristics can be overcome by more effective classrooms, the policy implications would be similar.

170. Social scientists who study human behavior usually consider that a policy innovation with what they term an "effect size" of 0.5 (a policy that moves performance from the 50th to about the 70th percentile in a normal distribution) to be a major accomplishment, rarely achieved in reform efforts. An innovation with an effect size of 0.3 (from the 50th to about the 62nd percentile) is considered respectable, the result of carefully designed reform. Even an innovation with an effect size of 0.1 (from the 50th to about the 54th percentile) is considered worthwhile. Policy makers in education who take their lead from Dr. Sanders believe that the achievement gap can be wiped out by adopting a policy (improving teacher quality) with an effect size of 1.3, a gain that is almost unprecedented.

171. DeNavas, Cleveland, and Roemer 2001, Table C.

172. The great Boston Red Sox of 1950 had a regular player average of .311. But even then, four regulars batted below .300, and the team could not sustain its unique performance. In 1951, with mostly the same regulars, the team average collapsed to .264. The 1950 team was a fluke, confirming that 90th percentile performance cannot be a model to emulate.

173. For example, on the 2003 National Assessment of Educational Progress, the black–white gap in mathematics at the fourth grade was 27 scale points, 216 vs. 243. In reading, the gap was 31 scale points, 198 vs. 229. NAEP 2004e.

174. Ballou 2002.

175. Rockoff 2003, Table 5.

176. Iatarola 2001.

177. Tames 2000.

178. There are currently about three million public school teachers. The estimate assumes that an additional $30,000 in salary represents about $35,000 in additional compensation, including payroll tax and pension benefit contributions. Matthew Miller (2003) claims that both liberal and conservative critics of education would agree to increasing the salaries of the best teachers by 50% if these teachers would agree to serve in the lowest-performing schools, provided that the increase were tied to a firm guarantee that these teachers were the most effective. He estimates the cost of his proposal to be $30 billion a year.

179. Defining the characteristics of the top quintile of teachers is a much more difficult task than defining the characteristics of teachers who are better than average. There is evidence that teachers who themselves have higher verbal test scores can generate better student achievement. (For a review of literature on teacher quality, see Rice 2003.) But the evidence is not sufficient to suggest that teachers with the top

quintile of test scores are also teachers who are in the top quintile of effectiveness. There is also evidence that, as discrimination against women in better-paying professions like law, medicine, and business has declined, fewer women with the very highest test scores become teachers, although the average test scores of teachers has not declined. See Corcoran, Evans, and Schwab 2002. But if competition from other fields has made teaching less attractive to the very top of the ability distribution, the cost of luring the best teachers back to the profession could be very high indeed.

180. Sanders and Rivers 1996.

181. Hanushek and Rivkin 2004.

182. See, for example, Ladd and Walsh 2002.

183. Olson 2004; Riley 2004.

184. McCaffrey et al 2003.

185. Carter 2000.

186. Allgood 1999.

187. And, on a test on which black children scored half a standard deviation below white students (not an unusual occurrence), in other words, in which black children were, on average, at about the 33rd percentile while white students were, on average, at about the 50th percentile, one-third of black children would score higher than the average-scoring white student.

188. Venezky 1998; Walberg and Greenberg 1998.

189. Carter 2000.

190. KIPP 2002.

191. KIPP 2003.

192. KIPP 2002.

193. KIPP 2003.

194. Levin, 2004.

195. Wilgoren 2000.

196. Jerald 2001.

197. D. Harris 2003.

198. For example, upon the release in 2002 of the Education Trust's list of "high flying schools," Williamson M. Evers of the Hoover Institution, a conservative "think tank" and a member of President Bush's committee to oversee federal education research, said that the Education Trust had now proven that it was "racist nonsense" to deny that accountability alone (for example, as enshrined in the No Child Left Behind law) could generate equal outcomes for poor and middle-class students. See Evers 2002.

199. Reeves 2000.

200. Reeves 2000.

201. Marshall 2003.

202. Orfield, Basa, and Yun 2001. The data should be treated with caution because they were collected and analyzed by the optometrists themselves, not by an independent reviewer.

203. Golden 1999.

204. Golden 1999; Viadero 2000; GAO 2001; Smrekar et al. 2001.

205. GAO 2001.

206. GAO 2001; Smrekar et al. 2001.

207. GAO 2001.

208. Smrekar et al. 2001.

209. Smrekar et al. 2001.

210. Golden 1999; Viadero 2000; GAO 2001; Smrekar et al. 2001.

211. Viadero 2000.

212. Golden 1999; Diekmann 2001; GAO 2001, Table 13.

213. Smrekar et al. 2001.

214. Smrekar et al. 2001.

215. Pyle 1998.

216. During the period that Mr. Esquith taught at Hobart Elementary School, and won national recognition for his efforts, ethnic enrollment percentages had a consistent pattern at the school. In the fall of 1990, Hobart Elementary School had these percentages: Asian, 18.4; black, 2.9; Filipino, 1.8; Hispanic, 76.1; white, 0.8; see LAUSD 1990, p. 143. In the fall of 1995, Hobart Elementary School had these percentages: Asian, 16.7; black, 2.3; Filipino, 0.5; Hispanic, 80.2; white, 0.3; see LAUSD 1996, p. 114.

217. These characterizations of Hobart parents are based on my discussions with Hobart administrators and faculty conducted on various dates in October 1991.

218. KIPP 2003.

219. Levin 2004; Yu 2004.

220. Levin 2004.

221. Freedman 2000.

222. The gap can be different for different ages, different subjects, and different tests. If white students' average score is at the 50th percentile, blacks' average score ranges from the 15th to the 35th percentile.

223. NAEP 2004b; NAEP 2004d.

224. Japan and Korea do have high proportions of eighth-graders close to proficiency in math and science as defined by the NAEP, although we cannot know how close students in these nations are to U.S. definitions of proficiency in other grade levels or subjects.

Two comparisons illustrate how far U.S. proficiency standards are from international norms.

First, on a 1990-91 reading test administered by the International Association for the Evaluation of Educational Achievement, America's nine-year-olds scored second highest in the world; Finnish nine-year-olds were first (Elley 1992). Yet on the NAEP, administered in 1992, the federal government determined that only 29% of U.S. nine-year-olds were proficient in reading (NAEP 2004c).

The other subjects and grade level in which direct comparisons are possible between U.S. proficiency levels and the performance of other nations is eighth grade mathematics and science. For these, the National Center of Education Statistics compared American students' performance on the NAEP, given in 1996, with the performance of students in the U.S. and other nations on the Third International Mathematics and Science Study (TIMSS), given in 1995 (Johnson 1998).

In mathematics, the average domestic NAEP score of 270 in 1996 was below the proficient level, defined as a score of 299 (NAEP 2004a; Loomis and Bourque 2001). Only 24% of U.S. eighth-graders were found to be proficient in mathematics, according to the government's definition (NAEP 2004b).

The U.S. average score on the TIMSS scale was 499 in 1995. This was not significantly different from the average scores of England (505) and Germany (508), somewhat below that of France (538), and considerably below that of Japan (605), Korea (608), and Singapore (642) (Johnson 1998, Table 18).

(The Singapore average score is not comparable, because Singapore, a city-state, educates relatively few lower-class children; much of its working class is imported daily from Malaysia, and children of these Singapore working-class fathers are educated in Malaysia, not Singapore.)

Thus, half or more of students in England and Germany score below what the U.S. government defines as proficiency in eighth grade mathematics. Nearly half (probably about 40%, assuming a normal distribution) of French students are below proficient. Even in Japan and Korea, about 10% of students would be below proficient as the United States defines it.

225. GAO 1993.

226. Shepard et al. 1993.

227. Pelligrino, Jones, and Mitchell 1999, p. 7.

228. Lapp 2002, pp. 14-15.

229. See, for example, Lapp 2002, Figure 2.3, p. 21.

230. Dillon 2003.

231. Horn et al. 2000.

232. Achieve Inc. 2003b.

233. Hoff 2002; Galehouse 2003; Portner and Folmar 2001; Schemo 2002.

234. Finn 2003.

235. Achieve Inc. 2003a.

236. Kane and Staiger 2002. (The version circulated in the summer of 2001 was an earlier draft of this published paper.)

237. Nonetheless, standardized tests may indirectly measure non-cognitive skills, associated with test-taking prowess, like the discipline to complete the exam or a willingness to solve problems that have no obvious relevance to students' interests. Private companies that coach students to get higher scores on college entrance exams teach how to identify with test developers' strategies, so students can provide answers which the test-developers want. Students who are skilled at test taking, for example, can often give a high proportion of correct answers to multiple choice questions without having read the passages on which the questions are based. Arguably, this relies upon a "non-cognitive" skill. See Owen 1985.

238. Johnson and Immerwahr 1994.

239. Rose and Gallup 2000.

240. Rose and Gallup 1998

241. Rose and Gallup 2000. I don't want to over-emphasize this point, however. Public opinion polling can generate different results if questions are asked in different ways. When Americans were asked which are the most "essential subjects" in a school's curriculum, they listed (in this order): math, English, civics and government, U.S. history, science, geography, physical education, and foreign relations. Only a minority considered music, foreign language, and art to be "essential" (Gallup 1979, p. 40). And in 2002, when asked if the schools have taken on too many "non-academic" responsibilities, 54% of respondents said they have, while 41% said they had not; see Rose and Gallup 2002.

242. Pipho 1999.

243. Jefferson's goals are cited often. See, for example, Hochschild and Scovronick 2003, p. 17.

244. *Pauley v. Kelley.*

245. Morgan et al. 1991.

246. Jencks 1979.

247. Carneiro and Heckman 2002. Underlying data provided by Masterov 2004. For definitions of the anti-social scale components, see BLS 2000, Appendix D.

248. College Board 1997.

249. Bowen and Bok 1998.

250. This was particularly true of black men, less so for black women, in the 1976 entering cohort. Then, black women who were admitted to these colleges were more likely than white admittees as adults to participate in community, alumnae, and religious activities, and less likely to participate in youth, educational, or cultural activities. Black men who were admitted to these colleges in 1976 were more likely than white admittees as adults to participate in each of these activity types. For the 1989 cohort, black men and women who were admitted to these colleges were more likely than white admittees to participate in each of these activity types.

251. Flacks 2004.

252. Card and Krueger 1996; Johnson and Stafford 1973.

253. Bowles and Gintis 2002.

254. Levin and Kelley 1994.

255. See, for example, Johnson and Neal 1998, who find that a one-standard-deviation test score gain corresponds to 18% higher earnings. This is still too small to explain much inequality. Consider this hypothetical: if workers with average I.Q. scores (of 100) earn median wages of $27,000 (in 2001, the 50th percentile male wage earner received $12.87 an hour, or about $27,000 annually for full-time work), then with an 18% wage gain for a one-standard-deviation test score increase, workers with I.Q.s of 115 would earn only $32,000. Yet if the 50th percentile male wage earner were to gain an increase in wages of a full standard deviation, he would then earn about $51,000. (Estimates of wage dispersion come from Mishel, Bernstein, and Boushey 2003, Table 2.6.)

256. Klein, Spady, and Weiss 1991.

257. Levin and Kelley 1994.

258. Cameron and Heckman 1993; Murnane and Levy 1993.

259. Richter 2000.

260. In 2001, 93% of whites, 16 to 24 years old, were either enrolled in school, had received a high school diploma, or had received a GED. For blacks, the share was 89%. NCES 2003b, Table 108.

261. Swanson 2004.

262. Mayer 1996.

263. Dunifon and Duncan 1998; Duncan and Dunifon 1998.

264. Murnane et al. 2001.

265. Dale and Krueger 2002.

266. Claude Steele (1997) has demonstrated that black students can do more poorly on tests because they have become convinced that black students are less able to do well on tests. Also see Steele and Aronson 1998.

267. Duncan and Dunifon 1998; Dunifon, Duncan, and Brooks-Gunn 2001.

268. Persico, Postelwaite, and Silverman 2003.

269. Dale and Krueger 2002.

270. The use of Thomas Edison, the "Tortoise and the Hare," and the "Little Engine That Could" in this context is taken from Heckman and Rubinstein 2001.

271. The appendix provides a summary of notable employer surveys during the last 20 years.

272. Moss and Tilly 2001.

273. Bowles, Gintis, and Osborne 2001.

274. Levin and Kelley 1994.

275. OTA 1990.

276. Ones, Viswesvaran, and Schmidt 1993.

277. Levin and Kelley 1994; Rotter 1966.

278. "Many integrity test publishers have conducted adverse impact research. Their studies report a variety of findings: in some cases, no statistically significant differences between groups' average test scores are found, in other cases there appears to be a favorable bias toward protected groups (minorities, women, and the elderly), and in other cases minority groups (i.e., Blacks and Hispanics) appear to do less well than whites. Based on the studies supplied by the authors and publishers of honesty tests, their instruments appear to be free of adverse impact" (OTA 1990, p. 68).

279. Sizer 1984, 1992.

280. Rothstein 2001.

281. Rushowy 2004.

282. Conference Board of Canada 2000.

283. U.S. Census Bureau 2002b. In 2000 37.2% of white (non-Hispanic) young adults voted compared with 33.9% of black young adults; 51.7% of eligible white (non-Hispanic) young adults were registered compared with 48.0% of eligible black young adults.

284. Voting participation gaps and test score gaps are not directly comparable, but while the black–white voting participation gap seems small, the history test score gap seems large. On the National Assessment of Educational Progress, 49% of white 12th graders scored above the "basic" level, while only 20% of black 12th graders were above "basic." There are similar gaps for eighth and fourth graders. See Lapp, Grigg and Tay-Lim 2002.

285. Frazer 2000; Langton and Jennings 1968; Torney-Purta et al. 2001; Niemi and Junn 1998; Greene 2000.

286. Lutkus et al. 1999, Table 5.8; Galston 2001; CHR 1999.

287. Torney-Purta et al. 2001.

288. Niemi and Chapman 1999; Youniss, McLellan, and Yates 1997; Hanks and Eckland 1998.

289. Lapp, Grigg, and Tay-Lim 2002, Figure 3.4; Hoffman, Llagas, and Snyder 2003, supplemental table 6.1.

290. Planty and Regnier 2003, Table 2. "High income" refers to families from the top quartile of the income distribution; "middle income" refers to families from the second and third quartiles of the income distribution; "low income" refers to families from the bottom quartile of the income distribution.

291. Planty and Regnier 2003, Table 2.

292. Planty and Regnier 2003, Table 1.

293. Planty and Regnier 2003, Table 4.

294. Planty and Regnier 2003, Table 1.

295. Test score advantages for white children in Head Start persist longer. See Currie and Thomas 1995; Garces, Thomas, and Currie 2000.

296. Schweinhart, Barnes, and Weikart 1993, Table 3.

297. Schweinhart, Barnes, and Weikart 1993.

298. Schweinhart, Barnes, and Weikart 1993, Tables 13 and 14.

299. Schweinhart, Barnes, and Weikart 1993; Barnett 1995.

300. Schweinhart, Barnes, and Weikart 1993, Table 9.

301. Schweinhart, Barne,s and Weikart 1993, Tables 22, 18, 24.

302. For a popularized discussion of learning theory, and how non-cognitive and cognitive development reinforce one another, see Stipek and Seal 2001.

303. Hacsi 2002.

304. Garces, Thomas, and Currie 2000; Currie and Thomas 1995.

305. Barnett 1995; Yoshikawa 1995.

306. Nye, Hedges, and Konstantopoulos 2002; Finn 1998; Finn and Achilles 1999; Krueger and Whitmore 1999; Krueger and Whitmore 2001.

307. Grissmer 1999.

308. It is beyond the scope of this book to engage the debate about whether colleges of education and teachers trained in them give either too much or too little emphasis to the development of children's motivation to learn, or to the different ways in which children may approach academic learning. Attacks on "progressive" pedagogy and demands that teachers focus more on developing children's basic academic skills have fueled contemporary policy's emphasis on tests of basic skills as the sole measure of learning. The concern of this chapter, however, has been not so much how non-cognitive characteristics do or do not contribute to cognitive development but rather about how the non-cognitive skills develop that we value in and of themselves – productivity, employability, good citizenship, socially responsible behavior, etc. – and what the role of schools might be in enhancing these skills.

309. For example, Crane 1991. Hanushek, Kain, and Rivkin 2004b find that, in Texas, if all schools were equally integrated (with similar proportions of black and white students), the black-white test score gap in mathematics in grades 5-7 would be reduced by 25%. For a review of claims about the importance of peer influences, see Kahlenberg 2001. There is a contrary view, however. See Jencks and Mayer 1990.

310. There is no clearly defined "tipping point" where student achievement plummets once a school's poverty concentration passes that point. A school's average student achievement appears to decline almost linearly as the school's percentage of children receiving subsidized lunches increases. But around the point where subsidized lunch eligibility exceeds 40%, the decline in average student achievement becomes slightly more precipitous. See Lippman, Burns, and McArthur 1996. Kahlenberg 2001 (see especially pp. 39-40 and 110-114) concludes, based on a careful review of "tipping point" literature, that preventing a precipitous decline in achievement requires that a school be "over 50%" white or middle class.

311. Smith 2003. In today's dollars, Mr. Moynihan was asking whether, to raise student achievement, Mr. Smith would rather spend nearly $5,000 in schools or in family income support.

312. Mosteller and Moynihan 1972.

313. In the wake of positive results from the Tennessee class size experiment, California adopted a statewide class size reduction program for the primary grades. There was already a teacher shortage in California, and the sudden implementation of the class size reduction program exacerbated that shortage. What was worse, it seems that some of the most experienced and qualified teachers who had been working in low-achieving schools took newly created jobs in suburban middle-class schools. With all schools competing for a small number of new teachers to staff the added primary school classrooms, schools in middle-class communities where working conditions were better had an edge in recruiting teachers during the implementation of the class size reduction program. The program may still have done some good for lower-class children, but not nearly as much as it might have done were it implemented only for schools serving such students. See Ross 1999; Jepsen and Rivkin 2002; Hacsi 2002; Bohrnstedt and Stecher 2002.

314. CBO 2003. Data from 2003 are not yet available.

315. CBO 2003. The most spectacular contrast, of course, is with the highest 1% of families, who had income growth exceeding 230% over the 1979-2002 period. However, the focus here is on the contrast between low- and middle-income families, because this is the relevant comparison for the educational achievement gap between lower- and middle-class children.

316. Mishel, Bernstein, and Boushey 2003, Table 5.2.

317. Mishel, Bernstein, and Boushey 2003, Table5.3.

318. Bernstein, Brocht, and Spade-Aguilar. 2000; Boushey et al. 2001, Table 3.

319. Mishel, Bernstein, and Boushey, Table 2.41.

320. Bernstein and Chapman 2002.

321. "Low income single mothers" are defined here as those whose earnings were below the median for all single mothers. Mishel, Bernstein, and Boushey 2003, Figure 5M.

322. A widely promoted reform, claimed to raise the achievement of lower-class children, is the provision of vouchers to pay the private school tuition for such children. However, such vouchers are usually designed only to enable these children to attend private schools that are similar in social class composition to the public schools that voucher recipients would leave. The result is that such voucher programs have no meaningful effect on lower-class children's achievement. See Krueger and Zhu 2003. Enthusiasts for school vouchers, however, do not similarly advocate housing vouchers that would permit lower-class children to attend middle-class schools where their achievement could rise. See Rothstein 2000b.

323. Sard and Fisher 2003.

324. Center on Budget and Policy Priorities 2003.

325. There are presently about 50 million children enrolled in public elementary and secondary schools.

326. Rosenbaum 1991; Kaufman and Rosenbaum 1992.

327. MTO differs from Gautreaux in that MTO tests the effect of moving out of predominantly low-income communities, whereas analyses of Gautreaux test the effect of moving out of predominantly minority communities. In practice, there is considerable overlap.

328. Jencks and Mayer 1990 observe: "From a scientific viewpoint, the best way to estimate neighborhood effects would be to conduct controlled experiments in which we assigned families randomly to different neighborhoods, persuaded each family to remain in its assigned neighborhood for a protracted period, and then measured each neighborhood's effects on the children involved. Fortunately, social scientists cannot conduct experiments of this kind."

329. Janofsky 1999.

330. In other respects, however, the program has still been controversial. Particularly in Baltimore, groups claiming to represent suburban residents complained that moving poor families into the suburbs would raise crime rates and reduce property values in these suburbs. As a result of these complaints, the federal government delayed commencement of the experiment, and then scaled it back (Dreier and Moberg 1995; Gordon 1997). Some conservative social critics attacked the program, claiming that recipients of vouchers who move to the suburbs will include not only the victims of inner-city social disorganization, "but the perpetrators as well, who may then spread social problems to marginal but stable working-class neighborhoods" (MacDonald 1997).

331. Jencks and Mayer 1990.

332. Ludwig et al. 2001.

333. Kling and Liebman 2004

334. Brooks-Gunn and Duncan 1997 cite evidence that low-income parents have worse physical and mental health than middle-class parents, and that parental mental health has an adverse effect on child outcomes.

335. NCES 2003b, Table 167. The average per pupil amount for 1999-2000, the most recent year reported, was $8,032.

336. This is based on a cost estimate of $2,600 per pupil in schools that had such clinics. The bases for this and subsequent estimates in this chapter, with program models and descriptions of service assumptions, will be published in a forthcoming working paper by Allgood and Rothstein. (The paper will be posted at www.epinet.org, the website of the Economic Policy Institute, by the end of 2004.) The numbers are still subject to revision. If we assume that these clinics should be placed in schools where at least 40% of the enrolled students were eligible for free and reduced lunch, clinics should be placed in schools serving 26% of all students; see Lippman et al. 1996, Table 1.7, p. A-9. This would increase the per-pupil spending, averaged for all children, rich and poor, by about $700.

337. Vandell and Wolfe 2000.

338. Lee, Brooks-Gunn, and Schnur 1988; Currie and Thomas 1995.

339. Garces, Thomas, and Currie 2000; Currie and Thomas 1995.

340. Barnett 1995.

341. NAEYC 1998.

342. NAEYC 1998. It is possible that advocacy groups wanting to enhance the importance of early childhood education might recommend higher qualifications for preschool teachers, and higher adult-child ratios than might be necessary to raise outcomes to desired levels. However, there is no experimental research that compares the outcomes generated by preschool teachers with different levels of educational attainment. And it seems reasonable that, if we require professionals to staff teaching positions for kindergartners and first-graders, similar qualifications might be required for preschool teachers as well. The recommendation for professional qualifications for preschool teachers was recently reinforced by Barnett et al. 2004.

343. See, for example, Donahue and Siegelman 1998.

344. Hacsi 2002; Vinovskis 1995.

345. Neuman 2003.

346. Olds et al. 1997; Olds et al. 1999.

347. It would increase average per-pupil costs nationwide by another $700 per pupil. See note 336.

348. Lareau 2002.

349. NIOOST 2000.

350. It would increase average per-pupil costs nationwide by another $1,400 per pupil. See note 336.

351. It would increase average per-pupil costs nationwide by another $700 per pupil. See note 336.

352. Enrollment in public elementary and secondary schools in 2001 was about 48 million (NCES 2003b, Table 37). Spending an additional $12,500 on 26% of these children would cost about $156 billion a year.

353. Rothstein 1997; Rothstein and Miles 1995.

354. This rough estimate assumes that average per-pupil spending is currently about $8,000 per pupil, that teacher salary and compensation represents 56% of that amount (NCES 2003b, Table 164), and that a class size reduction of 37% (from 24 to 15) would be applied to the first four of the 13 grades of elementary and secondary education. This calculation does not adjust for the fact that not all students finish high school, and it does not take account of the fact that costs are not identical at each grade level (i.e., it assumes that grades K-3 represent 4/13 of total costs).

355. Citizens for Tax Justice 2003. The total 10-year cost (to 2010) of federal tax cuts enacted from 2001 to 2003 is about $2.3 trillion, or an average of about $229 billion annually.

356. Winter 2004. The plaintiffs have proposed funding that, they claim, would enable all students to pass New York State's "Regents" exams, which signify the satisfactory completion of a college preparatory academic curriculum.

357. This appendix relies heavily upon reviews by Handel (forthcoming), Capelli 1995, and Barton 1990.

358. NACE 2004.

359. NAM 2001.

360. Teixeira 1998.

361. National Center on the Educational Quality of the Workforce 1995.

362. NCEE 1990. See also Marshall and Tucker 1992. The former labor secretaries thought that more employers should have been dissatisfied with high school mathematical and literacy levels, and that the employers were content with these levels only because they had failed to organize workplaces in the most productive ways to take advantage of higher cognitive skills. So the survey did not suggest that schools were doing an adequate job with academics.

363. Barton 1990.

364. CED 1985.

365. Barton 1990.

366. Barton 1990.

367. Levin, Rumberger, and Finnan 1990.

Bibliography

Abel, Ernest L. 1995. "An Update on Incidence of FAS: FAS Is not an Equal Opportunity Birth Defect." *Neurotoxicology and Teratology* 174:437-443.

Abel, Ernest L., and John H. Hannigan. 1995. "Maternal Risk Factors in Fetal Alcohol Syndrome: Provocative and Permissive Influences." *Neurotoxicology and Teratology* 17(4): 445-462.

Achieve Inc. 2003a. *All Tests Are not Equal: Why States Need to Give High Quality Tests.* Washington, D.C: Achieve Inc. <http://www.achieve.org>

Achieve Inc. 2003b. *State vs. NAEP Results 4th Grade Reading.* Washington, D.C: Achieve Inc. <http://www.achieve.org>

Allgood, Whitney C. 1999. "No Excuse for 'No Excuses'." Unpublished memorandum.

Allgood, Whitney C., and Richard Rothstein, forthcoming. "At-Risk Adequacy Calculations." Washington, D.C.: Economic Policy Institute.

Allington, Richard L., and Anne McGill-Franzen. 2003. "Summer Loss." *Phi Delta Kappan* 85(1): 68-75.

Altman, Lawrence K. 2004. "Doctors and Patients Start to Curb Use of Antibiotics." *New York Times,* March 2.

America's Second Harvest. 2003. *Differences in Nutrient Adequacy Among Poor and Non Poor Children.* <http://www.secondharvest.org>

Associated Press. 2003a. "Study: 1 in 4 Harlem Children Has Asthma." *New York Times*, April 21.

Associated Press. 2003b. "FDA Warns Consumers of Remedy With Lead." *Associated Press*, November 2.

Astley, Susan., 2003. "FAS/FAE: Their Impact on Psychosocial Child Development With a View to Diagnosis." In R.E. Tremblay, R.G. Barr, and R. DeV. Peters, eds., *Encyclopedia on Early Childhood Development* (online). Montreal, Quebec: Centre of Excellence for Early Childhood Development. http://www.escellence-earlychildhood.ca/documents/AstleyANGxp.pdf

Ballou, Dale. 2002. "Sizing Up Test Scores." *Education Next*, Summer: 10-15

Bankston, Carl L. III, and Min Zhou. 1995. "Religious Participation, Ethnic Identification, and Adaptation of Vietnamese Adolescents in an Immigrant Community." *The Sociological Quarterly* 36(3): 523-534.

Barnett, W. Steven. 1995. "Long-Term Effects of Early Childhood Programs on Cognitive and School Outcomes." *The Future of Children: Long-Term Outcomes of Early Childhood Programs* 5(3): 25-50.

Barnett, W.S., K.B. Robin, J.T. Hustedt, and K.L. Schulman. 2004. *The State of Preschool: 2003 State Preschool Yearbook*. National Institute for Early Education Research. <http://www.nieer.org/yearbook>

Barton, Paul E. 1990. *Skills Employers Need. Time to Measure Them?* Princeton, N.J.: Educational Testing Service, Policy Information Center.

Barton, Paul. 2003. *Parsing the Achievement Gap. Baselines for Tracking Progress.* Princeton, N.J.: Educational Testing Service, Policy Information Center.

Begag, Azouz. 1990. "The 'Beurs,' Children of North-African Immigrants in France: The Issue of Integration." *Journal of Ethnic Studies* 18(1): 1-14.

Berkowitz, Gertrud S., James G. Wetmur, Elena Birman-Deych, Josephine Obel, Robert H. Lapinski, James H. Godbold, Ian R. Holzman, and Mary S. Wolff. 2004. "*In Utero* Pesticide Exposure, Maternal Paraoxonase Activity, and Head Circumference." *Environmental Health Perspectives* 112(3): 388-391.

Bernstein, Jared, Chauna Brocht, and Maggie Spade-Aguilar. 2000. *How Much Is Enough: Basic Family Budgets for Working Families*. Washington, D.C.: Economic Policy Institute.

Bernstein, Jared, and Jeff Chapman. 2002. *Time to Repair the Wage Floor*. Washington, D.C.: Economic Policy Institute.

Bianchi, Suzanne M., and John Robinson. 1997. "What Did You Do Today? Children's Use of Time, Family Composition, and the Acquisition of Social Capital." *Journal of Marriage and the Family* 59(May): 332-344.

Bishop, John, et al. 2003. "Nerds and Freaks: A Theory of Student Culture and Norms." In Diane Ravitch, ed., *Brookings Papers on Education Policy 2003*. Washington, D.C.: Brookings Institution.

BLS (Bureau of Labor Statistics). 2000. *NLSY79 Child and Young Adults User's Guide, 2000*. Washington, D.C.: <http://www.bls.gov/nls/y79cyaguide/nlsy79cusg.htm>

Blum, Justin. 2004. "High Lead Levels Found in Water at 9 D.C. Schools." *Washington Post*, February 25.

Bohrnstedt, George W., and Brian M. Stecher, eds. 2002. *What Have We Learned About Class Size Reduction in California?* Sacramento: California Department of Education.

Boushey, Heather, Chauna Brocht, Bethney Gunderson, and Jared Bernstein. 2001. *Hardships in America : The Real Story of Working Families*. Washington, D.C.: Economic Policy Institute.

Bowen, William G., and Derek Bok. 1998. *The Shape of the River. Long-Term Consequences of Considering Race in College and University Admissions*. Princeton, N.J.: Princeton University Press.

Bowles, Samuel, and Herbert Gintis. 2002. "Schooling in Capitalist America Revisited." *Sociology of Education* 75(1): 1-18.

Bowles, Samuel, Herbert Gintis, and Melissa Osborne. 2001. "Incentive-Enhancing Preferences: Personality, Behavior, and Earnings." *American Economic Review* 19(2): 155-158.

Bracey, Gerald W. 2003. "The 13th Bracey Report on the Condition of Public Education." *Phi Delta Kappan* 85(2): 148-164.

Brennan, Patricia. 2003. "Tobacco Consumption During Pregnancy and Its Impact on Psychosocial Child Development. " Quebec, Canada: Centre of Excellence for Early Childhood Development. <http://www.excellence-earlychildhood.ca/documents/BrennanANGxp.pdf>

Brooks, E.C. 1916. "The Value of Home Study Under Parental Supervision." *Elementary School Journal* 17(3).

Brooks-Gunn, Jeanne, and Greg J. Duncan. 1997. "The Effects of Poverty on Children." *The Future of Children* 7(2): 55-71.

Brooks-Gunn, Jeanne, Pamela K. Klebanov, Judith Smith, Greg J. Duncan, and Kyunghee Lee. 2003. "The Black-White Test Score Gap in Young Children: Contributions of Test and Family Characteristics." *Applied Developmental Science* 7(4): 239-252.

Brown, Larry J. 2003. "Table. Low-Income Student Participation, by State, in the School Breakfast Program." (Provided by Dr. Brown, executive director, Center on Hunger and Poverty, Heller Graduate School, Brandeis University, July 9.)

Brown, Larry J., and Laura P. Sherman. 1995. "Policy Implications of New Scientific Knowledge." *Journal of Nutrition* 125: 2281S-2284S.

Brown, Michael K., Martin Carnoy, Eliott Currie, Troy Duster, David B. Oppenheimer, Marjorie M. Shultz, and David Wellman. 2003. *Whitewashing Race. The Myth of a Color-Blind Society*. Berkeley: University of California Press.

Bruno, James, and Jo Ann Isken. 1996. "Inter and Intraschool Site Student Transiency: Practical and Theoretical Implications for Instructional Continuity at Inner-City Schools." *Journal of Research and Development in Education* 29(4): 239-252.

Cameron, Stephen V., and James J. Heckman. 1993. "The Nonequivalence of High School Equivalents." *Journal of Labor Economics* 11(1) January.

Cameron, Stephen V., and James J. Heckman. 2001. "The Dynamics of Educational Attainment for Black, Hispanic, and White Males." *Journal of Political Economy* 109(3): 455-499.

Cappelli, Peter. 1995. "Is The 'Skills Gap' Really About Attitudes?" *California Management Review* 37(4): 108-124.

Card, David, and Alan B. Krueger. 1996. "Labor Market Effects of School Quality: Theory and Evidence." In Gary Burtless, ed. *Does Money Matter? The Effect of School Resources on Student Achievement and Adult Success*. Washington, D.C.: Brookings Institution.

Carneiro, Pedro, and James J. Heckman. 2002. "Human Capital Policy." Paper presented at the Alvin Hansen Seminar, Harvard University, April 25, revised August.

Carter, Samuel Casey. 2000. *No Excuses. Lessons from 21 High-Performing, High-Poverty Schools*. Washington, D.C.: Heritage Foundation.

Castles, Stephen, with Heather Booth and Tina Wallace. 1984. *Here for Good. Western Europe's New Ethnic Minorities*. London: Pluto Press.

CBO (Congressional Budget Office). 2003. *Effective Federal Tax Rates for All Households, by Household Income Category, 1979 to 2000*. Washington, D.C.: CBO. <ftp://ftp.cbo.gov/45xx/doc4514/08-29-Report.pdf>

CDC (National Center for Chronic Disease Prevention and Health Promotion). 2001a. *Women and Smoking. A Report of the Surgeon General – 2001. Pattern of Tobacco Use Among Women and Girls — Fact Sheet*. Centers for Disease Control and Prevention, U.S. Department of Health and Human Services. <http://www.cdc.gov/tobacco/sgr/sgr_forwomen/factsheet_tobaccouse.htm>

CDC (National Center for Chronic Disease Prevention and Health Promotion). 2001b. *Women and Smoking. A Report of the Surgeon General – 2001: Chapter 2. Patterns of Tobacco Use Among Women and Girls*. Centers for Disease Control and Prevention, U.S. Department of Health and Human Services. <http://www.cdc.gov/tobacco/sgr/sgr_forwomen/pdfs/chp2.pdf>

CDC (Centers for Disease Control and Prevention). 2002a. *Health, United States, 2002*. Table 71: Overweight children and adolescents 6-19 years of age, according to sex, age, race, and Hispanic origin: United States, selected years 1963-65 through 1999-2000. Washington, D.C.: Department of Health and Human and Human Services. <http://www.cdc.gov/nchs/data/hus/tables/2002/02hus071.pdf>

CDC (Centers for Disease Control and Prevention). 2002b. *National Health Interview Survey, 1997-2000*. Percent distribution of the drinking levels of females 18 years of age and older according to selected characteristics: United States. Washington, D.C.: U.S. Department of Health and Human Services. NHIS, 1997-2000.

CDC (Centers for Disease Control and Prevention). 2002c. *Pediatric Nutrition Surveillance 2001 Report*. Washington D.C.: U.S. Department of Health and Human Services.

CED (Committee for Economic Development). 1985. *Investing in Our Children. Business and the Public Schools. A Statement by the Research and Policy Committee of the Committee for Economic Development*. New York, N.Y.: author.

Center on Budget and Policy Priorities. 2003. *Introduction to the Housing Voucher Program*. Center on Budget and Policy Priorities, May 15.

Center on Hunger and Poverty. *Childhood Hunger, Childhood Obesity: An Examination of the Paradox* Medford: Center on Hunger and Poverty, School of Nutrition Science and Policy, Tufts University. 2003. <http://nutrition.tufts.edu/pdf/publications/hunger/hunger_and_obesity.pdf>

CHR (Center for Human Resources, Brandeis University). 1999. *Summary Report: National Evaluation of Learn and Serve America*. Waltham, Mass.: author.

Citizens for Tax Justice. 2003. Details on Bush Tax Cuts So Far (as of fall 2003). <http://www.ctj.org/pdf/gwbdata.pdf>

College Board. 1997. "Research Summary. Personal Qualities and Academic Experiences: Predictors of Academic Success." Office of Research and Development: College Board, RS-2, October. <http://www.collegeboard.com/repository/030205ressum02_21113.pdf>

Comer, James P. 1988. "Educating Poor Minority Children." *Scientific American* 259(5): 24-30.

Commission on the Skills of the American Workforce. 1990. *America's Choice: High Skills or Low Wages.* Rochester, N.Y.: National Center on Education and the Economy.

Conference Board of Canada. 2000. "Employability Skills 2000 +." May. 2000. <http://www.conferenceboard.ca>

Cook, Philip J., and Jens Ludwig. 1998. "The Burden of 'Acting White': Do Black Adolescents Disparage Academic Achievement?" including "Comment by Ronald F. Ferguson." In Christopher Jencks and Meredith Phillips, eds., *The Black-White Test Score Gap.* Washington, D.C.: Brookings Institution Press.

Corcoran, Sean P., William N. Evans, and Robert S. Schwab. 2002. *Changing Labor Market Opportunities for Women and the Quality of Teachers 1957-1992.* NBER Working Paper W9180. Cambridge, Mass.: National Bureau of Economic Research.

Covello, Leonard. 1936. "A High School and Its Immigrant Community: A Challenge and an Opportunity." *Journal of Educational Sociology* 9(February): 334.

Crane, Jonathan 1991. "Effects of Neighborhoods on Dropping Out of School and Teenage Childbearing." In Christopher Jencks and Paul Peterson, eds. *The Urban Underclass.* Washington, D.C.: Brookings Institution.

Currie, Janet, and Duncan Thomas. 1995. "Does Head Start Make a Difference?" *American Economic Review* 85(3): 341-364.

Dale, Stacy Berg, and Alan B. Krueger. 2002. "Estimating the Payoff to Attending a More Selective College: An Application of Selection on Observables and Unobservables." *Quarterly Journal of Economics* 117(4): 1491-1527.

Darity, William A. Jr., and Patrick L. Mason. 1998. "Evidence on Discrimination in Employment: Codes of Color, Codes of Gender." *Journal of Economic Perspectives* 12(2): 63-90

DeNavas-Walt, Robert W. Cleveland, and Marc I. Roemer. 2001. *Money Income in the United States: 2000.* Current Population Reports, P-60-213, September. Washington, D.C.: U. S. Department of Commerce, Economics and Statistics Administration, U.S. Census Bureau.

Denton, Kristen, and Elvira Germino-Hauskens. 2000. *America's Kindergartner's. Findings From the Early Childhood Longitudinal Study, Kindergarten Class of 1998-99, Fall 1998.* NCES 2000-070. Washington, D.C.: U.S. Department of Education, National Center for Education Statistics.

Diekmann, Michael. 2001. Superintendent, Department of Defense Dependents Schools, Japan District. Personal communication, February 17.

Dillon, Sam. 2003. "Citing Flaw, New York State Voids Math Scores." *New York Times*, June 25.

Donohue, John J. III, and Peter Siegelman. 1998. "Allocating Resources Among Prisons and Social Programs in The Battle Against Crime." *Journal of Legal Studies*, 27 J. Legal Stud. 1.

Doyle, Dennis. 1985. *Investing in Our Children. Business and the Public Schools.* New York, N.Y.: Committee for Economic Development.

Dreier, Peter, and David Moberg. 1995. "Moving From the 'Hood'." *American Prospect* 24(Winter): 75-79.

Dubay, Lisa, Jennifer Haley, and Genevieve Kenney. 2000. "Children's Eligibility for Medicaid and SCHIP: A View From 2000." *New Federalism: National Survey of America's Families.* Series B, No. B-41. March. Washington, D.C.: Urban Institute.

Duckman, Robert (College of Optometry, State University of New York). 2003. Interview with author, December 29.

Duncan, Greg J., and Jeanne Brooks-Gunn. 1997. "Income Effects Across the Life Span: Integration and Interpretation." In Greg J. Duncan and Jeanne Brooks-Gunn, eds. *Consequences of Growing Up Poor.* New York, N.Y.: Russell Sage Foundation.

Duncan, Greg J., and Rachel Dunifon. 1998. "'Soft Skills' and Long-Run Labor Market Success." *Research in Labor Economics.*

Dunifon, Rachel, and Greg J. Duncan. 1998. "Long-Run Effects on Motivation on Labor-Market Success." *Social Psychology Quarterly* 61(1): 33-48.

Dunifon, Rachel, Greg J. Duncan, and Jeanne Brooks-Gunn. 2001. "As Ye Sweep, So Shall Ye Reap." *AEA Papers and Proceedings* 91(2): 150-154.

Egbuonu, Lisa, and Barbara Starfield. 1982 "Child Health and Social Status." *Pediatrics* 69(May): 550-557.

Elley, W.B. 1992. *How in the World Do Students Read?* Hamburg, Germany: International Association for the Evaluation of Educational Achievement.

Entwisle, Doris, and Karl L. Alexander. 1992. "Summer Setback: Race, Poverty, School Composition, and Mathematics Achievement in the First Two Years of School." *American Sociological Review* 57(February): 72-84.

Entwisle, Doris R., Karl L. Alexander, and Linda Steffel Olson. 2000. "Summer Learning and Home Environment." In Richard D. Kahlenberg, ed., *A Notion At Risk. Preserving Public Education as an Engine for Social Mobility.* New York, N.Y.: Century Foundation Press.

Ermisch, John, Marco Francesconi, and David J. Pevalin. 2001. *Outcomes for Children of Poverty.* Research Report No. 158. London, England: Department for Work and Pensions.

Esquith, Rafe. 2003. *There Are No Shortcuts.* New York, N.Y.: Pantheon

Evers, Bill. 2002. "No More Excuses." *BrainstormNW*, January.

Fallon, Daniel. 2003. "Case Study of a Paradigm Shift. The Value of Focusing on Instruction." Speech to the Education Commission of the States, November 12.

Fergusson, David. 2003. "Tobacco Consumption During Pregnancy and Its Impact on Child Development." Quebec, Canada: Centre of Excellence for Early Childhood Development. <http://www.excellence-earlychildhood.ca/documents/FergussonANGxp.pdf>

Festinger, Trudy, and Robert Duckman. 2000. "Seeing and Hearing. Vision and Audiology Status of Foster Children in New York City." *Journal of Behavioral Optometry* 11(3): 59-67.

Figlio, David N., and Joshua Winicki. 2002. "Food for Thought: The Effects of School Accountability Plans on School Nutrition." NBER Working Paper W9319. Cambridge, Mass.: National Bureau of Economic Research.

Finn, Chester E. Jr. 2003. "Adequate Yearly Progress or Balloon Mortgage." *Education Gadfly* 3(4), January 30. http://www.edexcellence.net/foundation/gadfly/issue.cfm?id=9#367

Finn, Jeremy D. 1998. *Class Size and Students At Risk: What Is Known? What Is Next?* Washington, D.C.: U. S. Department of Education.

Finn, Jeremy D., and Charles M. Achilles. 1999. "Tennessee's Class Size Study: Findings, Implications, Misconceptions." *Educational Evaluation and Policy Analysis* 21(2): 97-109.

Flacks, Richard, et al. 2004 (in press). "Learning and Academic Engagement in the Multiversity. Results of the First University of California Undergraduate Experience Survey." University of California, Berkeley, Center for Studies in Higher Education, Student Experience in the Research University21st Century (SERU21) Project. <http://ishi.lib.berkeley.edu/cshe/seru21/>

Flanagan, Constance A., and Jacquelynne S. Eccles. 1993. "Changes in Parents' Work Status and Adolescents' Adjustment at School." *Child Development* 64: 246-257.

Fordham, Signithia, and John U. Ogbu. 1986. "Black Students' School Success: Coping With the 'Burden of Acting White'." *Urban Review* 18(3): 176-206.

Forrest, Christopher B., Barbara Starfield, Anne W. Riley, and Myungsa Kang. 1997. "The Impact of Asthma on the Health Status of Adolescents." *Pediatrics* 99(2): E1.

Frazer, Elizabeth. 2000. "'Civics' in American Schools." *Government and Opposition* 35(January): 123.

Freedman, Jonathan B. 2000. *Wall of Fame*. San Diego, Calif.: Avid Academic Press.

Fried, Peter A. 2002 "Tobacco Consumption During Pregnancy and Its Impact on Child Development." Quebec, Canada: Centre of Excellence for Early Childhood Development. <http://www.exellence-earlychildhood.ca/documents/FriedANGxp.pdf>

Frieden, Thomas R. 2003. "A Review of the Enforcement of Laws, Rules, Regulations and Surveillance Data Concerning Lead-Based Paint and Lead Poisoning Prevention." Testimony before the City Council Committees on Health and on Housing and Buildings, New York, N.Y., November 14.

Fryer, Ronald G. Jr., and Steven D. Levitt. 2002. "Understanding the Black-White Test Score Gap in the First Two Years of School." NBER Working Paper W8975. Cambridge, Mass.: National Bureau of Economic Research.

Galehouse, Maggie. 2003. "Academic Bar Lowered to Get Schools on Track." *Arizona Republic*, July 14.

Gallup, George H. 1979. "The Eleventh Annual Gallup Poll of the Public's Attitudes Toward the Public Schools." *Phi Delta Kappan* 61(1): 33-45.

Galston, William D. 2001. "Political Knowledge, Political Engagement, and Civic Education," *Annual Review of Political Science* 4(June): 217–234.

GAO (General Accounting Office). 1993. *Educational Achievement Standards: NAGB's Approach Yields Misleading Interpretations.* GAO/PEMD 93-12. Washington, D.C.: author.

GAO (U.S. General Accounting Office). 1994. *Elementary School Children: Many Change Schools Frequently, Harming Their Education.* GAO/HEHS-94-45. Washington, D.C.: author (ED 369-526).

GAO (U.S. General Accounting Office). 1999. *Lead Poisoning: Federal Health Care Programs Are Not Effectively Reaching At-Risk Children.* GAO/HEHS-99-18. Washington, D.C.: author.

GAO (U.S. General Accounting Office). 2000. *Oral Health in Low-Income Populations.* GAO/HEHS-00-72. Washington, D.C.: author.

GAO (U.S. General Accounting Office). 2001. *BIA and DOD Schools. Student Achievement and Other Characteristics Often Differ from Public Schools'.* GAO-01-934. Washington, D.C.: author.

Garces, Eliana, Duncan Thomas, and Janet Currie. 2000. "Longer Term Effects of Head Start." NBER Working Paper W8054, December. Cambridge, Mass.: National Bureau of Economic Research.

Gardner, Howard. 1999. *Intelligence Reframed.* New York. N.Y.: Basic Books.

Garner, Richard. 2004. "Chinese Perform Better in English Than White Children." *Independent Education*, February 25.

Geronimus, Arline T. 1997. "Teenage Childbearing and Personal Responsibility: An Alternative View." *Political Science Quarterly* 112(3).

Geronimus, Arline T. 2000. "To Mitigate, Resist, or Undo: Addressing the Structural Influences on the Health of Urban Populations." *American Journal of Public Health* 90(6): 867-872.

Gill, Brian P., and Steven L. Schlossman. 2000. "The Lost Cause of Homework Reform." *American Journal of Education* 109: 27-62.

Gitomer, Drew. 2003. "Preface." In Paul Barton, *Parsing the Achievement Gap. Baselines for Tracking Progress.* Princeton, N.J.: Policy Information Center, Educational Testing Service.

Golden, Daniel. 1999. "Pentagon-Run Schools Excel in Academics, Defying Demographics." *Wall Street Journal*, December 22.

Gordon, Larry. 1997. "A Social Experiment in Pulling Up Stakes." *Los Angeles Times*, September 23.

Gould, Marge Christensen, and Herman Gould. 2003. "A Clear Vision for Equity and Opportunity." *Phi Delta Kappan*, December.

Grant, Gerald. 1973. "Shaping Social Policy: The Politics of the Coleman Report." *Teachers College Record* 75(1): 17-54.

Greene, Jay P. 2000. "Review of *Civic Education* by Richard G. Niemi and Jane Junn." *Social Science Quarterly* 81: 696–697.

Grissmer, David. 1999. "Conclusion. Class Size Effects: Assessing the Evidence, Its Policy Implications, and Future Research Agenda." *Educational Evaluation and Policy Analysis* 21(2): 231-248.

Grissmer, David W., et al. 1994. *Student Achievement and the Changing American Family*. Santa Monica, Calif.: RAND.

Hack, Maureen, Nancy K. Klein, and H. Gerry Taylor. 1995. "Long-Term Developmental Outcomes of Low Birth Weight Infants." *The Future of Children* 5(1): 176-196.

Hacsi, Timothy A. 2002. *Children as Pawns. The Politics of Educational Reform*. Cambridge, Mass.: Harvard University Press.

Halfon, Neal, 2002. Personal correspondence.

Halfon, Neal, and Paul W. Newacheck. 1993. "Childhood Asthma and Poverty: Differential Impacts and Utilization of Health Services." *Pediatrics* 91(January): 56-61.

Handel, Michael J. (forthcoming). "Skills Mismatch in the Labor Market." Washington, D.C.: Economic Policy Institute.

Hanks, Michael, and Bruce K. Eckland. 1998. "Adult Voluntary Associations and Adolescent Socialization." *Sociological Quarterly* 19(Summer): 481–490.

Hanushek, Eric A., John F. Kain, and Steven G. Rivkin. 2004a. "Disruption Versus Tiebout Improvement: The Costs and Benefits of Switching Schools." *Journal of Public Economics*. Summer.

Hanushek, Eric A., John F. Kain, and Steven G. Rivkin. 2004b. "New Evidence About *Brown v. Board of Education:* The Complex Effects of School Racial Composition on Achievement." Revised draft, February, of paper presented at the Brookings Conference on Empirics of Social Interactions, January 2000.

Hanushek, Eric A., and Steven G. Rivkin. 2004. "How to Improve the Supply of High-Quality Teachers." In Diane Ravitch, ed. *Brookings Papers on Education Policy 2004*. Washington, D.C.: Brookings Institution.

Harris, Doug. 2003. "Beating the Odds or Losing the War?" Unpublished Working Paper, Economic Policy Institute.

Harris, Paul, 2003. Interview with author, December 12.

Harris, Paul. 2002. "Learning-Related Visual Problems in Baltimore City: A Long-Term Program." *Journal of Optometric Vision Development* 33(2): 75-115.

Hart, Betty, and Todd Risley. 1995. *Meaningful Differences*. Baltimore, Md.: Brookes Publishing.

Hart, Betty, and Todd Risley. 2003. "The Early Catastrophe. The 30 Million Word Gap by Age 3." *American Educator,* Spring.

Hauser, Robert M. 2000. "Response: Two Studies of Academic Achievement." In David W. Grissmer and J. Michael Ross, eds., *Analytic Issues in the Assessment of Student Achievement*. NCES, 2000-050. Washington DC: National Center for Education Statistics.

Hayes, Donald P., and Judith Grether. 1983. "The School Year and Vacations: When Do Students Learn?" *Cornell Journal of Social Relations* 17(1): 56-71.

Heath, Shirley Brice. 1983. *Ways With Words,* Cambridge, England: Cambridge University Press.

Heckman, James J. 1998. "Detecting Discrimination." *Journal of Economic Perspectives* 12(2): 101-116.

Heckman, James, and Yona Rubinstein. 2001. "The Importance of Noncognitive Skills: Lessons From the GED Testing Program." Papers and Proceedings of the Hundred Thirteenth Annual Meeting of the American Economic Association. *American Economic Review* 91(2): 145-149.

Herrnstein, Richard J., and Charles Murray. 1994. *The Bell Curve. Intelligence and Class Structure in American Life*. New York, N.Y.: Free Press.

Hilts, Philip J. 2000. "Study Finds Most States Lack System for Monitoring Asthma." *New York Times*, May 22.

Hochschild, Jennifer, and Nathan Scovronick. 2003. *The American Dream and the Public Schools*. New York, N.Y.: Oxford University Press

Hoff, David J. 2002. "States Revise the Meaning of 'Proficient'." *Education Week*, October 9.

Hoffereth, Sandra L., and John F. Sandberg. 2001. "How American Children Spend Their Time." *Journal of Marriage and the Family* 63(May): 295-308.

Hoffman, Kathryn, Charmaine Llagas, and Thomas Snyder. 2003. *Status and Trends in the Education of Blacks*. NCES 2003-034. Washington, D.C.: U.S. Department of Education, Office of Educational Research and Improvement.

Horn, Catherine, et al. 2000. *Cut Scores: Results May Vary*. Monograph Volume 1, Number 1, April. Boston, Mass.: National Board on Educational Testing and Public Policy.

Horvat, Erin McNamara, Elliot B. Weininger, and Annette Lareau. 2003. "From Social Ties to Social Capital: Class Differences in the Relations Between Schools and Parent Networks." *American Educational Research Journal* 40(2): 319-351.

Hudson Lisa. 2003. *Issue Brief. Racial/Ethnic Differences in the Path to a Postsecondary Credential*. NCES 2003-005. Washington D.C.: U.S. Department of Education, Office of Educational Research and Improvement.

Iatarola, Patrice. 2001. *Distributing Teacher Quality Equitably: The Case of New York City*. IESP Policy Brief, Spring. Institute for Education and Social Policy, New York University.

Jacobson, Sandra, and Joseph Jacobson. 2003. "FAS/FAE and Its Impact on Psychosocial Child Development." Quebec, Canada: Centre of Excellence for Early Childhood Development. <http://www.excellence-earlychildhood.ca/documents/ JacobsonANGxp.pdf>

Janofsky, Michael. 1999. "The Dark Side of the Economic Expansion. The Poor Wait Longer for Affordable Housing, Government Finds." *New York Times,* March 7.

Jencks, Christopher, 1979. *Who Gets Ahead?* New York, N.Y.: Basic Books

Jencks, Christopher. Forthcoming. "Should We Want a World in Which Family Background Doesn't Matter?" Working Paper, Kennedy School of Government, Harvard University, Cambridge, Mass.

Jencks, Christopher, and Susan Mayer. 1990. "The Social Consequences of Growing Up in a Poor Neighborhood." In Laurence E. Lynn and Michael G. H. McGeary, eds., *Inner-City Poverty in the United States.* Washington, D.C.: National Academy Press.

Jepsen, Christopher, and Steven Rivkin. 2002. *Class Size Reduction, Teacher Quality, and Academic Achievement in California Public Schools.* San Francisco, Calif.: Public Policy Institute of California.

Jerald, Craig, 2001. *Dispelling the Myth Revisited: Preliminary Findings From a Nationwide Analysis of "High-Flying" Schools.* Washington, D.C.: Education Trust.

Johnson, Eugene G. 1998. *Linking the National Assessment of Educational Progress (NAEP) and the Third International Mathematics and Science Study (TIMSS): A Technical Report.* NCES 98-499. Washington, D.C.: U.S. Department of Education, Office of Educational Research and Improvement.

Johnson, George E., and Frank P. Stafford. 1973. "Social Returns to Quantity and Quality of Schooling." *Journal of Human Resources* 8(2): 139-155.

Johnson, Jean, and John Immerwahr. 1994. *First Things First. What Americans Expect From the Public Schools. A Report from Public Agenda.* New York, N.Y.: Public Agenda.

Johnson, Kirk. 2003. "Looking Outside for Lead Danger." *New York Times*, November 2.

Johnson, William R., and Derek Neal. 1998. "Basic Skills and the Black–White Earnings Gap." In Christopher Jencks and Meredith Phillips, eds., *The Black–White Test Score Gap.* Washington, D.C.: Brookings Institution Press.

Kahl, Joseph A. 1953. "Educational and Occupational Aspirations of 'Common Man' Boys." *Harvard Educational Review* 23(Summer): 186-203.

Kahlenberg, Richard D. 2001. *All Together Now. Creating Middle-Class Schools Through Public School Choice.* Washington, D.C.: Brookings Institution Press.

Kalil, Ariel, Mary Pattillo, and Monique R. Payne. 2001. "Intergenerational Assets and the Black/White Test Score Gap." Delivered at "After the Bell: Education Solutions Outside the School," conference at Jerome Levy Economics Institute, Bard College, June 4-5.

Kane, Thomas J., and Douglas O. Staiger. 2002. "The Promise and Pitfalls of Using Imprecise School Accountability Measures." *Journal of Economic Perspectives* 16(4): 91-114.

Kao, Grace, Marta Tienda, and Barbara Schneider. 1996. "Racial and Ethnic Variation in Academic Performance." *Research in Sociology of Education and Socialization* 11: 263-297.

Karp, Robert, Roy Martin, Trevor Sewell, John Manni, and Arthur Heller. 1992. "Growth and Academic Achievement in Inner-City Kindergarten Children." *Clin Pediatr Phila* 31: 336-340.

Kaufman, Julie E., and James E. Rosenbaum. 1992. "The Education and Employment of Low-Income Black Youth in White Suburbs." *Educational Evaluation and Policy Analysis* 14(3): 229-240.

Kaufman, Leslie. 2003. "U.S. Finds New York Still Lags on Access to Food Stamp Program." *New York Times*. November 24.

Kaufman, Phillip, and Martha Naomi. 2000. *Dropout Rates in the United States 1998*. NCES 2000-022. Washington D.C.: U.S. Department of Education, Office of Educational Research and Improvement.

Keister, Lisa A. Forthcoming. "Family Structure, Race, and Wealth Ownership: A Longitudinal Exploration of Wealth Accumulation Processes." *Sociological Perspectives*.

Kerbow, David. 1996. "Patterns of Urban Student Mobility and Local School Reform." *Journal of Education for Students Placed at Risk* 12: 147-169.

KIPP (The KIPP Academies). 2002. *KIPP: Life. Lessons.* Author.

KIPP (The KIPP Academies). 2003. *2003 Report Card.* Author.

Klein, Roger, Richard Spady, and Andrew Weiss. 1991. "Factors Affecting the Output and Quit Propensities of Production Workers." *Review of Economic Studies*.

Kling, Jeffrey R., and Jeffrey B. Liebman. 2004. "Experimental Analysis of Neighborhood Effects on Youth." Working Paper 483; Industrial Relations Section, Princeton University, Princeton, N.J.

Kluegel, James, and Lawrence Bobo 2001. "Perceived Group Discrimination and Policy Attitudes: The Sources and Consequences of the Race and Gender Gaps." In Alice O'Connor, Chris Tilly, and Lawrence D. Bobo. *Urban Inequality: Evidence From Four Cities.* New York, N.Y.: Russell Sage.

Koch, Kathy. 2002. "Hunger in America." *CQ Researcher* 10(44): 1034-1055.

Kohn, Melvin L. 1969. *Class and Conformity. A Study in Values.* Homewood, Ill.: Dorsey Press.

Komaromy, Miriam, Kevin Grumbach, Michael Drake, Karen Vranizan, Nicole Lurie, Dennis Keane, Andrew B. Bindman. 1996. *The New England Journal of Medicine* 334(20): 1305-1310.

Krueger, Alan B., and Diane M. Whitmore. 1999. "The Effect of Attending a Small Class in the Early Grades on College-Test Taking and Middle School Test Results: Evidence From Project STAR." Working Paper 457. Industrial Relations Section, Princeton University, Princeton, N.J.

Krueger, Alan B., and Diane Whitmore. 2001. *Would Smaller Classes Help Close the Black–White Achievement Gap?* Working Paper 451. Industrial Relations Section, Princeton University, Princeton, N.J.

Krueger, Alan B., and Pei Zhu. 2003. *Another Look at the New York City School Voucher Experiment.* Working Paper 470, Industrial Relations Section, Princeton University, Princeton, N.J.

Ladd, Helen F., and Randall P. Walsh. 2002. "Implementing Value-Added Measures of School Effectiveness: Getting the Incentives Right." *Economics of Education Review* 21: 1–17.

Langton, Kenneth P., and M. Kent Jennings. 1968. "Political Socialization and the High School Civics Curriculum in the United States." *American Political Science Review* 62(September): 858–867.

Lapp, Michael, Wendy S. Grigg, and Brenda S.H. Tay-Lim. 2002. *The Nation's Report Card: U.S. History 2001.* NCES 2002-483. Washington, D.C.: U.S. Department of Education, Office of Educational Research and Improvement.

Lareau, Annette. 1989. *Home Advantage: Social Class and Parental Intervention in Elementary Education: Theory, Research, Practice.* Thousand Oaks, Calif.: Sage.

Lareau, Annette. 2002. "Invisible Inequality: Social Class and Childrearing in Black Families and White Families." *American Sociological Review* 67(October): 747-776.

Lareau, Annette. 2003. *Unequal Childhoods.* Berkeley: University of California Press.

LAUSD (Los Angeles Unified School District). 1990. *Fall 1990 Ethnic Survey Report.* Pub 114. Los Angeles: LAUSD Information Technology Division.

LAUSD (Los Angeles Unified School District). 1996. *Fall 1995 Ethnic Survey Report.* Pub 125. Los Angeles: LAUSD Information Technology Division.

Lee, Valerie, Jeanne Brooks-Gunn, and Elizabeth Schnur. 1988. "Does Head Start Work? A 1-Year Follow-Up Comparison of Disadvantaged Children Attending Head Start, No Preschool and Other Preschool Programs." *Developmental Psychology* 24(2): 210-222.

Lee, Valarie E., and David T. Burkam. 2002. *Inequality at the Starting Gate.* Washington, D.C.: Economic Policy Institute.

Lemke, Mariann, et al. 2002. *Outcomes of Learning. Results From the 2000 Program for International Student Assessment of 15-Year-Olds in Reading, Mathematics, and Science Literacy.* NCES 2002-115. Washington, D.C.: U.S. Department of Education, Office of Educational Research and Improvement.

Levin, David. 2004. Superintendent, Bronx KIPP Academy. Interview with the author, February 11.

Levin, Henry M., and Carolyn Kelley. 1994. "Can Education Do It Alone?" *Economics of Education Review* 13(2): 97-108.

Levin, Henry M., Russell Rumberger, and Christine Finnan. 1990. "Escalating Skill Requirements or Different Skill Requirements?" Paper prepared for the Conference on Changing Occupational Skill Requirements: Gathering and Assessing the Evidence. Brown University, June 5-6.

Lippman, Laura, Shelley Burns, and Edith McArthur. 1996. *Urban Schools, The Challenge of Location and Poverty.* NCES 96-184. U.S. Department of Education, Office of Educational Research and Improvement.

Loomis, Susan Cooper, and Mary Lyn Bourque, eds. 2001. *National Assessment of Educational Progress Achievement Levels. 1992-1998 for Mathematics.* Washington, D.C.: National Assessment of Educational Progress, National Assessment Governing Board, U.S. Department of Education.

Lu, Adrienne, 2004. "Agencies Say Hunger on Rise Outside Cities Across Region." *New York Times*, March 23.

Lu, Michael C. 2002. Personal correspondence.

Lu, Michael C., and Neal Halfon. 2003. "Racial and Ethnic Disparities in Birth Outcomes: A Life-Course Perspective." *Maternal and Child Health Journal* 7:13-30.

Ludwig, Jens, Helen F. Ladd, and Greg J. Duncan. 2001. "Urban Poverty and Educational Outcomes." *Brookings-Wharton Papers on Urban Affairs, 2001.* Washington, D.C.: Brookings Institution.

Lutkus, Anthony D., Andrew R. Weiss, Jay R. Campbell, John Mazzeo, and Stephen Lazer. 1999. *NAEP 1998. Civics Report Card for the Nation.* NCES 2000-457. Washington, D.C.: U.S. Department of Education, Office of Educational Research and Improvement.

MacDonald, Heather. 1997. "Comment on Sandra J. Newman and Ann B. Schnare's "'...And a Suitable Living Environment': The Failure of Housing Programs to Deliver on Neighborhood Quality." *Housing Policy Debate* 8(4): 755-62.

Marshall, Kim. 2003. "A Principal Looks Back. Standards Matter." *Phi Delta Kappan* 85(2): 105-113.

Marshall, Ray, and Marc Tucker. 1992. *Thinking for a Living.* New York, N.Y.: Basic Books.

Masterov, Dimitriy V. (Center for Social Program Evaluation, University of Chicago). 2004. January 30. Personal communication.

Mayer, Susan E. 1996. "From Learning to Earning." In Susan Mayer and Paul Peterson, eds., *Earning and Learning: How Schools Matter.* Washington, D.C.: Brookings Institution.

McCaffrey, Daniel F., J.R. Lockwood, Daniel M. Koretz, and Laura S. Hamilton. 2003. *Evaluating Value Added Models for Teacher Accountability.* Santa Monica, Calif.: RAND.

McKinnon, Jesse, and Karen Humes. 2000. *The Black Population in the United States: March 1999.* U.S. Census Bureau. Current Population Reports, Series P2-530. Washington, D.C.: U.S. Government Printing Office.

McLoyd, Vonnie C. 1990. "The Impact of Economic Hardship on Black Families and Children: Psychological Distress, Parenting and Socioemotional Development." *Child Development* 61: 311-346.

McLoyd, Vonnie C., Toby Epstein Jayaratne, Rosario Ceballo, and Julio Borquez, 1994. "Unemployment and Work Interruption among African American Single Mothers: Effects on Parenting and Adolescent Socioemotional Functioning." *Child Development* 65: 562-589.

Meyers, Alan F., Amy E. Sampson, Michael Weitzman, Beatrice L. Rogers, and Herb Kayne. 1989. "School Breakfast and School Performance." *American Journal of Diseases of Children* 143(October): 1234-1239

Mickelson, Roslyn Arlin. 1990. "The Attitude-Achievement Paradox Among Black Adolescents." *Sociology of Education* 63(January): 44-61.

Mikulecky, Larry. 1996. *Family Literacy: Parent and Child Interactions*. Washington, D.C.: U.S. Department of Education. <http://www.ed.gov/pubs/FamLit/parent.html>

Miller, Matthew. 2003. *The Two Percent Solution : Fixing America's Problems in Ways Liberals and Conservatives Can Love*. New York, N.Y.: Public Affairs.

Mills, Robert J., and Shailesh Bhandari. 2003. *Health Insurance Coverage in the United States: 2002*. U.S. Census Bureau. Current Population Reports. Washington, D.C.: Government Printing Office.

Mishel, Lawrence, Jared Bernstein, and Heather Boushey. 2003. *The State of Working America 2002 / 2003*. Ithaca, N.Y.: Cornell University Press.

Mishel, Lawrence, Jared Bernstein, and Edith Rasell. 1995.*Who Wins With a Higher Minimum Wage*. Briefing Paper. Washington, D.C.: Economic Policy Institute.

Moats, Louisa C. 2001. "Overcoming the Language Gap." *American Educator*, Summer.

Morbidity and Mortality Weekly Report. 2002. *Surveillance for Asthma United States, 1980-1999*. Washington D.C: U.S. Department of Health and Human Services.

Morgan, Alan D., et al. 1991. *Education Counts. An Indicator System to Monitor the Nation's Education Health. Special Study Panel on Education Indicators for the National Center for Education Statistics*. NCES 91-634. Washington, D.C.: U.S. Government Printing Office.

Moss, Philip, and Chris Tilly. 2001. *Stories Employers Tell. Race, Skill, and Hiring in America*. New York, N.Y.: Russell Sage Foundation.

Mosteller, Frederick, and Daniel P. Moynihan. 1972. "A Pathbreaking Report." In Frederick Mosteller and Daniel P. Moynihan, eds., *On Equality of Educational Opportunity*. New York, N.Y.: Random House.

Moynihan, Daniel P. 1968. "Sources of Resistance to the Coleman Report." *Harvard Educational Review* 38(1): 23-36.

Murnane, Richard J., and Frank Levy. 1993. "Why Today's High-School Educated Males Earn Less Than Their Fathers Did: The Problem and an Assessment of Responses." *Harvard Educational Review* 63(1).

Murnane, Richard J., John B. Willett, M. Jay Braatz, and Yves Duhaldeborde 2001. "Do Different Dimensions of Male High School Students' Skills Predict Labor Market Success A Decade Later? Evidence From the NLSY." *Economics of Education Review* 20(4): 311-320.

Murphy, J. Michael, Maria E. Pagano, Joan Nachmani, Peter Sperling, Shirley Kane, and Ronald E. Kleinman. 1998a. "The Relationship of School Breakfast to Psychosocial and Academic Functioning." *Archives of Pediatric and Adolescent Medicine* 152(September): 899-907.

Murphy, J. Michael, Cheryl A. Wehler, Maria E. Pagano, Michelle Little, Ronald E. Kleinman, and Michael S. Jellinek. 1998b. "Relationship Between Hunger and Psychosocial Functioning in Low-Income American Children." *Journal of the American Academy of Child Adolescent Psychiatry* 37(2): 163-170.

NACE (National Association of Colleges and Employers). 2004. *News Release. Employers Identify the Skills, Qualities of the 'Ideal Candidate.'* January 15.

NAEP (National Assessment of Educational Progress). 2004a. "Mathematics. The Nation's Report Card. Mathematics 2003 Major Results." <http://nces.ed.gov/nationsreportcard/mathematics/results2003/> Updated February 24, 2004.

NAEP (National Assessment of Educational Progress). 2004b. "Percentage of Students, by Mathematics Achievement Level, Grade 8: 1990–2003." <http://nces.ed.gov/nationsreportcard/mathematics/results2003/natachieve-g8.asp> Updated March 8, 2004.

NAEP (National Assessment of Educational Progress). 2004c. "Percentage of Students, by Reading Achievement Level, Grade 4: 1992–2003." <http://nces.ed.gov/nationsreportcard/reading/results2003/natachieve-g4.asp> Updated March 8, 2004.

NAEP (National Assessment of Educational Progress). 2004d. "Percentage of Students, by Reading Achievement Level, Grade 8: 1992–2003." <http://nces.ed.gov/nationsreportcard/reading/results2003/natachieve-g8.asp> Updated March 8, 2004.

NAEP (National Assessment of Educational Progress). 2004e. "NAEP Data. The Nation's Report Card." <http://nces.ed.gov/nationsreportcard/naepdata/getdata.asp> Updated October 31, 2003.

NAEYC (National Association for the Education of Young Children). 1998. *Accreditation Criteria & Procedures of the National Association for the Education of Young Children—1998 Edition.* Washington, D.C.: author.

NAM (National Association of Manufacturers). 2001. *The Skills Gap 2001.* Washington, D.C.: National Association of Manufacturers.

National Center on the Educational Quality of the Workforce. 1995. "First Findings From the EQW National Employer Survey." Philadelphia: University of Pennsylvania. http://www.hrpost.com/lib/training/eqwsrv2.html.

NCEE (National Center on Education and the Economy). 1990. *America's Choice: High Skills or Low Wages! The Report of the Commission on the Skills of the American Workforce.* New York, N.Y.: author.

NCES (National Center for Education Statistics). 2003a. "Condition of Education 2003." NCES 2003-067. Washington, D.C.: U.S. Department of Education, Office of Educational Research and Improvement.

NCES (National Center for Education Statistics). 2003b. *Digest of Education Statistics-2002*. NCES 2003-060. Washington, D.C.: U.S. Department of Education, Office of Educational Research and Improvement.

Neisser, Ulric, 1997. "Never a Dull Moment." *American Psychologist* 52: 79-81.

Neisser, Ulric, Gwyneth Boodoo, Thomas J. Bouchard Jr., A. Wade Boykin, Nathan Brody, Stephen J. Ceci, Diane F. Halpern, John C. Loehlin, Robert Perloff, Robert J. Sternberg, and Susana Urbina. 1996. "Intelligence: Knowns and Unknowns." *American Psychologist* 51: 77-101.

Neuman, Michelle J., and Shanny Peer. 2002. *Equal From the Start: Promoting Educational Opportunity for all Preschool Children - Learning from the French Experience*. New York, N.Y.: The French-American Foundation.

Neuman, Susan B. 2003. "From Rhetoric to Reality: The Case for High-Quality Compensatory Pre-Kindergarten Programs." *Phi Delta Kappan* 85(4): 286-291.

Neuman, Susan B., and Donna Celano. 2001. "Access to Print in Low-Income and Middle Income Communities: An Ecological Study of Four Neighborhoods." *Reading Research Quarterly* 36(1): 8-26.

Niemi, Richard G., and Chris Chapman. 1999. *The Civic Development of 9th- Through 12th- Grade Students in the United States: 1996*. NCES 1999-131. Washington, D.C.: U.S. Department of Education, Office of Educational Research and Improvement.

Niemi, Richard G., and Jane Junn. 1998. *Civic Education: What Makes Students Learn*. New Haven, Conn.: Yale University Press.

NIOOST (National Institute for Out of School Time). 2000. "Fact Sheet on School-Age Children's Out-of-School Time. <http://www.wellesley.edu/WCW/CRW/SAC/factsht.html>

Noguera, Pedro. 2001. "The Trouble With Black Boys." *Harvard Journal of African Americans and Public Policy* 3(Fall): 23-46.

Noguera, Pedro A. 2003. *City Schools and the American Dream. Reclaiming the Promise of Public Education*. New York, N.Y.: Teachers College Press.

Nord, Mark, Margaret Andrews, and Steven Carlson. 2003. *Household Food Security in the United States, 2002*. Food Assistance and Nutrition Research Report No. FANRR35. Washington D.C.: U.S. Department of Agriculture.

Nunberg, Geoff. 2002. "A Loss for Words." *Fresh Air* Commentary. September 3. <http://www-csli.stanford.edu/~nunberg/vocabulary.html>

Nye, Barbara, Larry V. Hedges, and Spyros Konstantopoulos. 2002. "Do Low-Achieving Students Benefit More From Small Classes? Evidence From the Tennessee Class Size Experiment." *Educational Evaluation and Policy Analysis* 24(3): 201-217.

O'Donnell, Fran. 2001. New York State Department of Education. Interview by author, July 10.

OFSTED (Office for Standards in Education). 1999. *Raising the Attainment of Minority Ethnic Pupils.* HMI 170. London, England: OFSTED Publications Centre. Author.

Ogbu, John. 1990. "Minority Status and Literacy in Comparative Perspective." *Daedalus* 119(2): 141-168.

Ogbu, John. 1992a. "Understanding Cultural Differences and School Learning." *Educational Libraries* 16(3): 7-11.

Ogbu, John, 1992b. "Understanding Cultural Diversity and Learning." *Educational Researcher* 21(8): 5-14, 24.

Ogbu, John. 2003. *Black American Students in an Affluent Suburb. A Study of Academic Disengagement.* Mahwah, N.J.: Lawrence Erlbaum Associates.

Olds, David L., et al. 1997. "Long-Term Effects of Home Visitation on Maternal Life Course and Child Abuse and Neglect: Fifteen-Year Follow-Up of a Randomized Trial." *Journal of the American Medical Association* 278 (8): 637-643.

Olds, David L., et al. 1999. "Prenatal and Infancy Home Visitation by Nurses: Recent Findings." *Future of Children* 9(1): 44-65.

Olneck, Michael R., and Marvin Lazerson. 1974. "The School Achievement of Immigrant Children: 1900-1930." *History of Education Quarterly*, 453-482.

Olson, Lynn. 2004. "Tennessee Reconsiders Tennessee Value-Added Assessment System." *Education Week* 23(25): 9

Ones, Deniz S., Chockalingam Viswesvaran, and Frank L. Schmidt. 1993. "Comprehensive Meta-Analysis of Integrity Test Validities. Findings and Implications for Personnel Selection and Theories of Job Performance." *Journal of Applied Psychology* 78(4): 679-703.

Orfield, Antonia. 2003. Interview with author. November 11.

Orfield, Antonia, Frank Basa, and John Yun. 2001. "Vision Problems of Children in Poverty in an Urban School Clinic: Their Epidemic Numbers, Impact on Learning, and Approaches to Remediation." *Journal of Optometric Vision Development* 32(Fall): 114-141.

OECD (Organization for Economic Cooperation and Development). 2001. *Knowledge and Skills for Life: First Results from the OECD Programme for International Student Assessment PISA 2000.* Paris, France: OECD.

OTA (U.S. Congress, Office of Technology Assessment). 1990. *The Use of Integrity Tests for Pre-Employment Screening.* OTA-SET-442. Washington, D.C.: U.S. Government Printing Office.

Owen, David, 1985. *None of the Above: Behind the Myth of Scholastic Aptitude.* Boston, Mass.: Houghton Mifflin.

Pager, Devah. 2003. "The Mark of a Criminal Record." *American Journal of Sociology* 108(5): 937-975.

Pauley v. Kelly, 255 S.E.2d 859 (W.Va. 1979).

Pelligrino, James W., Lee R. Jones, and Karen J. Mitchell, eds. 1999. "Grading the Nation's Report Card. Evaluating NAEP and Transforming the Assessment of Educational Progress." Washington, D.C.: National Academies Press.

Persico, Nicola, Andrew Postelwaite, and Dan Silverman. 2003. "The Effect of Adolescent Experience on Labor Market Outcomes: The Case of Height." <http://www.econ.lsa.umich.edu/~dansilv/height.pdf>

Phillips, Meredith. 2000. "Understanding Ethnic Differences in Academic Achievement: Empirical Lessons From National Data." In David W. Grissmer and J. Michael Ross, eds., *Analytic Issues in the Assessment of Student Achievement.* NCES 2000-050. Washington DC: U.S. Department of Education.

Phillips, Meredith, Jeanne Brooks-Gunn, Greg J. Duncan, Pamela Klebanov, and Jonathan Crane. 1998. "Family Background, Parenting Practices, and the Black–White Test Score Gap." In Christopher Jencks and Meredith Phillips, eds., *The Black-White Test Score Gap.* Washington, D.C.: Brookings Institution Press.

Pipho, Chris 1999. "Public Opinion and Public Education." *Phi Delta Kappan*, April: 565-566.

Planty, Mike, and Michael Regnier, 2003. *Statistics in Brief. Volunteer Service by Young People From High School Through Early Adulthood.* NCES 2004-365. Washington, D.C.: U.S. Department of Education, Institute of Education Sciences.

Portas, Carole A. 2004. "Early Childhood Care and Education and Its Relationship to Reading Achievement at the Start of Kindergarten." Paper prepared for the annual meeting of the American Education Finance Association, Salt Lake City, Utah, March 12.

Portner, Jessica, and Kate Folmar. 2001. "Most Ninth Graders Flunked High-Stakes Test on Their First Try. Education Board Sets Bar for Exam; 70% Correct Deemed Too High." *San Jose Mercury-News*, June 8.

Pyle, Amy. 1998. "Public Education: California's Perilous Slide; Escalante's Formula Not Always the Answer." *Los Angeles Times,* May 4.

Rathburn, Amy, and Jerry West. 2003. *Young Children's Access to Computers in the Home and at School in 1999 and 2000.* NCES 2003-036. Washington, D.C.: U.S. Department of Education, Office of Educational Research and Improvement.

Rebello Britto, Pia, and Jeanne Brooks-Gunn. 2001. "Beyond Shared Book Reading: Dimensions of Home Literacy and Low-Income African American Preschoolers' Skills." *New Directions for Child and Adolescent Development* 92(Summer): 73-89.

Reeves, Douglas B. 2000. *Accountability in Action. A Blueprint for Learning Organizations.* Denver, Colo.: Center for Performance Assessment.

Rice, Jennifer King. 2003. *Teacher Quality; Understanding the Effectiveness of Teacher Attributes.* Washington, D.C.: Economic Policy Institute.

Rich-Edwards, Janet, Nancy Krieger, Joseph Majzoub, Sally Zierler, Ellice Lieberman, and Mathew Gillman. 2001. "Maternal Experiences of Racism and Violence as Predictors of Preterm Birth: Rationale and Study Design." *Paediatric and Perinatal Epidemiology* 15(Suppl 2): 124-135.

Richardson, Gale A., et al. 2002. "Prenatal Alcohol and Marijuana Exposure: Effects on Neuropsychological Outcomes at 10 Years." *Neurotoxicology and Teratology* 24(3): 309-320.

Richter, Paul. 2000. "Army Launches Bid to Recruit School Dropouts." *Los Angeles Times*, February 4.

Riley, Claudette. 2004. "Lawmakers Plan Forum for Value-Added Test Scores." *Nashville Tennessean,* February 18

Ritter, Scott. 2004. "Asthma Hits Record Rates Among Minority Kids." *Chicago Sun-Times*, January 8.

Rockoff, Jonah E. 2003. "The Impact of Individual Teachers on Student Achievement: Evidence From Panel Data." Unpublished paper, March. http://www.people.fas.harvard.edu/~rockoff/rockoff_individual_teachers_march_03.pdf

Rose, Lowell C., and Alec M. Gallup. 1998. "The 30th Annual Phi Delta Kappa/Gallup Poll of the Public's Attitudes Toward the Public Schools." *Phi Delta Kappan*, September: 41-56.

Rose, Lowell C., and Alec M. Gallup. 2000. "The 32nd Annual Phi Delta Kappa/Gallup Poll of the Public's Attitudes Toward the Public Schools." *Phi Delta Kappan* 82(1): 41-58.

Rosenbaum, James E. 1991. "Black Pioneers: Do Their Moves to the Suburbs Increase Economic Opportunity for Mothers and Children?" *Housing Policy Debate* 2(4): 1179-1213.

Ross, Randy, 1999. "How Class-Size Reduction Harms Kids in Poor Neighborhoods." *Education Week* 18(37): 48, 30.

Rosso, Randy, and Lisa Fowler. 2000. *Characteristics of Food Stamp Households: Fiscal Year 1999*. U.S. Department of Agriculture, Food and Nutrition Service, Office of Analysis, Nutrition and Evaluation. Alexandria, Va.: FSP-00-CHAR.

Rothstein, Richard 1997. *Where's the Money Going? Changes in the Level and Composition of Education Spending, 1991-96*. Washington, D.C.: Economic Policy Institute

Rothstein, Richard. 1998. *The Way We Were? The Myths and Realities of America's Student Achievement*. New York, N.Y.: Century Foundation Press.

Rothstein, Richard. 2000a. "When Culture Affects How We Learn." *New York Times*, October 11.

Rothstein, Richard. 2000b. "Better Than a Voucher, a Ticket to Suburbia." *New York Times*, October 18.

Rothstein, Richard. 2001. "A Worthwhile Substitute for the Regents Exams." *New York Times*, February 21.

Rothstein, Richard, Martin Carnoy, and Luis Benveniste. 1999. *Can Public Schools Learn From Private Schools? Case Studies in the Public & Private Nonprofit Sectors.* Washington, D.C.: Economic Policy Institute.

Rothstein, Richard, with Karen Hawley Miles. 1995. *Where's The Money Gone? Changes in the Level and Composition of Education Spending.* Washington, D.C.: Economic Policy Institute.

Rotter, Julian B. 1966. "Generalized Expectancies for Internal Versus External Control of Reinforcement." *Psychological Monographs* 80(1).

Rushowy, Kristin. 2004. "Certificate Rewards Job Skills, not Marks. Toronto Board to Issue 200 in June. Seen as Alternative to Dropping Out." *Toronto Star*, February 20.

Sanders, William L., and June C. Rivers. 1996. *Cumulative and Residual Effects of Teachers on Future Student Academic Achievement.* Knoxville: The University of Tennessee Value-Added Research and Assessment Center.

Sanders, William L., et. al. 1997. "The Tennessee Value-Added Assessment System. A Quantitative, Outcomes-Based Approach to Educational Assessment." In Jason Millman, ed., *Grading Teachers, Grading Schools: Is Student Achievement a Valid Evaluation Measure?* Thousand Oaks, Calif.: Corwin Press.

Sanderson, Allen, et al. 1996. *National Education Longitudinal Study: 1988-1994. Descriptive Summary Report.* NCES 1996-175. Washington D.C.: U.S. Department of Education, Office of Educational Research and Improvement.

Sard, Barbara, and Will Fisher. 2003. *Senate Committee Bill May Avert Cuts to Housing Vouchers Despite Inadequate Appropriation.* Washington, D.C.: Center on Budget and Policy Priorities, September 23.

Schemo, Diana Jean. 2002. "Few Exercise New Right to Leave Failing Schools." *New York Times*, August 28.

Schweinhart, Lawrence J., Helen V. Barnes, and David P. Weikart (with W. Steven Barnett and Ann S. Epstein). 1993. *Significant Benefits: The High/Scope Perry Preschool Study Through Age 27.* Ypsilanti, Mich.: High/Scope Press.

Sciolino, Elaine. 2004. "France Seems to Try Acting Affirmatively on Muslims." *New York Times*, January 15.

Shepard, Lorrie A., et al. 1993. *Setting Performance Standards for Student Achievement. Report of the NAE Panel on the Evaluation of the NAEP Trial State Assessment: An Evaluation of the 1992 Achievement Levels.* Stanford, Calif.: National Academy of Education.

Shonkoff, Jack P., and Deborah A. Phillips, eds. 2000. *From Neurons to Neighborhoods. The Science of Early Childhood Development.* Washington, D.C.: National Academy Press.

Simmons, Roger E., et al. 2002. "Fractionated Simple and Choice Reaction Time in Children With Prenatal Exposure to Alcohol." *Alcoholism: Clinical and Experimental Research* 26(September): 1412-1419.

Sizer, Theodore R. 1984, 1992. *Horace's Compromise. The Dilemma of the American High School.* Boston, Mass.: Houghton Mifflin.

Smith, Marshall S. 2003. "Education Reform: A Report Card." *Bulletin of the American Academy of Arts and Sciences* 56(2): 38-48.

Smrekar, Claire, James W. Guthrie, Debra E. Owens, and Pearl G. Sims. 2001. *March Toward Excellence: School Success and Minority Student Achievement in Department of Defense Schools.* Washington, D.C.: National Education Goals Panel.

Snow, Catherine, and Patton Tabors. 1996. "Intergenerational Transfer of Literacy." Washington, D.C: U.S. Department of Education. <http://www.ed.gov/pubs/FamLit/transfer.html>

Solan, Harold A., John Shelley-Tremblay, Anthony Ficarra, Michael Silverman, and Steven Larson. 2003. "Effect of Attention Therapy on Reading Comprehension." *Journal of Learning Disabilities* 36(6): 556.

Sowell, Thomas. 1994. *Race and Culture: A World View.* New York, N.Y.: Basic Books.

Starfield, Barbara. 1982. "Child Health and Socioeconomic Status." *American Journal of Public Health* 72(June): 532-534.

Starfield, Barbara. 1997. "Health Indicators for Preadolescent School-Age Children." In Robert M. Hauser, Brett V. Brown, and William R. Prosser, eds. *Indicators of Children's Well-Being.* New York, N.Y.: Russell Sage Foundation.

Steele, Claude M. 1997 "A Threat in the Air. How Stereotypes Shape Intellectual Identity and Performance." *American Psychologist* 52(6): 613-629.

Steele, Claude M., and Joshua Aronson. 1998. "Stereotype Threat and the Test Performance of Academically Successful African Americans." In Christopher Jencks and Meredith Phillips, eds., *The Black–White Test Score Gap.* Washington, D.C.: Brookings Institution Press.

Steinberg, Laurence. 1996. *Beyond the Classroom. Why School Reform Has Failed and What Parents Need to Do.* New York, N.Y.: Simon and Schuster.

Stipek, Deborah, and Kathy Seal. 2001. *Motivated Minds. Raising Children to Love Learning.* New York, N.Y.: Henry Holt and Company.

Streissguth, A., et al. 1994. "Maternal Drinking During Pregnancy: Attention and Short-Term Memory in 14-Year Old Offspring – A Longitudinal Prospective Study." *Alcoholism Clinical and Experimental Research* 18: 202-218.

Swanson, Christopher B. 2004. *Who Graduates? Who Doesn't? A Statistical Portrait of Public High School Graduation, Class of 2001.* Washington, D.C.: Urban Institute, Education Policy Center. <http://www.urban.org/UploadedPDF/410934_WhoGraduates.pdf>

Tames, Howard, Executive Director, Division of Human Resources, New York City Board of Education. 2000. Interview with author. August 29.

Teixiera, Ruy. 1998. "Rural and Urban Manufacturing Workers: Similar Problems, Similar Challenges." *Agriculture Information Bulletin* 736-02, January. U.S. Department of Agriculture, Economic Research Service.

Thernstrom, Stephen, and Abigail Thernstrom. 1997. *American in Black and White. One Nation, Indivisible.* New York, N.Y.: Simon and Schuster.

Thernstrom, Stephen, and Abigail Thernstrom. 2003. *No Excuses. Closing the Racial Gap in Learning.* New York, N.Y.: Simon and Schuster.

Torney-Purta, Judith, Rainer Lehman, Hans Oswald, and Wolfram Schulz. 2001. *Citizenship and Education in Twenty-Eight Countries: Civic Knowledge and Engagement at Age Fourteen.* Amsterdam, the Netherlands: International Association for the Evaluation of Educational Achievement.

Tourangeau, Karen, et al. 2002. *User's Manual for the ELCS-K First Grade Public-Use Data Files and Electronic Code Book.* NCES 2002-135. Washington, D.C.: U. S. Department of Education, Office of Educational Research and Improvement.

U.S. Census Bureau. 2002a. *Average Number of People per Family Household by Race and Hispanic Origin, Marital Status, Age, and Education of Householder: March 2002.* U.S. Census Bureau, Population Division. Washington, D.C.: Government Printing Office. <http://www.census.gov/population/socdemo/hh-fam/cps2002/tabAVG2.pdf>

U.S. Census Bureau. 2002b. *Table A-1. Reported Voting and Registration by Race, Hispanic Origin, Sex and Age Groups: November 1964 to 2000.* U.S. Census Bureau, Population Division. Washington, D.C.: Government Printing Office. <http://www.census.gov/population/socdemo/voting/tabA-1.xls>

U.S. Conference of Mayors – Sodexho. 2003. *Hunger and Homelessness Survey*, December. http://www.usmayors.org/uscm/home.asp

Vandell, Deborah Lowe, and Barbara Wolfe. 2000. "Child Care Quality: Does it Matter, and Does it Need to be Improved?" Washington, D.C.: U.S. Department of Health and Human Services. http://aspe.hhs.gov/hsp/ccquality00/index.htm

Vaughan, Roger D. (Associate Professor, Mailman School of Public Health, Columbia University). 2003. Personal correspondence, April 22.

Venezky, Richard L. 1998. "An Alternative Perspective on Success for All." In Kenneth Wong, ed., *Advances in Educational Policy: Perspectives on the Social Functions of Schools.* Stamford, Conn.: JAI Press.

Viadero, Debra. 2000. "Minority Gaps Smaller in Some Pentagon Schools." *Education Week* 19(29): 1, 20-21.

Vinovskis, Maris A. 1995. "School Readiness and Early Childhood Education." In Diane Ravitch and Maris A. Vinovskis, eds. *Learning From the Past. What History Teaches Us About School Reform.* Baltimore, Md.: Johns Hopkins University Press.

Wadhwa, Pathik D., Jennifer F. Culhane, Virginia Rauh, Shirish S. Barve, Vijaya Hogan, Curt A. Sandman, Calvin J. Hobel, Alexsandra Chicz-Demet, Christine Dunkel-Schetter, Thomas J. Garite, and Laura Glynn. 2001. "Stress, Infection, and Pre-Term Birth: A Biobehavioural Perspective." *Paediatric and Perinatal Epidemiology* 15(Suppl 2): 17-29.

Walberg, Herbert J., and Rebecca C. Greenberg. 1998. "The Diogenes Factor." *Education Week*, April 8.

Wang, M.C., G.D. Haertel, and H. J. Walberg. 1994. "Educational Resilience in Inner Cities." In Wang, M.C., and E. W. Gordon, eds., *Educational Resilience in Inner-City America: Challenges and Prospects*. Hillsdale, N.J.: Lawrence Erlbaum Associates.

Welfare Law Center. 2000. "New York City Admits Monitoring Insufficient to Establish Proper Processing of Applications for Food Stamps, Medicaid, and Cash Assistance: Court Bars Opening of More Job Centers." *Welfare News*. September. http://www.welfarelaw.org/monitoring.htm

Whitman, Steven, Cynthia Williams, and Ami Shah. 2004. *Improving Community Health Survey: Report 1*. Chicago, Ill.: Sinai Health System.

Whyatt, Robin M., et al. 2002. "Residential Pesticide Use During Pregnancy Among a Cohort of Urban Minority Women." *Environmental Health Perspectives* 110(5): 507-514.

Whyatt, R. M., et al. 2004. "Prenatal Pesticide Exposures, Birth Weight and Length Among an Urban Minority Cohort." *Environmental Health Perspectives OnLine*, March 22. <http://dx.doi.org>

Wilgoren, Jodi. 2000. "After Success With Poor, Schools Try Cloning." *New York Times*, August 16.

Wilson, James Q. 2002. "Slavery and the Black Family." *Public Interest*, Spring: 3-23.

Winter, Greg. 2004. "$4 Billion More Is Needed to Fix City's Schools, Study Finds." *New York Times*, February 5

Yoshikawa, Hirokazu. 1995. "Long-Term Effects of Early Childhood Programs on Social Outcomes and Delinquency." *Future of Children: Long-Term Outcomes of Early Childhood Programs* 5(3): 51-75.

Youniss, James, Jeffrey A. McLellan, and Miranda Yates. 1997. "What We Know About Engendering Civic Identity." *American Behavioral Scientist* 40(March–April): 620–631.

Yu, Ron. 2004. Director of Training. KIPP Foundation, San Francisco office. Interview with the author, January 29.

Zajonc, R. B. 1976. "Family Configuration and Intelligence." *Science* 192(April 16): 227-236.

Zajonc, R. B. 1983. "Validating the Confluence Model." *Psychological Bulletin* 93: 457-480.

Zeller, Tom. 2004. "Of Fuzzy Math and 'Food Security'." *New York Times*, January 11.

Zhou, Min, and Carl L. Bankston III. 1998. *Growing Up American. How Vietnamese Children Adapt to Life in the United States*. New York, N.Y.: Russell Sage.

Acknowledgments

I delivered the core of this book as a series of public lectures at Teachers College, Columbia University in the winter of 2004. I am grateful to Arthur Levine, president of the college, for inviting me to spend the 2003-04 academic year as the "Julius and Rosa Sachs Distinguished Lecturer."

Some of the material in Chapter 1 relating to the early childhood and health conditions that contribute to children's different levels of academic achievement draws on a working paper for the Economic Policy Institute, being developed under my supervision by Whitney C. Allgood, a Ph.D. candidate at Vanderbilt University. Calculations of the cost of early childhood, health, summer, and after-school programs, briefly described in Chapter 5, come from a model that Ms. Allgood and I developed, initially at the request of the Institute for Wisconsin's Future as part of its design of an "adequate" school system for that state. Ms. Allgood has been a superb colleague and it is impossible to identify which of the ideas in Chapters 1 and 5 were originally hers or my own.

Chapter 1 is also the latest step in the gradual development of my ideas regarding the social class characteristics that influence student achievement. I began working on them in a paper, "Finance Fungibility," commissioned by the Ball Foundation in 1998. Professor James W. Guthrie of Peabody College, Vanderbilt University, coordinated the Ball Foundation's research agenda in this area; without his early encouragement, I would never have tried to think systematically about these issues. I developed the analysis further in a paper for the Finance Project and the Center on Education Policy; Carol Cohen and Jack Jennings, respectively, were also encouraging. Finally, Ellen Lagemann, then president of the Spencer Foundation, invited me to deliver the keynote address for the foundation's 30th anniversary celebration in 2002; preparing that address was an additional opportunity to develop these themes. Paul Goren, then acting president of Spencer, supported further work in this area.

Other analyses included in this volume were originally conceived for columns I wrote as *The New York Times*' national education columnist from 1999 to 2002. There, I had the benefit of an insightful and supportive editor, Ethan Bronner. When I began this assignment, his first instruction to me was, "Remember, only one idea per column." It was great advice, I tried to adhere to it, and it worked well for a brief column. This volume, however, gives me the chance to bring some of these separate ideas together and show how they connect in a bigger picture.

Chapter 3 draws heavily on an article I wrote for *The American Prospect* (February 2004), "Testing Our Patience." It was improved by two terrific editors, Robert Kuttner and Rhea Wilson.

Material in Chapter 4 about the impact of history classes, service learning, and volunteerism on adult civic participation was originally developed for
an article, "We Are Not Ready to Assess History Performance," in the March
2004 issue of the *Journal of American History*.

Much of the material in this book is also part of a larger project, commissioned by the Century Foundation, to calculate all the costs of an adequate
education. Most of my work on this larger project has been sponsored by the
Economic Policy Institute, with financial support from the William and Flora
Hewlett Foundation. I am grateful to Richard Leone and Greg Anrig of the
Century Foundation for their patience and understanding as I put the project
aside while I was writing the *Times* education column, and then as I carved out
a small part of the project to publish separately as the present volume. Lawrence
Mishel, the Economic Policy Institute's president, was not only patient and
understanding as well, but also, as always, my most reliable intellectual com-
panion and supporter. I also benefited from frequent discussions of these ideas
with David Grissmer at RAND; his influence has been wide-ranging, and in
particular, he pressed me to think more seriously about non-cognitive school
outcomes. Chapter 4 was the result.

I could not have completed this project without the help of Lauren M.
Wells, my research assistant at Teachers College in 2003-04. She not only
tracked down sources and took care of details, but wrote thorough memoranda
to me summarizing several areas of research with which I was unfamiliar.

In the fall of 2003, I taught a seminar at Teachers College to explore several ideas that appear in this volume. It would be more accurate to say that the
students in this seminar taught me. Some of them will notice that formulations
from their term papers crop up at various points in this volume. Papers by Juan
Diego Alonso (on how family structure affects student learning), Rebecca
Jacobsen (on the non-cognitive outcomes of the Perry Preschool experiment),
Shawn Sadjatumwadee (on cultural differences between immigrant groups that
affect student learning), and Kara VanderKamp (on how parental use of language affects children's intellectual development) were particularly helpful.

Professors James Guthrie, Christopher Jencks (at the Kennedy School of
Government at Harvard), and Ray Marshall (at the LBJ School of Public Affairs at the University of Texas at Austin), as well as Lawrence Mishel, Whitney
Allgood, Lauren Wells, and Ross Eisenbrey read a draft of the manuscript and
made numerous helpful suggestions, many of which caused me to modify and
correct earlier formulations. My debt to them is enormous but, of course, they
are not responsible for my stubborn refusal to follow all their advice and correct errors that remain.

For final editing, the volume was turned over to Patrick Watson who, as
always, did a superb job, and I am grateful to him.

The biggest intellectual debts I owe for this volume are reflected in the
published sources referenced in the endnotes and bibliography. Often, however, I contacted scholars and practitioners for additional information or guid-

ance, beyond what may have appeared in their published work. These experts who advised me during the six years that these ideas were developing are too numerous to list here, but I am deeply appreciative of their help and apologize for not being able to thank them by name.

About EPI

The Economic Policy Institute was founded in 1986 to widen the debate about policies to achieve healthy economic growth, prosperity, and opportunity.

In the United States today, inequality in wealth, wages, and income remains historically high. Expanding global competition, changes in the nature of work, and rapid technological advances are altering economic reality. Yet many of our policies, attitudes, and institutions are based on assumptions that no longer reflect real world conditions.

With the support of leaders from labor, business, and the foundation world, the Institute has sponsored research and public discussion of a wide variety of topics: trade and fiscal policies; trends in wages, incomes, and prices; education; the causes of the productivity slowdown; labor market problems; rural and urban policies; inflation; state-level economic development strategies; comparative international economic performance; and studies of the overall health of the U.S. manufacturing sector and of specific key industries.

The Institute works with a growing network of innovative economists and other social science researchers in universities and research centers in the U.S. and abroad who are willing to go beyond the conventional wisdom in considering strategies for public policy.

Founding scholars of the Institute include Jeff Faux, distinguished fellow and former president of EPI; Lester Thurow, Sloan School of Management, MIT; Ray Marshall, former U.S. secretary of labor, professor at the LBJ School of Public Affairs, University of Texas; Barry Bluestone, Northeastern University; Robert Reich, former U.S. secretary of labor; and Robert Kuttner, author, editor of *The American Prospect,* and columnist for *Business Week* and the Washington Post Writers Group.

For additional information about the Institute, contact EPI at 1333 H Street NW, Suite 300, East Tower, Washington, DC 20005, (202) 775-8810, or visit www.epinet.org.

About Teachers College

Teachers College, the graduate school of education at Columbia University, supports the advancement of teaching and learning through its exceptional faculty, institutes, conferences, and outreach, its dialog with the local and international community, and its embrace of new technologies. The College's dedication to academic excellence is known worldwide, and Teachers College consistently ranks among the top four graduate schools of education in the nation, according to *U.S. News & World Report*.

Teachers College carries out its essential mission in five ways: engaging in research on the central issues facing education; preparing the next generation of leaders for education; educating the current generation of leaders in practice and policy to meet the challenges they face; shaping the public debate and public policy in education; and improving practice in educational institutions.

Inclusion and diversity have been embedded in Teachers College's educational mission from its beginnings as an institution in 1887, and its student population comes from across the United States and around the world. Throughout the 20th century, Teachers College opened its classrooms to teachers, administrators, and educators of all races and backgrounds, and its faculty continues to lead the way in studying and celebrating diverse perspectives on culture and learning. The College's legacy of forward-thinking policies of equity and inclusion keeps it at the forefront of promoting social progress, through research, scholarship, and a commitment to high-quality education for all.

Index

Abel, Ernest L., 159n108, 159n110, 159n118
absenteeism, 40, 42, 143
Achieve, Inc., 167n232, 167n235
achievement gap, *passim*, and 13, 15, 19, 20, 89, 92, 95, 97, 103, 107, 153n5,164n173
Achilles, Charles M., 171n306
adaptability to change, 152
adequacy lawsuits, 96, 144, 145–146, 175n356
adoption studies, 17–18
adult-student ratio. *See* class size
Aesop's fable, 113
affirmative action, 51, 79, 82, 103–107
African students in Britain, 20
after-school programs, activities, 19, 26, 56–59, 61, 79, 81–2, 83, 101, 113, 127, 130, 142–3
alcohol use. *See* drinking (alcohol)
Alexander, Karl L., 163n160, 163n164
Algerian students in France, 20
Allen, Woody, 113
allergic reactions, 40
Allgood, Whitney C., 159n126, 165n186, 173n336
Allington, Richard L., 163n160
Altman, Lawrence K., 158n81
ambition, 103, 126, 130
America's Second Harvest, 159n124
Andrews, Margaret, 160n128
anemia, iron deficiency, 44
anti-social score, 99–102, 116
appearance, 152
application of knowledge, 86
Armed Forces Qualifying Test, 156n59
Army, 109, 112. *See also* Pentagon schools
Aronson, Joshua, 169n266
art, 74, 97, 143
Asian students, 33
assets, family, 49–50, 52, 53, 61. *See also* wealth distribution
Associated Press, 158n89, 158n91
asthma, 40, 43, 45, 61, 79, 158n99
Astley, Susan, 159n106, 159n111
attainment, 30, 98, 107–113, 125, 169n260. *See also* diploma, high school
auto exhaust, 39
averages, 16, 27, 72, 153n5, 165n187
AVID, 79, 83, 131

ballet, 74
Ballou, Dale, 164n174
Baltimore, 136, 173n330
band and orchestra, 113
Bangladeshi students in Britain, 20
Bankston, Carl L. III, 155n53
Barnes, Helen V., 171nn296–301

Barnett, W. Steven, 171n299, 171n305, 174n340
Barnett, W. Steven, et al., 174n342
Barton, Paul E., 158n86, 175n357, 175n363, 175nn365–366
Basa, Frank, 157n71, 157n73, 157n75, 166n202
baseball, 65
basic skills, 22, 86, 92, 93. 96
Begag, Azouz, 153n15
Bell Curve, The, 52
benchmark, 75, 76, 87
Benveniste, Luis, 155n52
Berkowitz, Gertrud S., et al., 159n116
Bernstein, Jared, 161n148, 169n25, 172nn316–321
Bhandari, Shailesh, 158n101
Bianchi, Suzanne M., 153n10
birth weight, 43, 45, 52, 61
Bishop, John et al., 157n69
BLS (Bureau of Labor Statistics), 168n247
Blum, Justin, 158n86
Bobo, Lawrence, 156n65
Bohrnstedt, George W., 172n313
Bok, Derek, 104–106, 168n249
books in the home, 19, 22, 52, 58, 153n12
Booth, Heather, 153n15
Boston Red Sox, 164n172
Boston, 77, 136
Bourque, Mary Lyn, 167n224
Boushey, Heather, 161n148, 169n255, 172nn316–319, 172n321
Bowen, William, 104–106, 168n249
Bowles, Samuel, 169n253, 169n273
Boys and Girls Clubs, 143
Bracey, Gerald W., 155n40
Britto, Pia Rebello, 154n21
Brocht, Chauna, 172n317
Brock, William E., 152
Bronx High School of Science, 82
Bronx, 74
Brooks, E.C., 155n37
Brooks-Gunn, Jeanne, 154n21, 158n84, 160n139,160nn141–142, 169n267, 173n334, 174n338
Brown vs. Board of Education, 13, 129
Brown, Larry J., 159n120, 159n123, 160n132
Brown, Michael K., et al., 159n103, 161n150
Bruno, James, 160n135, 160n137
Buraku in Japan, 20
Burkam, David, 54–55, 161nn154–155, 161n162
Burns, Shelley, 171n310
Bush, President George W., 82, 94, 141
business school, 104

207